S0-BHY-317

The Urban Experience

The Urban Experience

DAVID HARVEY

The Johns Hopkins University Press
Baltimore and London

HT
321
.H3732
1989

Barnard

Copyright © 1989 David Harvey

Original volumes © 1985 The Johns Hopkins University Press

The Urban Experience is an abridged version of *The Urbanization of Capital:
Studies in the History and Theory of Capitalist Urbanization* and *Consciousness
and the Urban Experience: Studies in the History and Theory of Capitalist Urbanization*,
both volumes originally published in hardcover editions by The Johns Hopkins
University Press, 1985

All rights reserved

First published in the United States of America by
The Johns Hopkins University Press
2715 North Charles Street
Baltimore, Maryland 21218-4363

4 6 8 9 7 5 3

ISBN 0–8018–3849–5

Library of Congress Catalog Card Number 88–46118

Printed in the United States of America on acid-free paper

A catalog record for this book is available from the British Library.

Contents

List of Figures

Preface

This book is an abridged and slightly modified version of *The Urbanization of Capital* and *Consciousness and the Urban Experience*, both originally published in 1985 under the imprimatures of the Johns Hopkins Press in the United States and Blackwell Publishers in the United Kingdom. I have chosen the essays for this paperback version with an eye to their theoretical coherence and utility in providing an interpretation of why the urban experience under capitalism takes the forms it does. I have added one essay not included in the original volumes because I think it helps illustrate some of the ways in which the theory might be put to work to interpret recent trends. I also felt it useful to transform the original "Preface" into a lengthier "Introduction" and to engage in an extensive re-write of the essay on "The Urbanization of Consciousness" which here appears as chapter 8. Otherwise, the original texts remain unchanged, except for minor alterations to ensure consistency and to eliminate duplication.

Personal and intellectual debts are always hard to tabulate. I had institutional support from the Department of Geography and Environmental Engineering in the Johns Hopkins University and I want to thank Professor Wolman for that. Carol Ehrlich of the Johns Hopkins Press was a delight to work with and Alison Richards of Blackwell Publishers did a sterling job at the production stage. John Davey has been most helpful in advising on and guiding the paperback version. Many good friends in Baltimore helped me to see, understand, and participate in things that might otherwise have passed me by. It is invidious to choose, perhaps, but let me extend personal thanks to Barbara Koeppel, Ric Pfeffer, Vicente Navarro, Cliff DuRand, and Chester Wickwire. And among those associated with Hopkins I want to mention Lata Chatterjee, Gene Mumy, Jorn Barnbrock, Amy Kaplan, and Erica Schoenberger and to give very special thanks to Dick Walker, Neil Smith, and Beatriz Nofal. I owe them all a tremendous debt.

Acknowledgements

Chapter 2, "The Urban Process under Capitalism: a Framework for Analysis," first appeared in the *International Journal of Urban and Regional Research* 2 (1978), published by Edward Arnold; Chapter 3 on "Land Rent under Capitalism" has been revised out of an article of the same title in *Antipode* 14, no. 3 (1982); Chapter 4, "Class Structure and the Theory of Residential Differentiation," is taken from *Bristol Essays in Geography*, edited by M. Chisholm and R. Peel and published by Heinemann Press; "Monument and Myth: the Building of the Basilica of the Sacred Heart" was first published in the *Annals, Association of American Geographers*, 69, no. 3 (1979) and "Flexible Accumulation through Urbanization: Reflections on 'Post-Modernism' in the American City," is taken from *Antipode*, 19, no. 3 (1987). I would like to thank all of the editors and publishers of these books and journals for permission to republish these articles here. Figure 10 is taken with permission from B.J.L. Berry and E. Neils, "Location, Size, and Shape of Cities as Influenced by Environmental Factors: The Urban Environment Writ Large," in the *Quality of the Urban Environment*, ed. H. Perloff (Baltimore, 1969) Figures 12, 13, 14, and 16 are printed with permission from the Musée Carnavelet, 15 from the *Illustrated London News* and Figure 17 is reproduced, with permission, from the *Collections d'affiches politiques* of Alain Gesgon.

Introduction

Who among us will refuse the opportunity on arriving in some unfamiliar city, to ascend to a convenient high point and look down upon the intricate landscape of streets and buildings and the restless flow of human activity among them? Why do we feel so curious to do what long-term residents rarely consider (except when visitors arrive) and what do we gain by it? Michel de Certeau (1984) suggests an intriguing answer when he recounts his thoughts on ascending to the heights of New York's World Trade Center. The ascent, he writes, lifts us out of the city's grasp, out of the feverish motion of street life and allows us to become, if only for a while, "voyeurs". The elevation "transforms the bewitching world by which one was 'possessed' into a text that lies before one's eyes. It allows one to read it, to be a solar Eye, looking down like a God." We can, from such a vantage point, possess the city in imagination instead of being possessed by it.

The relation between such a "God-like" vision of the city and the turbulence of street life is interesting to contemplate. Both perspectives, though different, are real enough. Nor are they independent, in fact or in mental construction. The seeing eye, when it scans the city as a whole, brings to its task a whole set of prejudices, concepts (such as that of the city itself) and even theories built up laboriously out of street experience. We thereby burden our interpretations from on high with a variety of associations and assumptions, hopes and fears, wants and desires. The eye is never neutral and many a battle is fought over the "proper" way to see. Yet, no matter what the associations and aspirations, a special satisfaction attaches to contemplating the view from on high, for we have seen the city as a whole, taken it into our minds as a totality. Afterwards, the experience of street life cannot help acquiring new meaning.

The essays assembled in this book are about ways of seeing the city, of reading its text and finding an interpretive frame within which to locate the million and one surprises that confront us on the street. The construction of a vantage point from which to see urban processes and from which to "possess the city in imagination" involves us, however, in the hardest of intellectual labors. It amounts to the building of a theoretical apparatus through which we might understand the city as a whole while appreciating the multiple confusions to which daily urban experience is always prone.

The formation of concepts and the construction of theories have always been vital aspects of human activity. It is through such practices that we grasp who, what, where and (sometimes) why we are in the world. Theories provide cognitive maps for finding our way in a complex and changeable environment. The cognitive map may not be stable or even coherent. Experience leads us to construct, transform and modify it all the time. Purposeful theory construction, in much the same way, seeks an ordered and consistent though never entirely closed map, to improve our understanding and command of daily practices (social, political, economic or technological). Sophisticated or unsophisticated, the urge to construct and the need for some kind of cognitive map is a basic human attribute.

Fortunately, we do not have to start upon such labors from scratch, since the work of generations of thinkers and scholars provide us with a rich fund of ideas and theoretical constructs upon and within which to build. The choice of theoretical frame is by no means easy, however, since each mixes strengths with limitations. Not all the ways of seeing are mutually exclusive of course. An architect looking upon an urban landscape may appreciate the rules of architectural design, the visual rhythms and the historical references. A traffic engineer might think of street design and traffic flow and think of ways to improve the phasing of traffic lights. The historian might contemplate the palimpsest of urban forms, superimposed upon each other over many years, each reflecting the technical, economic and political circumstances of its time, while the urban planner might wonder how to impose the next layer of that palimpsest in such a way as to meet future requirements without being too destructive of what went before. The property developer typically looks at the buildings in terms of rents per square foot, zoning regulations, set-backs, and height limitations. These are all perfectly valid, though obviously partial and technically grounded ways of seeing the city; and all of them are at least potentially reconcilable with each other.

The problems become more acute when we seek some meta-theory of the urban process, by which I mean a theoretical framework that has the potential to put all such partial views together not simply as a composite vision but as a cognitive map that shows how each view can itself be explained by and integrated into some grander conception of what the city as a whole, what the urban process in general, is all about. The choices here are more limited – shall we privilege Marx, Weber, Durkheim, Simmell or the Chicago sociologists? If we adopt one of these particular meta-theories we will almost certainly see the urban process in general through a lens that has been shaped and ground by the beliefs of the maker and the predominant preoccupations of his or her times. Equally, our own framework for seeing and understanding will be political and social, influenced by beliefs and purposes as well as by the endless struggle to achieve more powerful tools for explanation.

In my own case, I turned to the Marxian meta-theory in the early 1970s in part because I found (and still find) it the most powerful of all the explanatory schemas available. It had the potentiality – largely unrealized in actual work – to get at matters as diverse as built environment formation and architectural design, street culture and micro-politics, urban economy and politics as well as the role of urbanization in the rich and complex historical geography of capitalism. The political foundation and purpose of this science also made sense to me as its orientation is critical and progressive and aims not only to enhance the conditions of life of the least privileged but to probe the frontiers of human emancipation in general. Science can never be neutral in human affairs (it would otherwise be irrelevant); attempts to put ourselves outside history and politics at best produce well-meaning pseudo-sciences (of which positivism is one example) and at worst so break the chain of moral connection between what scientists do and what society does as to sanction the grossest forms of political and social irresponsibility. Conversely, political rhetoric unbacked by scientific understanding is only by accident non-vacuous. Marx founded his struggle to define an alternative to the evils of capitalism on a deep study of how capitalism works and how these workings tend to generate certain states of political and social consciousness. He saw capitalism as a revolutionary force, a fount of perpetual revolutionary change. He perceived that the question was not whether, but how and to what purposes change will occur. In order to intervene in that process, we too have to understand it. But how are we to understand it; who is to educate the educators? New understandings of the world cannot come from passive contemplation, Marx argues, but arise through active struggle. But that process cannot be understood onesidedly either. Critical reflection on our understandings, perceptions and ideology, struggle to make concepts and ways of seeing both plain and hegemonic, and the evaluation of our own experience of historical and geographical change are as important as political and social engagement on the barricades. That is why Marx wrote *Capital*. And that is why the Marxist tradition is so rich in its attachment to writing, theorizing and analyzing.

What I am seeking to describe here is the dialectical quality of the Marxian approach to understanding and participating in social change. We think before we act but learn to think through doing. The view from the commanding heights of theory, like that from the top of the World Trade Center, may be "God-and voyeur-like" but it is neither uninformed by nor irrelevant to experience and action. At the same time there is bound to be a tension between the encompassing vision that meta-theory entails and the rich diversity of urban experience. While the tension may inspire creativity (in both imagination and practice) it is by no means easy to keep the two modes of seeing at once distinct and mutually informative.

Individual works, such as this, almost certainly lean to one or the other side of this dialectic. Given the limitations of the human mind and the benefits which always derive from a division of labor, it is indeed both inevitable and proper that they should. Intellectual life, furthermore, is as prone to fashions as any other. Students of the human and social sciences can hardly have failed to notice this. Different disciplines will (usually successively) lay claim to all the answers and different styles of work (meta-theoretical, deconstructionist, hermeneutical, ethnoscientific or just plain empiricist) will be proclaimed as the unique path to knowledge. Such shifts of emphasis need not in themselves be bad. The difficulty is to convert them from the mere swings of the pendulum of fashion into some kind of spiral of growing understanding. If my recent interventions on the matter as it concerns the study of urban processes (see Dear et al., 1988) have been somewhat acerbic, this is because I see the current backing away from Marxian meta-theory and its historical materialist grounding less as a move into a new phase of understanding and creative political action and more as a hasty retreat into emasculated and relatively powerless formats for research and action.

To seek, as I do in these essays, an understanding of capitalist urbanization in Marxian terms is to resort, however, to a framework of understanding that is controversial, incomplete, and in some respects highly problematic. I sought to do something about the incompleteness in *The Limits to Capital*. I there tried to fill in all kinds of "empty boxes" in Marxian theory, such as the formation of fixed capital and built environments; the appropriation of rent; the workings of money, finance, and credit; the production of monetary and financial crises; and the like. I needed to theorize such phenomena if I was ever to construct a comprehensive theory of urbanization. But, curiously, most reviewers passed by what I thought to be the most singular contribution of that work – the integration of the production of space and spatial configurations as an active element within the core of Marxian theorizing. That was the key theoretical innovation that allowed me to shift from thinking about history to historical geography and so to open the way to theorizing about the urban process as an active part of the historical geography of class struggle and capital accumulation.

I readily confess, of course, that much of my fascination with the spatial dimension of human affairs comes out of my disciplinary background in geography. But if, as Anthony Giddens (1981) insists, time-space relations are "constitutive features of social systems," then the question of space is surely too important to be left exclusively to geographers. Social theorists of all stripes and persuasions should take it seriously. Yet there has been a strong and almost overwhelming predisposition to give time and history priority over space and geography. Marx, Weber, Durkheim, and Marshall all have that in common. We consequently lack, as Giddens goes on to observe, the conceptual apparatus "which would make space, and control of space, integral to social theory." That lack is doubly disturbing. To begin with, the insertion of concepts of space and space relations, of place, locale, and milieu, into any social theory has the awkward habit of paralyzing that theory's central propositions. Microeconomists working with perfect competition find only spatial monopoly and prices that fail to produce equilibrium; macroeconomists find as many economies as central banks and a great deal of guesswork affecting relations between them; sociologists find all sorts of "space-time edges" that disturb otherwise coherent processes of structuration; and Marxists, employing a vocabulary appropriate to universal class relations, find neighborhoods, communities, and nations that partition class struggle and capital accumulation into strange configurations of uneven geographical development. Whenever social theorists actively interrogate the meaning of geographical and spatial categories either they are forced to so many ad hoc adjustments that their theory splinters into incoherency or they are forced to rework very basic propositions. Small wonder, then, that Peter Saunders (1981, 278), in a recent attempt to save the supposed subdiscipline of urban sociology from such an ugly fate, offers the extraordinary proposition that "the problems of space . . . must be severed from concern with specific social processes."

Marxists cannot, unfortunately, claim any superior virtue on this score. One searches the major Marxist journals in vain for serious discussion of spatial concepts and geographical dimensionality. Marx himself is partly to blame for this state of affairs. He certainly gave priority to time over space and was not averse to dismissing the question of geographical variation as an "unnecessary complication." To be sure, he sometimes admitted the importance of space and place (see my *The Urbanization of Capital*, Chapter 2), but this does not compensate for a meta-theory that is powerful with respect to time but weak with respect to space. Historical materialism appeared to license the study of historical transformations while ignoring how capitalism produces its own geography. This left Lenin and later theorists of imperialism with a huge gap to fill. Unfortunately they did so by ad hoc adjustments that permitted discussion of the development of capitalism in, say, Russia and India (as if such units made inherent sense) and provoked an alternative rhetoric of exploitation in which centers exploit peripheries, the First World subjugates the Third, and capitalist power blocs compete for domination of space (and hence of markets, labor supplies, raw materials, production capacity etc.). But how can we reconcile the idea that people in one place exploit or struggle against those in another place with Marx's view of a capitalist dynamic powered by the exploitation of one class by another? Such concessions to spatial questions as Lenin, Luxembourg, and the other theorists of imperialism introduced merely made the theoretical foundations of Marxism-Leninism ambiguous, sparking savage and often destructive disputes over the national question and the right to national self-determination, the significance of the urban-rural contradiction, the prospects for socialism in one country, the appropriate response to urban social movements, the importance of geographical decentralization, and the like. The ad hoc adjustments treated, unfortunately, of capitalism in space without considering how space is produced and how the process of production of space integrates into the capitalist dynamic and its contradictions. Historical materialism has to be upgraded to historical-geographical materialism. The historical geography of capitalism must be the object of our theorizing.

This in part explains my choice of the urban as a distinctive focus for analysis. The urban is, however, one of several spatial scales at which the production of spatial configurations, social organization and political consciousness might be examined — regions, nation-states and power blocs being others. Indeed, there are many social theorists, including not a few Marxists, who reject the idea of urbanization as a "theoretically specific object of analysis." Examination of the urban process, it is said can at best yield "real but relatively unimportant insights" into the workings of civil society (Saunders 1981). Even Anthony Giddens (1981, 147), who, as we have seen, takes the problem of spatial organization seriously argues that "with the advent of capitalism, the city is no longer the dominant time-space container or 'crucible of power'; this role is assumed by the territorially bounded nation state." Only occasional mavericks like Jane Jacobs (1984) insist on prioritizing the urban as a unit of analysis.

By focusing on urbanization I do not intend that it should be considered a theoretically specific object of analysis separate from the historical geography of capitalism as a whole. Capital, Marx insists, must be conceived of as a process and not reified as a thing. The study of urbanization is a study of that process as it unfolds through the production of physical and social landscapes and the production of distinctive ways of thinking and acting among people who live in towns and cities. The study of urbanization is not the study of a legal, political entity or of a physical artifact. It should be concerned with processes of capital circulation; the shifting flows of labor power, commodities, and capital; the spatial organization of production and the transformation of time-space relations; movements of information; geopolitical conflicts between territorially-based class alliances; and so on. The fact that cities in the legal sense have lost political power and clear geopolitical influence, that urban economies now assume megalopis-type forms of spread outwards across rambling suburbs into rural fringes is but part of this urban process. And if this appears somewhat ambiguous it is to some extent deliberately so. The ambiguity allows us to study urbanization as a process; there is no point in setting down apparently secure reifications that conceal rather than reveal the fluid processes at work. This way we can better integrate an understanding of the urban process into a broader conception of the dynamics of capitalism and understand how each is part and parcel of the other.

Yet, by the same token, concentration upon the specifics of the urban process allows the construction of yet another distinctive vantage point within the overall corpus of Marxian meta-theory from which to analyse all manner of phenomena that might otherwise remain obscure.

That immediately poses the problem of the proper relation between historical geography (actually experienced) and theory. Much critical ado has been made about the supposed Marxist shortcomings in this regard, chiefly focusing on the enclosure of theory and evidence within such a coherent frame as to preclude "independent" verification. More recently, post-modernist writers like Lyotard (1984) and Rorty (1979) have questioned whether any kind of meta-theory (such as that proposed by Marx) is legitimate at all. These same ideas have now filtered into urban studies, giving comfort to those who prefer a more empiricist approach to research.

There are various levels of response to such criticisms. Firstly, anyone who thinks that there is no problem in the way language of any sort captures experience and represents structures in the external world is preaching in the wind. Knowledge, Bourdieu (1977) reminds us, does not merely depend "on the particular standpoint an observer 'situated in space and time' takes up on the object," but entails a "much more fundamental and pernicious alteration." In withdrawing from action in order to "observe it from above and from a distance," we constitute "practical activity as *an object of observation and analysis, a representation.*" Even the representations of ordinary language constitute objectifications, the power and significance of which, lie "not in the language itself but with the group that authorizes it and invests it with authority." The particular representations that we call "facts" and "data" are by no means independent of the theories which inform them and to which they may be applied. The choice is between different modes of approach to this universal problem. Secondly, there are good reasons for preferring one kind of approach to another. The abstract theories of positivism, for example, must first be translated into working models (an exercise that necessarily encloses a representation of theory and data within the same frame) and then tested against data that are supposed to be samples of repetitive and independent events. Such a procedure may be reasonable in relation to certain limited arenas of enquiry. But it is not obviously relevant to historical geography, which is a complex configuration of interdependent events in space and time. Measuring the growth of cities as if each of them is an "independent event," as if there were no trade, capital flow, migration, or cultural and political influence between them makes little sense. For that reason, many historians, humanists, and historical geographers prefer to bury their theoretical and political orientations in the broad ambiguities of everyday language. This may produce some good stories but in terms of rigor even positivism may appeal by comparison.

As a Marxist I am always seeking coherent and consistent theory to explain unique configurations of historical-geographical processes. The building of such a theory entails a continuous dialogue between experience, action, concept formation, and dialectical theorizing. Since there is considerable and often heated debate among Marxists as to what constitutes theoretical rigor and explanatory power — including the celebrated polarization between the Althusserian structuralists and historians like E.P. Thompson — I should perhaps explain, as simply as I can, what I construe the Marxist approach to be.

One of the central precepts of Marx's historical materialism is that we have to eat in order to live, think, argue, raise children, fight, enjoy ourselves, or whatever. How basic wants and needs are fulfilled has varied historically and continues to vary geographically. It is by way of a study of daily life that we can begin upon the task of theory construction. For example, if I were to trace back where my dinner came from, I would become aware of the myriads of people involved in putting even the simplest of meals upon the table. Yet I can consume my repast without having to know anything about them. Their conditions of life and labor, their joys, discontents and aspirations remain hidden from me. This masking arises because our social relations with those who contribute to our daily sustenance are hidden behind the exchange of things in the market place. Marx calls this masking effect of market exchange "the fetishism of commodities." We cannot use only the experience of shopping in the supermarket as a way to understand how daily life is reproduced. There is no trace of exploitation upon the lettuce, no taste of apartheid in the fruit from South Africa. We have to get behind the surface appearances, unmask the fetishism of commodities in the market place and build a general theory of how commodities are produced, traded and consumed in order to better appreciate the technical conditions and social relations which put our daily bread upon the table.

It is tempting to ascend immediately to the heights of Marxian theory since *Capital* is precisely about a way of seeing that unmasks the fetishisms. But it is useful to go back to the method Marx employs to build his theory to get some sense of how secure a construction it really is. If we look at all the varied elements that make up, say, a typical breakfast, then we find that most of them were produced as commodities under a similar system of circulation of capital. The latter is defined, in its standard form, as a system in which money (held by "capitalists") is used to buy raw materials, intermediate input, machinery and labor power (in the possession of "workers") in order to combine them through an organized production process into a fresh commodity for human use. That commodity is typically sold upon the market for the initial money value plus an increment called profit. The concepts used to describe this process – money, raw materials, machinery and other means of production, work, buying and selling, and profit – are *concrete* abstractions. By this I mean that the concepts are available to us in everyday speech as descriptions of how goods are produced, sold and consumed and that we use money, commodities and means of production in concrete ways while responding to the demands of work, market exchange, profit seeking and the like in equally practical ways (see Chapter 6). The analysis so far seems secure: it should not be hard to persuade any reasonable person that most of the things that lie on the breakfast table have been produced by way of a capital circulation process of this kind. Of course, some items get there by other means (the tomatoes grown in the back garden or surplus butter given away by the state). But the defining characteristic of living under capitalism (as opposed to living under some other mode of production) is that most of what we consume is produced by way of this very standard capital circulation system.

We have thus far taken what Marx calls (to reverse the metaphor of the view from the World Trade Center) the path of *descent* from the complexity of everyday life to a simple set of concrete representations of the way material life is reproduced. There is very little that is problematic in this. But Marx takes matters further. He postulates abstract and non-observable concepts that help us see how all the myriad circulation processes of capital, undertaken by many individuals working under all manner of special conditions, intersect and interact to generate certain dynamics within the social system of capitalism conceptualized as a whole. These concepts, such as value and surplus value, class relations and productive forces, are qualitatively different from concrete abstractions such as money, work, and commodity. Their validity cannot be established in the same way and they are, therefore, much more problematic – so much so that some Marxists feel justified in dispensing with even the most basic concepts like "value". We can propose rough correspondence rules between, for example, wages and the value of labor power, money and value, profits and surplus value, but it is precisely Marx's point that if, for example, price is "the money name of value" then price is not value itself nor even necessarily an adequate representation of value. The proof of this conceptual apparatus lies in the using, i.e. by showing how the underlying concepts can, when put in motion, help us understand all kinds of surface occurencies that would otherwise remain incomprehensible. Explanatory power becomes the central criterion of acceptability.

From this point on, the strategy of enquiry is reversed from that of *descent* from daily life and the construction of abstract underlying categories to an *ascent* through elaboration of these categories step by step to the point where they can, in Marx's words, come to "reflect daily life as in a mirror."

Marx's strategy is similar to that in most scientific endeavors. Theory in physics does not deal with observable entities but uses abstract and non-observable theoretical concepts to grasp observable events. Freud takes a similar tack (with concepts like ego, id and super-ego) and so do most other proponents of social theory. There is nothing special about this aspect of Marx's method though he was undoubtedly a pioneer in pushing social-theoretical abstraction to new levels of sophistication. His admonition that "if everything were as it appears on the surface then there would be no need for science" signalled an important break with radical empiricism and has helped to define the way in which what are sometimes now pejoratively referred to as "meta-theories" of society might be produced.

The special qualities of Marx's theoretical method mostly derive from his dialectical mode of argument. This is often viewed as a legacy from Hegel. While it would be foolish to deny that influence, I think Marx's dialectical argument has a different grounding. Let us go back to his description of the circulation of capital. The early chapters of *Capital* contain a careful analysis of each of the concrete abstractions which comprise the circulation of capital. The commodity, for example, is seen as a single unitary object; but it has both a use value and an exchange value. Most people would recognize that the houses they live in have both use and exchange value and readily perceive the tensions that can arise in how they behave because of the difference between these two considerations. Even more obvious is the inevitable opposition of interests between buyers and sellers in the market place. In labor markets we frequently find that opposition raised to a level of such downright antagonism over wage rates and conditions of work (length of the working day or week, intensity of work schedules, etc.) that it is hard to avoid seeing class struggle as a vital force in the historical geography of capitalism. In other words, we can go back to the concrete abstractions which describe the circulation of capital and discover all kinds of contradictions, antagonisms and oppositions. What Marx does in effect, is to carry over this dialectical sense into the world of abstract theorizing and to use it there as the means to represent how capitalism is constituted as a socio-economic system.

The open-ended and dialectical reasoning Marx adopts is as a guiding thread through a potential maze of interrelations and abstractions. The inner logic of such a technique deserves to be understood in its own terms. The oppositions implanted within the abstract conceptual apparatus are used to spin out new lines of argument. We reach out dialectically (rather than inwardly and deductively) to probe uncharted seas from a few seemingly secure islands of known concepts. Different starting points yield different perspectives. What appears as a secure conceptual apparatus from one vantage point turns out to be partial and one-sided on further investigation. The construction of theory from opposing perspectives helps us map (in much the same way that triangulation is fundamental to cadestral mapping) the rich complexity of a socio-economic system like capitalism with greater accuracy. For example, Marx builds an elaborate picture of the historical dynamic of capitalism (the accumulation of capital over time) purely from the standpoint of production in the first volume of *Capital* but then analyses that same system from the perspective of market exchange and aggregate patterns of production, consumption and circulation in the second volume. The conclusions derived from the second volume (for example, the idea that the value of labor power and, by extension, the total wage bill must tend towards some equilibrium level in relation to capital accumulation) look very different from those derived in the first (for example, the thesis of progressive impoverishment of the proletariat). Both accounts are equally true, but together they make up a dialectical and multidimensional picture of capitalist reality. Bringing the perspectives together (a project that Marx never completed) gives us a fuller picture of the workings of a capitalist mode of production and its internal contradictions (its tendency, for example, to engage in "accumulation for accumulation's sake, production for production's sake beyond levels consistent with labor supply or profitability and to accelerate technological innovation so as to likewise undermine the possibility of sustained profitability). Pursuing an argument in this way allows us to follow how antagonisms get resolved under capitalism and how each contradiction gets internalized a-fresh in new realms, such as the financial and credit system and the apparatus of the state, and through the historical geography of uneven development. These are some of the theoretical and practical issues I explored in *The Limits to Capital*.

In preparing this abridged and consolidated paper-back edition of *The Urbanization of Capital* and *Consciousness and the Urban Experience* (to which I have added a further essay on "post-modernism" in the contemporary city), I have decided to select and arrange the essays so as to illustrate how such a theoretical argument might be brought to bear on the phenomena of capitalist urbanization.

After an initial historical sketch (chapter 1) of the differentiated role of urban processes in the history and geography of capitalist development, I look at the ways in which surpluses of capital and labor power are produced then used in the production of physical and social infrastructures. I focus in particular on the circulation of capital (and value) through the production and use of built environments, since this is one very important aspect of what urbanization is about. I think it useful to look upon the geographical landscape of capitalism as the expression of flows of capital. These flows can often switch directions (sectorally and geographically), and can be implicated in the formation and resolution of various crises. Phenomena like post-war suburbanization, deindustrialization or the contemporary trend to inner city renewal (London's Docklands or Baltimore's inner harbor) can usefully be looked at in this way. The spatial dimension is, however, rather weakly developed in this chapter and so the next two focus on the theories of land rent and residential differentiation in order to understand how the spatial organization of a city is produced by the intersection of capital flows into land development, on the one hand, and the requirements on the other of the reproduction of labor power (of different skills and qualities) and class relations.

The issue of localized labor markets leads into consideration of how urban regions can acquire unstable, often fuzzy but nevertheless potent "structured coherence" in their political and economic organization (chapter 5). This forms a basis for the creation of territorially-based class alliances which turn the urban region into a quasi-competitive unit within a geographical division of labor. Examining the political strategies of inter-urban competition gives some real insights into the role of cities in the creation of an uneven geography of capitalist development. We can, thereby, more clearly see how the historical dynamic of capitalism is expressed in geographical terms.

In chapter 6, I reflect on the ways in which money, time and space are linked together and given special significance under conditions where the circulation of capital is dominant in social life. I wish to show that what appear to be separate categories with which we typically describe the world are fundamentally interrelated — that money cannot be understood independently of time or space and that the latter take on special meanings in a monetized economy. This essay may appear at first to be rather different from those that precede it. Yet despite stylistic difference and the appeal to more literary forms of evidence, I am here merely trying to make explicit themes of the integration of money, time, space and capital accumulation and class struggle already broached in earlier essays. This allows me to build a firmer basis upon which to construct a theory of the historical geography of capitalism in general and the role of the urban process under capitalism in particular.

In chapter 7, I try to use the insights of theory to understand a particular instance of urban transformation. I examine the construction of the Basilica of Sacré Coeur in Paris and how it was caught up in the class struggles that arose out of the peculiar problems of capital accumulation in Second Empire Paris (examined at length in chapter 3 of *Consciousness and the Urban Experience*). The basilica can readily be seen as a product and a symbol of class struggle; and indeed it remained so mired in controversy for many years that its completion was seriously threatened. In chapter 8, I speculate further on why the urban experience leads us to see the urban process and society in general in such contradictory ways and what the social and political implications might be of so doing. The last essay is on flexible accumulation, urbanization, and post-modernism. Here I seek to show how a major shift in the political economy of capitalism, particularly since the slump of 1973, has been associated with rapid transformations of urban processes, particularly in the United States, and brought into being a quite different set of cultural and political symbols to represent what capitalist urbanization is about. I also here seek to understand why post-modern style and rhetoric (be it in architecture, philosophy, or whatever) have become so popular and commonplace. The explanation lies, I suggest, in alterations in daily life generated by the shift in the pattern of accumulation away from the relatively stable Keynesian and Fordist configuration of the post-war period to a much more "flexible" system promoted by heightened competition, entrepreneurialism and neo-conservativism.

Though theoretically inclined, most of the essays presented here contain sufficient illustrative material to indicate how and when the way of seeing proposed might reasonably be deployed. While helpful as corroborative evidence, such materials scarcely constitute proof sufficient to convince sceptics of the veracity of the theoretical propositions here advanced. What constitutes proof of a meta-theory like that of Marx is not a simple matter. A few comments on that problem may be helpful. Proof cannot be reduced (as many critics of Marxian meta-theory appear to propose) to a simple test procedure against a supposedly pristine set of factual data. The imposition of positivist standards of proof upon Marxian theory means accepting positivism not Marxism as a working base. From the Marxian standpoint, proof is constituted in part out of the confidence that arises from the mode of concept formation and in part through explanatory power. The latter implies the capacity to interpret historical geography in coherent and compelling ways. It was with such an end in view that I undertook the long study of Second Empire Paris in *Consciousness and the Urban Experience*. The broader problem, however, is to bring the theory into contact with experience (political and practical) in a diversity of ways and circumstances. Confidence in the power of theory can that way be built up incrementally.

I find the idea that there is something called "experience" unmediated by imagination as unacceptable as the equally misguided view that facts and data exist independently of theory. We typically approach the world with some well-honed conceptual apparatus – the capital equipment of our intellect – and interpret events and experiences broadly in those terms. Yet there are moments, events, people, and experiences which impinge upon imagination in unexpected ways, that jolt and jar received ways of thinking and doing, that demand some extra imaginative or theoretical leap to give them meaning. Experience comes in many guises. Casual street interactions and observations, the reading of the local press and all the pamphlets that get thrust into one's hands at street corners, local political action and attempts at more national and international political collaboration all hang together in a muddle of often conflicting impressions. And then there is the literature – vast, rambling, diverse, sometimes rhetorical and polemical (and no less interesting for that) and at other times making claims to dry-as-dust science. The analyst has to sample all of that, wrestle with the ideas and information advanced, sometimes fight in intellectual combat with those who advance them. The literature is not purely academic either. Novels, plays, poems, songs, paintings, graffiti, photographs, architectural drawings and plans . . . all of these give clues, contain potential surprises. My thinking on the urban process has been as much influenced by Dickens, Zola, Balzac, Gissing, Dreiser, Pynchon, and a host of others as it has been by urban historians.

I find myself most deeply drawn to those works – of which I regard Engels' *Condition of the Working Class in England in 1844* as an outstanding example – that function both as literature and social theory, as history and contemporary commentary. It was, I suspect, out of that admiration that I began with detailed studies of the Baltimore housing market and later on of the transformation of Paris after 1848 and the production of the Commune of 1871. Both offered opportunities to extract new insights with which to challenge theory. Yet those studies depended crucially upon the prior formulation of some kind of theoretical and conceptual frame upon which the historical and geographical reconstructions could be mounted. Engels provided the frame for the Baltimore housing studies, and *The Limits to Capital* gave me a basis to investigate the transformation of Paris in Haussmann's time.

Historical and geographical studies form one proving ground on which to test the power of Marxian meta-theory. Contemporary political relevance provides another, arguably more important given the Marxist commitment to human emancipation through political and economic change. The considerable frustration experienced over the last decade with respect to the feasibility of the Marxist project and the powers of Marxian meta-theory to inspire and guide it have resulted in a marked withdrawal from Marxist commitments and burgeoning scepticism within the Marxist camp as to the political relevance of theory construction. I think it important to distinguish between the good and bad reasons for that scepticism. Among the bad reasons I would cite trends in fashion, the rather too easy cave-in to right wing pressures (I am not talking of Chile but of social democracies where neo-conservativism has come to life and flexed its muscle in government, the media, and education), a certain 'ennuie' with Marxian theory that set in after the socialist millennium failed to materialize in the five years after the high wave of revolt in 1968, and the usual struggles within the intelligentsia for power and influence by setting new trends and denigrating the old.

Consideration of the good reasons suggests a strong case for more rather than less attention to theory construction. The vast surge of Marxist work from the mid-1960s on, first had to recuperate a tradition of thinking that had been emasculated by fascism and the Cold War in the West and Stalinism in the East and to invent for itself new traditions appropriate to contemporary conditions. In the course of this work it became apparent that there were many empty rooms in the house of Marxian theory and that a lot of thought had to be given as to how best they might be furnished. Urban analysts, for example, had to take up questions of the significance of spatial organization, the powers of the local state apparatus, urban social movements, problems of collective consumption in urban settings, and the like, and somehow integrate them into the corpus of Marxian theorizing. This was no easy task and the fact that it has taken so long to bring us close to any kind of consenus as to how this might be done continues to be politically damaging.

No one, probably, would argue that action has to wait upon improved theory, but in retrospect I think it evident that theory was not robust enough, even when handled skillfully, to provide anything other than a rudimentary guide to action in the tumultuous years of the late 1960s. The subsequent failure of working class movements to respond radically to the slump of 1973–75, the rising tide of deindustrialization, the switch away from Fordism-Keynesian to what I call more "flexible" modes of accumulation (see chapter 9), the rise of neo-conservativism, and the resurgence of an "entrepreneurial culture" in the 1980s, created difficulties for theoretical concepts that had broadly been shaped in response to the conditions of the long post-war boom. Many of the presuppositions of prevailing theory had to be challenged – for example, the implied teleology in the path from competitive through monopoly to state monopoly capitalism with socialism as its inevitable next step. While the recent period has been rather dismal with respect to political action (with working class movements everywhere on the defensive and in any case confused over issues of occupation, gender, race, ethnicity and localism), I think it has been salutary from the standpoint of theory building, precisely because we have been forced to evaluate and reformulate our ways of thinking in the light of two decades of experience.

The reader will find passages of commentary on the political relevance of theory in various of the essays that follow (particularly chapter 9). But I would want to emphasize that the new-found strength of Rainbow-Coalition politics in the United States, with its rediscovery of the rhetoric of class and its concern to establish a broad coalition of forces across many of the divides that have splintered the working class movement in the past, is a most encouraging signal. But the difficulties of building bridges from place to place and from group to group ought not to be minimized. It is in this context that I hope the analysis of the confusions of political practice and consciousness that arise out of the urban experience might be helpful. I certainly think the evidence is strong that the time has never been more appropriate for the application of Marx's conceptual apparatus to understanding processes of capitalists development and transformation. I also believe that the claim of Marxian theory to provide the surest guide to the construction of radical theory and radicalizing practices still stands. The task within the Marxian camp is, in short, to deepen and sharpen theory so that it can reach into realms that have hitherto remained opaque and define new social practices that can integrate into an emancipatory socialist project. The political proving ground may be the most difficult of all terrains to work upon. But, in the final analysis, it is the only one that counts.

1

The Urbanization of Capital

The language of any question has the awkward habit of containing the elements of its own response. For this reason I have always attached particular importance to Marx's comment that "frequently the only possible answer is a critique of the question and the only possible solution is to negate the question" (*Grundrisse*, 127). The eternal skepticism of Marxian scientific endeavor resides precisely in that methodological prescription.

The question I began with, more than a decade ago now, was roughly this: can we derive a theoretical and historical understanding of the urban process under capitalism out of a study of the supposed laws of motion of a capitalist mode of production? I quickly became convinced that the answer was yes, provided those laws could be specified more rigorously in terms of temporal and spatial dynamics. But was this the right question? A decade of thinking and writing on the subject points to a reformulation. I now ask, how does capital become urbanized, and what are the consequences of that urbanization? The answer to that question has, I submit, profound implications for understanding the future of capitalism as well as the prospects for transition to some alternative mode of production.

But let me begin with some remarks on how we might conceptualize urbanization in the context of a predominantly capitalist mode of production.

I. THE PRODUCTION OF URBANIZATION UNDER A CAPITALIST MODE OF PRODUCTION

The use values necessary to the reproduction of social life under capitalism are basically produced as commodities within a circulation process of capital that has the augmentation of exchange values as its primary goal. The standard form of this circulation process can be symbolized as follows:

$$M \to C \begin{cases} LP \\ MP \end{cases} \ldots P \ldots C' \to M + \triangle m \to \text{etc.}$$

where M stands for money; C and C' for commodities; MP for all kinds of means of production, including machinery, energy inputs, raw materials, and partially finished products; LP for labor power; P for production; and $\triangle\, m$ for profit. This was the system that Marx scrutinized so thoroughly in order to establish its inherent laws of motion. He showed, among other things, that capitalism had to be both expansionary and technologically dynamic; that profit depended on the exploitation of living labor power in production; and that this defined the central class relation and line of class struggle between buyers (capitalists) and sellers (workers) of labor power as a commodity. He also showed that the necessary expansion ("accumulation for accumulation's sake, production for production's sake") often conflicted with the impulsion to revolutionize the productive forces under such a system of class relations. The system is therefore unstable, degenerating into periodic crises of overaccumulation, a condition in which surpluses of capital and labor power exist unused side by side. Overaccumulation leads to devaluation and destruction of both capital and labor power unless some way can be found profitably to absorb them (cf. Harvey 1982).

The study of urbanization under such a mode of production requires much closer attention to spatial and temporal dynamics than Marx was prepared to give (though, Marx was quite aware of these aspects of the process). We can begin on the path toward some kind of integration by scrutinizing the different moments of money, commodities, labor power (and its reproduction), and production within the circulation of capital and the transitions (metamorphoses, Marx called them) between one moment and the other. We immediately see that each moment has a different capacity for geographical mobility and that the transitions inevitably entail some kind of spatial movement.

Let us look more closely at the point of commodity exchange ($M \rightarrow C$ and $C' \rightarrow M + \triangle\, m$). The intervention of money in exchange, Marx comments, permits the separation of purchases and sales in space and time. But how much separation? The analysis of the circulation of capital cannot really proceed without some kind of answer to that question. The spatial and temporal horizons of exchange are evidently socially determined. Investments in new systems of transport and communications reduce spatial barriers and roll back the possible geographical boundaries of exchange relations. Revolutions in the credit system relax and roll back temporal constraints, making long-term investments both possible and compatible with other production systems of radically different turnover times (between, for example, the production of power stations, corn, and short-order meals). Nevertheless, the buying and selling of commodities (including the purchase of machinery and other intermediate goods) entails the loss of time and money in overcoming spatial separation. This means that commodity markets become articulated into distinctive geographical trading patterns in which the efficiency of coordinations in space and time is a vital consideration.

The details of this are horrendously complex. Though the movement of commodities is constrained by the cost and time of transportation, credit money now moves as fast and with as few spatial constraints as information. Furthermore, each commodity has a different potentiality for movement (given its weight, perishability, and value), while time and cost introduce two dimensions often very different from physical distance. The social and geographical division of labor is in part an adaptation to these possibilities as well as an outcome of the general sociotechnical conditions prevailing in production. But the general point remains: when looked at from the standpoint of exchange, the circulation of capital is a geographical movement in time. I shall later seek to show that the geographical structures of commodity markets are more than mere reflections of capital circulation and function as real determinants of capitalism's dynamic.

The buying and selling of labor power deserves special scrutiny. Unlike other commodities, labor power has to go home every night and reproduce itself before coming back to work the next morning. The limit on the working day implies some sort of limit on daily travel time. Daily labor markets are therefore confined within a given commuting range. The geographical boundaries are flexible; they depend on the length of the working day within the workplace, the time and cost of commuting (given the modes and techniques of mass movement), and the social conditions considered acceptable for the reproduction of labor power (usually a cultural achievement of class struggle). A prima facie case exists, therefore, for considering the urban process in terms of the form and functioning of geographically integrated labor markets within which daily substitutions of labor power against job opportunities are in principle possible. The history of the urbanization of capital is at least in part a history of its evolving labor market geography.

The labor market is perpetually in the course of modification. Vast capital investments are directed to achieve relatively minor increases in the range of daily commuting possibilities. In-migration and population growth augment the supply of labor power but also entail considerable and sometimes vast capital investments for housing, food, and care. Investment in skills is a long-drawn-out process and also often absorbs large quantities of resources. The aspirations and demands of the laborers, particularly when enhanced by labor scarcity or organized class struggle, affect the quantities and qualities of labor supply in very particular ways, thus affecting the prospects for both accumulation and sociotechnical change in production. The result is considerable differentiation between geographically distinct labor markets. That, too, is what much of capitalist urbanization reflects.

Consider, now, the moment of production. With the singular but important exception of transport and communications, labor processes are pinned down to a particular place for the length of the working period (the time taken to produce the finished commodity). But even the short-order cook who has a very short working period may make use of fixed capital equipment that has an economic lifetime of several years. And some of that fixed capital cannot be moved without being destroyed. Production cannot change location in the middle of a working period without destroying some of the capital engaged, while the relative immobility and economic lifetime of the fixed capital used also severely constrain geographical mobility. The ability to move also depends, however, upon the sociotechnical conditions of production. The general Marxist approach is to see the evolution of those sociotechnical conditions of production as an outcome of intercapitalist competition and class struggle supplemented by spillover needs and effects from one sector of industry to another. But here I shall have to introduce a fundamental modification of the general Marxian account. I insist that intercapitalist competition and class struggle spark spatial competition for command of favorable locations and that the choice of sociotechnical mix is in part a response to the particularities of geographical situation. Viewing things this way helps us get a better handle on relations between the social and spatial divisions of labor in society.

We see immediately, for example, that the sociotechnical forms of the labor process are not independent of the geographical possibilities within structured labor and commodity markets and vice versa. The splitting of production into many specializations permits much greater sensitivity to geographical variation, thus allowing capitalists to exploit the differentials and accumulate capital faster than before. Detail functions can also be split up over space under the planned control of the corporation. This applies not only to the separation of design, planning, production, and marketing functions but also to the elements of a complex production system which can be produced in many different locations throughout the world before assembly into the final product. Such geographical separations have major impacts upon trading patterns and become feasible only to the degree that integrated production schedules can be organized efficiently over space. The general result is an evident tension between the virtues of geographical concentration to minimize spatial separation (the assembly of detail functions within the factory or the agglomeration of many firms within one urban center) and geographical dispersal, which has the virtue of providing opportunities for further accumulation by exploiting particular geographical advantages (natural or created). How that tension is resolved has important implications for the shape and form of the urban system. But the latter, insofar as it is shaped to facilitate tight temporal coordinations of flows in space, affects the way in which the tension is played out. The benefits to be had from conjoining the social with the geographical division of labor can then be parlayed into accelerating accumulation.

Production is typically separated from consumption under capitalism by market exchange. This has enormous implications for urbanization and urban structure. Work spaces and times separate out from consumption spaces and times in ways unknown in an artisan or peasant culture. The moment of consumption, like that of production, stands to be further fragmented. Vacation, leisure, and entertainment places separate from spaces of daily reproduction, and even the latter fragment into the lunch counter near the office, the kitchen, the neighborhood drugstore or bar. The spatial division of consumption is as important to the urban process as is the spatial division of labor — the qualities of New York, Paris, and Rome as well as the internal organization of these and other cities could not be understood without consideration of such phenomena. This is, however, a theme that remains underexplored in Marxian theory, in part because of the tendency to focus exclusively on production because it is the hegemonic moment in the circulation of capital.

Consumption also has to be looked at from another standpoint. The circulation of capital when viewed in aggregate presupposes the continuous expansion of effective demand in order to realize in the marketplace the value created through production. Where, then, does the effective demand come from? (cf. Harvey 1982, chap. 3). There are three broad sources: workers purchase wage goods (depending upon their achieved standard of living), the bourgeoisie purchases necessities and luxuries, and capitalists purchase investment goods (machinery and plant) and intermediate products. Each one of these markets has its own particular qualities and geographical sensitivities. The spatial division of labor puts a premium on continuous flow so that tight temporal and spatial coordinations and cost-minimization are mandatory pressures. Final consumption, particularly of luxuries for the bourgeoisie, is much less sensitive on these scores, though in the case of the wage laborers much depends upon customary living standards (the real wage) and the cost matrix within which the social reproduction of labor power takes place. However, we must also bear in mind that final consumption entails the use of a certain amount of fixed capital equipment. To the degree that this is fixed and of long life (housing, for example), so the "mode of consumption" tends to become fixed quantitatively, qualitatively, and geographically. The spatial division of consumption entails relatively permanent structurations of social and physical spaces both within and between urban centers.

Consider, finally, the moment of money itself. Money takes many forms, from the tangible commodity gold to the vague imprecision of an open line of credit. Money also has the peculiar quality of concentrating in time and space a form of universal power that is an expression of the world market in historical time. Money represents the greatest concentration of social power in the midst of the greatest possible dispersal. It can be used to overcome the geographical limitations of commodity and labor markets and fashion ever-greater dispersal of the spatial division of labor and of consumption. It can also transcend all other limits of geographical concentration and allow the assembly of massive social power in a few hands in a few places. It can be deployed over long time-horizons (as state debt, stocks and shares, mortgages, and so forth) or pulled together at particular moments for particular purposes. As a higher form of social power, it can dominate not only ownership of other means of production but also space and time as sources of social power (see *Consciousness and the Urban Experience,* chap. 1). The holding and command of money confers tremendous social power. But under capitalism that power is contingent upon the continuous use of money as capital.

Money, finance, and credit form a hierarchically organized central nervous system regulating and controlling the circulation of capital as a whole and expressing a class interest, albeit through private action (see Harvey 1982, chaps. 9 and 10). Financial markets separate out from commodity and labor markets and acquire a certain autonomy vis-à-vis production. Urban centers can then become centers of coordination, decision-making, and control, usually within a hierarchically organized geographical structure.

Let me summarize. An inspection of the different moments and transitions within the circulation of capital indicates a geographical grounding of that process through the patterning of labor and commodity markets, of the spatial division of production and consumption (under sociotechnical conditions that are in part an adaptation to geographical variations), and of hierarchically organized systems of financial coordination. Capital flow presupposes tight temporal and spatial coordinations in the midst of increasing separation and fragmentation. It is impossible to imagine such a material process without the production of some kind of urbanization as a "rational landscape" within which the accumulation of capital can proceed. Capital accumulation and the production of urbanization go hand in hand.

This perspective deserves modification on two counts. Profit depends upon realizing the surplus value created in production within a certain time. The turnover time of capital (the time taken to get back the initial outlay plus a profit) is a very important magnitude – hence derives the old adage "time is money." Competition produces strong pressures to accelerate turnover time. That same pressure has a spatial manifestation. Since movement across space takes time and money, competition forces capitalism toward the elimination of spatial barriers and "the annihilation of space by time". Building a capacity for increased efficiency of coordination in space and time is one of the hallmarks of capitalist urbanization. Considerations derived from a study of the circulation of capital dictate, then, that the urban matrix and the "rational landscape" for accumulation be subject to continuous transformation. In this sense also, capital accumulation, technological innovation and capitalist urbanization have to go together.

II. CITIES, SURPLUSES, AND THE URBAN ORIGINS OF CAPITALISM

The connection between city formation and the production, appropriation, and concentration of an economic surplus has long been noted (see Harvey 1973, 216–26). The circulation of capital also presupposes the prior existence of surpluses of both capital and labor power. But closer inspection of its dynamic shows that capital circulation, once set in motion, produces capital surpluses (in the form of profit) coupled with relative labor surpluses produced through labor-saving revolutions in the sociotechnical conditions of production. Much of the history of capitalism can be written around this theme of the production and absorption of capital and labor surpluses. Strong phases of balanced and seemingly self-sustained growth occur when capitalism produces exactly those surpluses it needs in order to continue on its expansionary path. But the tendency toward overaccumulation poses the problem of how to absorb or dispose of the surpluses without the devaluation or destruction of both capital and labor power. This tension between the need to produce and to absorb surpluses of both capital and labor power lies at the root of capitalism's dynamic. It also provides a powerful link to the history of capitalist urbanization. I shall, in what follows, make that link the pivot of much of my analysis.

In the early stages of capitalism, the surpluses were largely produced by processes external to the direct circulation of capital. The violent expropriation of the means of production through primitive accumulation or more subtle maneuvers of appropriation put capital surpluses in the hands of the few while the many were forced to become wage laborers in order to live. Capital exists potentially in many forms, however, so it was the various moves of appropriation of money, goods, productive assets (land, built environments, means of communication, and so forth), and rights to labor power and the conversion of all of these into commodities with exchange value that really counted. The appropriation, mobilization, and geographical concentration of these surpluses of capital and labor power in commodity form was a vital moment in capitalism's history in which urbanization played a key role (cf. Braudel 1984). The urban concentration of wealth by merchants (looting the world of both money and commodities through unfairly or badly structured exchange); the transformation of landed property into a commodity for the production of urban-based wealth through direct monetization or subversion by usurers; and the direct extraction of surpluses from the countryside through money rents, state taxation, and other mechanisms of redistribution (such as that organized through the church) were some of the means whereby surplus capital was mobilized and geographically concentrated in a few hands. The use of these surpluses to build physical infrastructures, communication systems, and market centers formed a potential basis for capital circulation at the same time as the assembly of commodity use values (including wage laborers) in the urban centers created the prior conditions under which the circulation of capital could be more easily launched.

Urbanization, together with money rent, usurers' interest, merchants' profit, and state taxation, had to appear on the historical stage before the standard form of circulation of capital through production could begin (cf. *Capital* 1:165). The historical sequence was exactly the reverse, therefore, of the analytical and logical sequence we would now use to analyze the relations of production and distribution and of long-term investment in physical and social infrastructures in their urban context. A built environment potentially supportive of capitalist production, consumption, and exchange had to be created before capitalism won direct control over immediate production and consumption. Social infrastructures for the control of civil society, most particularly with respect to labor markets, also had to be put in place before capital accumulation through production could freely develop. The political power and authority of the state had to be deployed in ways favorable to primitive accumulation and the mobilization of capital and labor surpluses before the material base existed for capitalist domination of the state or even for the formation of some urban-based class alliance in which capitalists had an important role. The rise of urban centers with a ruling class acquisitive of wealth and specie, mercantilist in philosophy, and possessed of superior authority and military power was, Braudel (1984) shows, a crucial moment in the rise of capitalism. The maturation of capitalism rested on a process of gradual and sometimes revolutionary role reversal in which political processes; class alliances; the categories of rent, interest, merchants' profit, and taxation, and the assets of physical and social infrastructures were converted from interdependent though interlinked preconditions and determinants of political-economic processes into pure servants of capital accumulation. The role of the urban process, as well as the mechanisms of its development, shifted dramatically with this role reversal.

Primitive accumulation and other processes of appropriation do not guarantee, however, that the surpluses can be assembled in time and space in exactly the right proportions for strong capital accumulation to proceed. In eighteenth-century Britain, for example, the strong capital surpluses more than matched the surpluses of labor power. Wages rose, and much of the surplus was absorbed in consumption projects. In contrast, much of contemporary Africa, Asia, and Latin America is faced with a situation in which immense quantities of labor power have to be dispossessed to release very little capital, creating massive and chronic surpluses of labor power in a context of serious capital shortage. Situations can arise and even persist, therefore, in which surpluses of one sort cannot be absorbed because surpluses of another sort are not present in the requisite quantities and qualities. Under contemporary conditions, this means that either capital or labor power is devalued, but not both. To the degree that the dominant power relations favor capital and that the qualities of the latter can quickly adapt to shortages of labor power through technological innovation, so the likely persistent (as opposed to occasional) condition will be that of capital shortage and labor power surpluses. This is, for example, the hallmark of much of contemporary Third World urbanization.

The urban assembly of such surpluses does not guarantee, however, that they will be used capitalistically. We here encounter a historical problem of considerable political, social, and economic complexity. The most successful of the urban centers from the standpoint of assembling the surpluses often used their political power in ways inimical to the direct flowering of capital accumulation through production. The latter, after all, meant a major transformation of class power and structure and cutting loose any controls over technological innovations that might threaten, as they nearly always do, the value of any existing base of assets. In addition, the purpose of appropriation of surpluses was the building of wealth as a basis for conspicuous consumption, and it was not immediately apparent to those who held that wealth that the best way to preserve it was to use it as capital. The more powerful urban-based class alliances often used their class and monopolistic power to organize against the capitalism they helped spawn.

Unfortunately for the city states, the very methods employed in the assembly of much surpluses tended in the end to undermine their powers of monopolistic control over money, space, and commodity flow. Trade and commerce meant monetization, and that always has a dissolving effect upon the coherence of community (*Grundrisse*, 224–25; *Consciousness and the Urban Experience*, chap. 1). Anyone who holds money is perpetually tempted to use it for personal gain outside of the controlling powers of some urban-based class alliance. Trade also entailed the formation of other trading centers that could ultimately become rivals. And to the degree that new products and military technology were important facets of a city's power, so innovation became a vital force that no urban-based class alliance could afford to stifle if it was to prosper and survive. Competition between urban centers became a major check on internal monopoly controls and tended to create conditions of instability out of which the circulation of capital through production could more easily gain a foothold.

The separation of laborers from control over their means of production (through physical or legalized violence in some instances and out of attraction to the opportunities of urban life in others) and their conversion into wage laborers forms the other half of the conditions necessary to the rise of capital as a hegemonic mode of production and circulation. But again, there was no guarantee that displaced laborers would become wage laborers. The processes of displacement and socialization into the proletariat were anything but idyllic (Pollard 1965). The habituation of the worker to wage labor, the inculcation of a work discipline and all that went with it, and the formation of freely functioning labor markets were not, and still are not, easy matters. The workers themselves often sought and acquired corporatist powers that checked the liberty of labor and in so doing learned to support mercantilist and monopolistic practices on the part of their rulers. The urban-based guilds and the corporatist organization of labor also formed a powerful barrier to free capital accumulation (this remained a serious problem in France, for example, throughout the whole of the nineteenth century as the case of Second-Empire Paris clearly demonstrates – see *Consciousness and the Urban Experience,* chap. 3). The labor process tended to stagnate into monopolistic mosaics of craft control at the same time as labor markets froze into rigid configurations.

But again, there were processes at work that undermined guild, artisan, and craft controls. Immigration of displaced rural labor into urban centers meant that the pressure of labor surpluses was never absent. Competition between urban centers for new products and new technologies meant pressure (sometimes organized by the ruling class and therefore a major point of class struggle) to open up the labor process to new possibilities. And the wage laborers themselves, particularly if they aspired, as many did, to become small masters and entrepreneurs, could often undermine the corporatist logic. The original qualities of labor power and labor's powers of organization in the different industries nevertheless had deep impacts upon the prospects for using surplus wealth as capital in production. Hardly surprisingly, the pace of accumulation and technological innovation varied greatly from one urban center to another. Without the force of interurban competition, the pace of capitalist penetration into production would certainly have been much slower and may even have been blocked altogether.

For these sorts of reasons it proved easier for capitalist industrialization to emerge in entirely new urban centers in which the politics of monopoly control and the tactics of mercantilism were less firmly entrenched. In some instances the capitalist penetration of agriculture, coupled with technological innovation in the countryside, proved the cutting edge of capitalist development. The circumstances that gave free rein to the circulation and accumulation of capital through production, that allowed labor markets to function freely and new technologies and forms of labor organization to be deployed without restraint, were evidently diverse even if rather restricted (Merrington 1975; Holton 1984). The urban centers had, nevertheless, crucial advantages in relation to accumulation. The vast assembly of assets in the built environment, though oriented primarily to trade, consumption, and political-military dominance, could be converted almost costlessly into assets for capital accumulation – the consumption fund could be transformed into fixed capital in the built environment simply by changing patterns of use. The transport and communications systems built to facilitate appropriation, trade, consumption, and military control could likewise be used by capitalist producers. Countries like Britain and France in the eighteenth century that had vast assets of this sort were, therefore, in a far better situation for capitalist development than many contemporary Third World countries whose asset base is extremely limited. Furthermore, the sociopolitical institutions, private property rights, and systems of command of money (banking and treasuries) could also be mobilized behind the geopolitics of capital accumulation as command centers for the circulation of capital. The breakthrough into a predominantly capitalist mode of production and circulation was not, therefore, a purely urban or a purely rural event. But without the urban accumulation of surpluses of both capital and labor power, one of the crucial necessary conditions for the rise of capitalism would not have been fulfilled.

The transition to a capitalist mode of production was signaled by a shift from the production of capital and labor surpluses by processes external to the circulation of capital to an internalization of surplus production within the circulation of capital itself. That shift was also signaled, I have argued, by a role reversal in which rent, interest, merchants' profit, state powers and functions, and the production of built environments became servants of capital accumulation and subservient to its dominant logic.

Consider, for example, the manner of production and use of the physical and social landscape necessary to capital accumulation. The story of how that landscape is produced and used is central to my theorization of the urban process. I focus upon it because it is the product of a process – or a set of processes, for we here confront matters of great intricacy and complexity – that gives definite shape and form to a capitalist urbanization process that would otherwise appear far more flexible and fluid than is in fact the case. The transition from a historical condition in which that landscape is produced by forces outside the logic of accumulation to one in which it is integrated within that logic is signaled when the circulation of capital produces the necessary surpluses and the sufficient conditions for the shaping of physical and social space within its confines. And that occurs when overaccumulation begins to grab hold of immediate production and consumption – when, in short, crises become clear manifestations of the internal contradictions of capitalism rather than being reasonably attributable to external circumstances of natural calamity (such as harvest failures) or social breakdown (wars of aggrandizement or internal civil and political strife). Though hints of that occurred before, 1848 was perhaps the first indisputable and unambiguous manifestation of that kind of crisis within the capitalist world.

The production of the physical and social landscape of capitalism was thereafter increasingly caught up in the search for solutions to the over-accumulation problem through the absorption of capital and labor surpluses by some mix of temporal and geographical displacement of surplus capital into the production of physical and social infrastructures (the "secondary" and "tertiary" circuits depicted in fig. 3). I have dwelt at length in *The Urbanization of Capital*: see also Harvey 1982, 1985) on the potentialities and limitations of that process. Suffice it to remark that the problems of overaccumulation and devaluation are thereby imparted to the physical and social landscape so that its whole historical evolution dances to their tune. For that to happen, however, a whole set of preconditions has to be realized, including, of course, that most essential precondition of all, the command of immediate production and consumption by the industrial capitalist. It is then, to that issue and its requisite form of urbanization that we now turn.

III. THE CAPITALIST PRODUCTION OF SURPLUSES AND THE INDUSTRIAL FORM OF URBANIZATION

The rise of the industrial city signaled the penetration of capital circulation into the heart of immediate production and consumption. The shift from the appropriation of surpluses through trade, monopoly, and military control to the production of surpluses through command over labor processes in production was slowly wrought. Not all sectors were immediately captured, of course (agriculture remained notoriously recalcitrant, finally succumbing in the advanced capitalist countries only after World War II and then often unevenly). But for those sectors subsumed, there was a dramatic transformation in the organization of the sociotechnical conditions of production and in the functioning of labor and commodity markets.

This meant that the whole basis of urbanization had to change. The preindustrial city had to be disciplined, weaned away as it were from its mercantilist proclivities, its monopolistic practices, and its assertion of the primacy of place over a capitalist organization of space in which relative rather than absolute locations had to dominate. The incorporation of the city state within the broader configurations of nation states – a tension that Braudel (1984) makes much of – was one important step in the direction that allowed the freer functioning of labor, commodity, and credit markets as well as the freer flow of capital and labor power between sectors and regions. Industrial capitalists, seeking out new resource bases and new sociotechnical conditions of production within entirely new urban areas outside the monopoly controls so prevalent in preexisting urban centers, could do so only in a context where a relatively strong nation state had secured the political and institutional basis for private property and that sort of control over the means of production which allowed the exploitation of labor power. Where industrial capitalism was grafted on to older structures (as in Paris and London), it assumed qualities quite different from those of the burgeoning capitalist industrialism of a Manchester or a Birmingham. There are, indeed, those who attribute the relative stagnation of capitalism in France to the inability to break with preexisting patterns of urbanization and the political power of prevailing urban-based class alliances (St. Etienne was the only new major city opened up in the nineteenth century). The story in Britain, Germany, and the United States was very different – new industrial centers opened up all over the place under the watchful institutional and legal eye of strong state power.

The industrial city was a new centerpiece of accumulation. The production of surpluses through the direct exploitation of living labor in production was its trademark. This meant the geographical concentration of labor power and productive force (epitomized in the factory system) and open access to the world market, which, in turn, meant the consolidation of universal money and credit. It meant, in short, the firm implantation of all those features of geographical and temporal organization of the circulation of capital that I began by describing. The geographical patterning of labor and commodity markets, of spatial and social divisions of production and consumption, and of differentiated sociotechnical mixes within the labor process became much more pronounced within the urban landscape. Intercapitalist competition and class struggle pushed the whole dynamic of urbanization toward the production of rational physical and social landscapes for capital accumulation. The search for profitable trade-offs between command over and creation of advantageous locations, coupled with adaptations in the sociotechnical conditions of production, became a much more visible moving force within the urban process.

The capacity of any urban-based class alliance to wield monopoly control, either internally or on the world stage, diminished. This is not to say that certain of the more important industrial centers – like Manchester in the nineteenth century and Detroit in the twentieth – did not assemble sufficient power to mimic for a while the behavior of urban-based class alliances in preceding eras. But such delusions of geopolitical grandeur soon foundered on the dynamics of growth and geographical expansion, technological change and product innovation, class struggle, international competition within a shifting frame of relative space shaped by revolutions in transport and communications, and the growing disruptions of crises of overaccumulation. Although the industrial city was a centerpiece of accumulation and surplus production, it has to be seen as a distinctive place within the spaces of the international division of labor, a mere element within a more and more generalized capitalist system of uneven geographical development.

But urban organization was vital to the working out of such a process. Though individual cities (like individual firms) exercised less and less control over aggregate processes and outcomes, their individual performance in the context of interurban competition set the tone, pace, and direction of historical-geographical development. The industrial city became, in short, a concrete means toward the definition of abstract labor on the world market (see Harvey 1982, 422–26). Value on the world market then became the standard against which every industrial center's performance was judged. The conception of the industrial city as a competitive unit within the uneven geographical development of global capitalism made more and more sense under such conditions.

Denied the grandeur of geopolitical posturing (a role increasingly reserved for nation states or capital cities like Paris), the tasks of urban politics within the industrial city had to shift toward more mundane concerns. The problems of organization and control, of management of physical and social infrastructures, were radically different from anything that had gone before, while the context of class alliance formation changed because class structures were redefined. Class warfare between capital and labor and the drive to reproduce that basic class relation of domination became the pivot of urban politics. The formation of physical and social infrastructures adequate to support the reproduction of both capital and labor power while serving as efficient frameworks for the organization of production, consumption, and exchange surged to the forefront of political and managerial concerns. Such problems had to be approached with an eye to efficiency and economy because that was the way to assure growth, accumulation, innovation, and efficiency in interurban competition. Public investments also had to be organized on an increasing scale and on a more and more long-term basis and in such a way as to compensate for individual capitalists' underproducing collective infrastructures.

It was precisely around such themes that Joseph Chamberlain built such a powerful class alliance in Birmingham in the 1860s, comprising representatives of industry, commerce, and the professions, with a great deal of solid working-class support. The emergence of a distinctive civic tradition in Leeds, Manchester, and Birmingham during the nineteenth century – a process ultimately paralleled in many a new industrial city – was part of a search to define a new urban politics appropriate to new circumstances. Older cities, like Haussmann's Paris (see *Consciousness and the Urban Experience*, chap. 3), had to acquire the same virtues of efficiently organized capitalist modernity by a far more tortuous route. The bases for class-alliance formation and confrontation were very different and the objectives equally so. But the common problems faced (from debt-financing infrastructure investments to finding ways to rationalize urban space as a whole) and the common techniques employed (engineering skills merging into rational urban planning) also induced a certain tactical convergence toward a distinctively capitalist kind of urban managerialism.

Industrial capitalism also wrought far-reaching transformations of all aspects of civil society. Traditional social relations of work were altered or destroyed and new social structures forged against the background of freely functioning labor markets and powerful currents of technological change. Integrating immigrants and absorbing the shocks of technological change posed key questions of socioeconomic policy and political management. The role of women changed in both labor markets as well as in the household, and the family had to adapt and reconstitute itself to the buying and selling of labor power as a way of life. At the same time, social reproduction processes had to incorporate mechanisms directed toward the production of labor supply with the right qualities and in the right quantities. Attention had to be paid to such questions at a time when the bonds of civil society threatened to break asunder under the strain of the alienations of class conflict, the anomie of individualistic labor markets, and the sheer rage at the new regimes of domination. It took real political talent and much subtle maneuvering to keep the urban pot from boiling over under the best of conditions, and the new bourgeoisie had to find new ways to keep the revolutionary turmoil under control. Bourgeois surveillance of the family and interventions in the cultural, political, and social milieu of the working classes began in earnest. Above all, the ruling-class alliance had to find ways to invent a new tradition of community that could counter or absorb the antagonisms of class. This it did in part by accepting responsibility for various facets of social reproduction of the working class (health, education, welfare, and even housing provision) and mobilizing sometimes brutal and sometimes subtle means of social cooptation and control – police, limited democratization, control of ideology via the churches or through the newly emerging organs of mass communication, and the manipulation of space as a form of social power. And the working class, as part of its own tactic of survival, also sought a new definition of community for itself. With its help, industrial capitalism in fact forged, with amazing rapidity, new traditions of urban community out of conditions of social disintegration and class conflict.

So strong did the popular attachments become that they formed a major barrier to further urban transformations within the short space of a generation.

But that sense of urban community, along with the "structured coherence" of the sociotechnical conditions of production and consumption and of labor supply in relation to industrial capitalism's needs, could never become a stable configuration. The dynamics of accumulation and overaccumulation, of technological change and product innovation, of shifting international competition in a rapidly changing structure of relative space (transformed through revolutions in transport and communications), kept even the best-managed and the most efficiently organized industrial city under a perpetual cloud of economic uncertainty. The mobilities of capital and labor power could not be controlled — this was, after all, the essence of free-market capitalism — nor could the context of wage or profit opportunities elsewhere. Each and every participant in or supporter of some urban-based class alliance faced the temptation of abandoning or undermining it for individual gain.

It was within this space of relative uncertainty and insecurity that a relatively autonomous urban politics made its mark. A charismatic leadership (sometimes collective and sometimes individual) could build its reputation on successful strategies for progress and survival in an uncertain and highly competitive world. Strategies could vary from ruthless creative destruction of anything that stood in the way of capitalist rationality, modernity, and progress to attempts to insulate against or even break out from under the coercive laws of competition through movements toward municipal socialism. But the latter could always be checked by two reserve powers. The discipline of competition and of "abstract labor" on the world market could not for long be held at bay without lapsing into an isolationism that could destroy much that had been achieved. Political experience taught the bourgeoisie another lesson that could be used to check the undue radicalism of any urban-based political movement: superior control over space provided a powerful weapon in class struggle. The Parisian revolutions of 1848 and 1871 were put down by a bourgeoisie that could mobilize its forces across space. Control over the telegraph and flows of information proved crucial in disrupting the rapidly spreading strike of 1877 in the industrial centers of the United States. Those who built a sense of community across space found themselves with a distinct advantage over those who mobilized the principle of community in place. Politically, this meant increasing ruling-class reliance upon national and, ultimately, international power sources and the gradual reduction of the sphere of relative autonomy of urban-based class alliances. It was no accident, therefore, that the nation state took on new roles and powers during that period of the late nineteenth century when diverse movements toward municipal socialism and machine politics with a working-class or immigrant orientation gathered momentum. The more the bourgeoisie lost control over urban centers, the more it asserted the dominant role of the nation state. It reinforced the authority of the spaces it could control over the places it could not. This was the political lesson that the bourgeoisie learned from the rise of the industrial city as a powerhouse of accumulation and a crucible of class struggle.

The industrial city was, therefore, an unstable configuration, both economically and politically, by virtue of the contradictory forces that produced it. On the one hand it sought and sometimes achieved a rational internal ordering to facilitate space-time coordinations in production, in flows of goods and people, and in necessary consumption coupled with the ordered construction of social spaces for the reproduction of labor power and well-managed patterns of social provision, built-environment production, and urban political management. From this standpoint it appeared as a relatively efficient corporation geared for competition on the stage of world capitalism. On the other hand, the industrial city was beset with the social anarchy generated by crises of overaccumulation, technological change, unemployment and de-skilling, immigration, and all manner of factional rivalries and divisions both within and between social classes. Interurban competition to some degree exacerbated the difficulties, since it increased the pressures toward product innovation and technological change. The industrial city had to consolidate its function as an innovation center if it was to survive. But innovation brought disruption and also lay at the root of the overaccumulation problem. The industrial city, as a powerhouse of accumulation and innovation, had to be the prime vehicle for the production of overaccumulation.

How were the prodigious surpluses of capital, and to a lesser extent of labor power, to be absorbed without devaluation and destruction? The periodic crises of industrial capitalism indicated no easy answer to that question. Surpluses could be and were in part absorbed by deepening productive forces (including those of labor power) within the industrial city through an increasing flow of investments into long-term physical and social infrastructures. They were also absorbed through geographical expansion. The search for a "spatial fix" for the overaccumulation problem spawned industrial development in far-off lands and the increasing linkage of urban industrialism into a system of urban places through movements of money, capital, commodities, productive capacity, and labor power. That way the threat of overaccumulation could be staved off, sometimes at the cost of primitive accumulation from precapitalist societies or forcible implantation of capitalist industrialization on societies (like the United States) that had sought a radically different path to social progress. The industrial city had to be, therefore, an imperialist city. And if it wanted to retain is hegemonic competitive position within a proliferating world market, it had to be prepared to conjoin political and military imperialism with an economic imperialism that rested on technological superiority and innovation coupled with superior organization of production, capital markets, and trade within the social and geographical divisions of labor. Joseph Chamberlain even made such themes central to the ideology of the class alliance (including many workers) that he kept together in Birmingham in the troubled depression years of the 1880s and 1890s.

But interurban competition, spiraling technological innovation and over-accumulation, and geographical expansionism constituted an unstable mix. Indeed, this was the kind of underlying pressure that produced national geopolitical rivalries and two world wars, the second of which inflicted enormous and uneven geographical destruction on urban assets — a neat but hideously violent resolution to capitalism's overaccumulation problem. Was there any way to avoid such a paralyzingly destructive resolution of capitalism's internal contradictions?

IV. THE ABSORPTION OF SURPLUSES: FROM FORDISM TO THE KEYNESIAN CITY

Underconsumption seemed to be, and in a sense was, the reverse side of the coin to overaccumulation. If that was so, then why could not the contra-dictions of capitalism be resolved by closer attention to the expansion of consumption, particularly on the part of the working masses of the population who were, in any case, not only economically needy but politically aggressive? The search for a solution of that sort underlay a shift in focus from production to distribution and consumption. Capitalism shifted gears, as it were, from a "supply-side" to a "demand-side" urbanization. Let us consider the elements of that transition.

The rise of the corporation from the ashes of the family firm, coupled with major reorganizations of labor processes in many industries, liberated many aspects of production from reliance upon access to particular natural or urban assets. Industry became increasingly footloose, not above the calculus of local advantages of labor supply or social and physical infrastructures, but more able to exploit their uneven availability within the urban system. This did not automatically produce geographical decentralization of production under unified corporate control. Precisely because much of the impetus toward the formation of large corporations, trusts, and cartels came from the need to curb excessive competition, the emphasis lay on the joys of monopoly rather than the rigors of competition. And monopoly powers could be used geopolitically, either to further concentrate production geographically or to protect geographical concentrations already achieved. The distortion of relative space imposed by the United States steel companies through their "Pittsburgh plus" system of steel pricing was one example of many sustained attempts to use monopoly power to protect a particular urban region against external competition. It took many years, and in some cases deep financial trauma, for large corporations to learn how to internalize competition (between, for example, regional branch plants) and use their power to command space and manipulate geographical dispersal to their own advantage. In this they were always limited, of course, by the need to assure internal economies of scale and continuous flow in production while sustaining reasonable proximity to networks of subcontractors and adequate labor supplies.

Relieved of the burden of excessive competition in production, the large corporations became much more sensitive to the control of labor power and markets as the basis for a constant and secure flow of revenues and profits (Gramsci 1971). Their attachment to large-scale production also led them to direct their attention to mass rather than privileged and custom markets. And the mass market lay within the working class. This was the basis for Fordism. Increased productivity in the workplace was compensated by higher wages that would allow the workers to buy back a larger share of the commodities they helped produce. Ford himself was quite explicit about that strategy when he inaugurated the eight-hour, five-dollar work day at his auto plant in 1914. But to the degree that workers are never in a position to buy back the whole of the output they create, so the large corporations were forced into strategies of geographical dispersal in order to ensure market control on an expanding basis. And it was not long before the advantages of decentralization of component production as well as of final assembly became apparent. But these adjustments were slowly wrought, depending to a considerable degree upon the changing space relations created by new systems of transport and communications.

The more corporations used their powers of dispersal, however, the less urban regions competed with each other on the basis of their industrial mix and the more they were forced to compete in terms of the attractions they had to offer to corporate investment as labor and commodity markets and as bundles of physical and social assets that corporations could exploit to their own advantage. The corporations became less and less place-bound and more and more representative of the universality of abstract labor on the world market. Innovation likewise tended to shift its breeding ground from the interstices of the urban matrix into government and corporate research labs, though new product innovation still retained some of its more traditional urban bases.

The growing power of the credit system added its weight to these shifts. The centralization of credit power was nothing new – the Barings and the Rothschilds early learned that superior information and capacity to deploy money power over space gave them the power to discipline even nation states throughout much of the nineteenth century. But they had largely confined their operations to government debt and selected large-scale projects, like railroads, leaving commercial and industrial credit and consumer loans (if they existed at all) to other, more fragmentary sources. The manifestation of crises in the nineteenth century as credit and commercial crises – 1847–48 being a particularly spectacular example – prompted major changes in capital and credit markets. The stock market and the reorganization of banking changed the whole context of credit and finance by the end of the nineteenth century. The rise of finance capital (see Harvey 1982, chap. 10) had all manner of implications. It facilitated the easier movement of money capital from one sector of production or geographical region to another and so allowed the much finer tuning of the relations between the social and geographical divisions of labor. It made the debt-financed production of urban infrastructures that much easier, as well as facilitating the production of long-term investments that reduced spatial barriers and helped further annihilate space with time. It therefore meant a smoother and accelerating flow of capital into the deepening and geographical widening of urban infrastructures at the very moment when increasingly footloose corporations were looking to tap into the particular advantages to be derived from those sorts of investments. The effect, however, was to tie the production of urban infrastructures more tightly into the overall logic of capital flow, primarily through movements in the demand and supply of money capital as reflected in the interest rate. The "urban construction cycle" therefore became much more emphatic, as did the rhythmic movement of uneven urban development in geographic space.

But the credit system also seemed to pack another punch, one that could virtually annihilate the overaccumulation problem at one blow. The proper allocation of credit to production and consumption held out the prospect of balancing both within the constraints of continuous profit realization. The flow of money and credit into production had simply to be matched by the flow of money and credit to support consumption in order that self-sustained growth continue in perpetuity. There were, of course, many problems to be resolved. Balanced growth could not be achieved through any pattern of production and consumption if accumulation was to be achieved and profits realized. The proper balance between productive consumption (investments that enhanced the capacity of the productive forces) and final consumption (investments and flows that enhanced the living standards of the bourgeoisie as well as of the working class) had to be struck. But the credit system nevertheless seemed to have the potential power to do what individual corporations seeking a Fordist compromise set out to do but could not because of their limited power to affect distribution. To the degree that the credit system became oriented to these tasks it became the major vehicle for the transformation to demand-side as opposed to supply-side urbanization.

But there were two interrelated problems. First, financial markets, like money itself, embody immense powers of centralization in the midst of the greatest possible dispersal of powers of appropriation. This permits the concentration of key decision-making functions for global capitalism in a few hands (like J. P. Morgan) in a few urban centers (like New York and London). This poses the threat of private perversion of this immense centralized social power for personal gain or the use of monopoly power for narrow geopolitical ends. It also tends to consolidate the hierarchical geographical ordering of financial centers into a system of authority and control that is as much self-serving as it is facilitative of balanced accumulation. Worse still, and this brings us to the second objection, the formation of "fictitious capital" (all forms of debt) has somehow to be regulated if it is not to spiral out of control into orgies of speculation and unchecked debt creation (see Harvey 1982, chaps. 9 and 10). How, for example, was the debt on urban infrastructures to be paid off if the latter did not enhance surplus value production? And if such investments were productive, would not that merely exacerbate the overaccumulation problem? Periodic financial crises indicated that overaccumulation could all too easily be translated into an overaccumulation of debt claims on nonearning assets.

It is against this background that we have to understand the increasing pressure toward state intervention in macro-economic policy. It was, of course, to the nation state that the bourgeoisie turned, in part because this was the space they could most easily control but also because the nation state was the institutional frame within which fiscal and monetary politics were traditionally formulated. It was the switch into Keynesian strategies of fiscal and monetary management that consolidated the turn to demand-side urbanization. The trauma of 1929–45 provided the catalyst. When the depression hit in the United States, Ford, true to his colors, saw it as an underconsumption problem and tried to raise wages. Forced within six months by the logic of the market to back down, Fordism failed and had to convert itself (often reluctantly) into state-managed Keynesianism and New Deal institutional reforms and politics. For more than a generation, capitalist urbanization (particularly in the United States) was shaped after the added trauma of World War II into a state-organized response to what were interpreted as the chronic underconsumption problems of the 1930s.

The implications for the urbanization of capital were profound. The Keynesian city was shaped as a consumption artifact and its social, economic, and political life organized around the theme of state-backed, debt-financed consumption. The focus of urban politics shifted away from alliances of classes confronting class issues toward more diffuse coalitions of interests around themes of consumption, distribution, and the production and control of space. The "urban crisis" of the 1960s bore all the marks of that transition. The shift also provoked a serious tension between cities as "workshops" for the production of surplus value and cities as centers of consumption and realization of that surplus value. There was a tension between the circulation of capital and the circulation of revenues, between the spatial division of labor and the spatial division of consumption, between cities and suburbs, and so forth. Keynesian policies radically changed, in fact, the manner and style of temporal (debt-financed) and spatial displacement of the overaccumulation problem. Let us see how.

Unlimited temporal displacement could be achieved to the degree that state-backed credit allowed the unlimited creation of fictitious capital. Keynes had meant deficit financing as a short-run managerial device, but permanent and growing deficits were built up as the business cycle was kept under control and the urban construction cycle that had been so powerfully present before 1939 was all but eliminated. Overaccumulated capital and labor power were switched into the production of physical and social infrastructures; and if such investments helped produce more surpluses, then another round of switching could take place. The prospect arose, for urban regions as well as for nations, of a permanent upward spiral of economic growth, provided, of course, the targets of debt-financing were well chosen. Investments in transportation, education, housing, and health care appeared particularly appropriate from the standpoint of improving labor qualities, buying labor peace, and accelerating the turnover time of capital in both production and consumption. But the process rested on unlimited debt creation no matter how it was worked out. By the 1970s, the United States was weighed down by what even *Business Week* conceded was a "mountain" of public, private, and corporate debt, much of it wrapped up in urban infrastructures. The accumulation of debt claims posed a problem. The attempt to monetize them away produced strong surges of inflation, thus demonstrating that the threat of devaluation of commodities and other assets could be converted into the devaluation of money (cf. Harvey 1982, chap. 10). But any counterattack against inflation could only put a great deal of urbanized capital at risk. The collapse of the property market worldwide in 1973 (and the collapse of banking and financial institutions heavily caught up in property finance) and the New York fiscal crisis of 1974–75 were opening gambits in a whole new mode of the urban process based on non-Keynesian approaches.

The temporal displacement of overaccumulation through debt-financed infrastructure formation was accompanied by strong processes of spatial reorganization of the urban system. Long reduced to a commodity, a pure form of fictitious capital, land speculation had also been a potent force making for urban sprawl and rapid transitions in spatial organization, particularly in the United States. The means of further dispersal – the automobile – had also been on hand since the 1920s. But it took the rising economic power of individuals to appropriate space for their own exclusive purposes through debt-financed homeownership and debt-financed access to transport services (auto purchases as well as highways), to create the "suburban solution" to the underconsumption problem (Walker 1976, 1981). Though suburbanization had a long history, it marked post-war urbanization to an extraordinary degree. It meant the mobilization of effective demand through the total restructuring of space so as to make the consumption of the products of the auto, oil, rubber, and construction industries a necessity rather than a luxury. For nearly a generation after 1945, suburbanization was part of a package of moves (the global expansion of world trade, the reconstruction of the war-torn urban systems of Western Europe and Japan, and a more or less permanent arms race being the other key elements) to insulate capitalism against the threat of crises of underconsumption. It is now hard to imagine that postwar capitalism could have survived, or to imagine what it would have now been like, without suburbanization and proliferating urban development.

The whole process rested, however, on continuous and radical restructurings of the space-time matrices that frame economic decisions as well as social and political life. The revolution in space relations overwhelmed the punctiform settlement patterns of industrial capitalism and replaced them with "space-covering" and "space-packing" patterns of labor and commodity markets merging into pure megalopolitan sprawl. The urban-rural distinction was swamped with respect to production in the advanced capitalist societies, only to be reproduced as an important consumption option. Geographical dispersal and space-packing had its limits, however. The more investments crystallized into fixed spatial configurations, the less likely it became that space could be further modified without being devalued. This was not a new problem. The reshaping of the industrial city to fit Keynesian requirements imposed economic costs and sparked social resistance, often on the part of working-class communities that had forged their identity from the industrial experience. Greater attachment to that sense of community (and a reluctance to treat land as pure fictitious capital) slowed the pace of suburbanization in Europe, perhaps slowing overall growth as a result. But even in the United States, the erosion and occasional destruction of the preexisting bases of community in older areas became widely seen as the negative side of the golden currency of suburbanization. As the processes of spatial transformation gathered pace, so those problems became more widespread, affecting middle and even upper-income communities with much more power to resist.

The Keynesian city put much greater emphasis upon the spatial division of consumption relative to the spatial division of labor. Demand-side urbanization depended on the mass mobilization of the spirit of consumer sovereignty. Surpluses were, in effect, widely though unevenly distributed, and the choice of how to spend them was increasingly left to the individual. The sovereignty, though fetishistic (in Marx's sense), was not illusory and had important implications (see *Consciousness and the Urban Experience*, chap. 5). Since there are no natural breaks on the continuum of money power, all kinds of artificial distinctions could be introduced. New kinds of communities could be constructed, packaged, and sold in a society where who you were depended less and less on class position and more and more on how you spent money in the market. Living spaces were made to represent status, position, and prestige. Social competition with respect to life-style and command over social space and its significations became an important aspect of access to life chances. Fierce struggles over distribution, consumption rights, and control over social space ensued. Once largely confined to the upper layers of the bourgeoisie, such struggles now became part of urban life for the mass of the population. It was largely through such struggles and the competition they engendered that demand-led urbanization was organized to capitalistic ends.

Urban politics had to change its spots. The success of the Keynesian project depended upon the creation of a powerful alliance of class forces comprising government, corporate capital, financial interests, and all those interested in land development. Such an alliance had to find ways to direct and channel a broadening base of consumer sovereignty and increasing social competition over consumption and redistribution. It had to shape and respond to the quest for new life-styles and access to life chances so as to create patterns of temporal and spatial growth conducive to sustained and reasonably stable capital accumulation. But the basis of popular legitimacy (at both the local and national levels) had to rest on performance with respect to distribution and satisfaction of consumer wants and needs. While there were phases of concordance of these two aims, there were also serious points of tension.

The attempt to use the urban process as a vehicle of redistribution ran up against the realities of class structure, income differentials, and minority deprivation. The strong processes of spatial reorganization of consumer landscapes left behind growing pockets of abandonment and deprivation, for the most part concentrated in inner cities. It was almost as if creative destruction split into the physical and social destruction of the inner cities and the creation of the suburbs. But all was not necessarily well at the other end of the social scale. As consumers, even upper echelons of the bourgeoisie could demand protection against developers and others who wanted to shape space for growth and profit. Peculiar kinds of "consumer socialism," built around the power of the local government to check growth-machine politics, could take root even in affluent areas (such as Santa Monica). Consumer sovereignty, if taken seriously, presupposes a certain popular empowerment to shape the qualities of urban life and construct collective spaces in an image of community quite different from that embodied in the circulation of capital. The production of space tended to run up against sensitivity to place. The boundary between consumerist innovation promoted by capitalism and attempts to construct community in the image of real self-fulfillment became exceedingly fuzzy.

It was in exactly such a context that the inner-city uprisings of the 1960s (and some of the later urban unrest in Europe) coupled with no-growth and environmentalist movements on the fringes checked the accelerating trajectory of urban transformation typical of the Keynesian city. The urban social movements of the 1960s focused strongly on distribution and consumption issues, and urban politics had to adjust from a pure growth machine track to redistributive issues. The circulation of revenues had to be managed so as to ensure economic and political inclusion of a spatially isolated under-class and a socially just distribution of benefits within the urban system. The city was increasingly interpreted as a redistributive system. Questions of jobs and employment and of the city as an environment for production, though never excluded from consideration, were viewed as minor elements in a complex matrix of forces at work within the urban process. Rivalry over the circulation of revenues and redistributions tended, however, to exacerbate intercommunity tensions and geopolitical conflicts (between, for example, cities and suburbs). And there was nothing about such a strategy that necessarily assured smooth sailing for the circulation of capital either.

Three problems were central to the temporal and spatial displacement of overaccumulation through demand-side urbanization. First, temporal displacement led to increased indebtedness and strong inflationary pressures. A return to classic forms of devaluation would, however, have put vast urban investments at risk and would have destroyed well-established patterns of redistribution, thus making such a policy reversal harder and harder to confront as time went by. Second, investment in suburban sprawl and the "space-covering" style of urbanization entailed the fixation of fragmented spaces within which the drive toward local empowerment and community formation created barriers to the further pursuit of the suburban solution and the spatial fix. The process of spatial displacement either slowed or was forced to ever more intense levels of creative destruction and contentious devaluation. Third, demand-led urbanization (with all of its concerns for individualism, consumer sovereignty, life-style and status, and social competition for command over space) pushed the focus of concern away from the direct circulation of capital toward the circulation of revenues. It emphasized the production of preconditions for the spatial division of consumption rather than of production. This shift was as dangerous as it was provocative. It assumed an automatic and apropriate supply-side response to match the debt-financed growth of effective demand. The tension between cities as "work-shops" for production and as centers for consumption was not easy to contain. Investment in the physical and social infrastructures for consumption, coupled with the politics of redistribution, does not necessarily create a favorable climate for capitalist production. And since corporations now possessed increased powers of geographical mobility, and since finance capital had by now become extraordinarily mobile, cities became much more vulnerable to job loss, capital flight, and corporate disinvestment. This was to be the dilemma of the 1970s, though evidence of it could be seen much earlier.

This account of demand-side urbanization and its inner tensions is, admittedly, highly simplified and rather biased toward the American case. It is also rather superficial to the degree that it does not pay sufficient attention to the necessary unity of production and consumption within the logic of the production and realization of surplus value. That question was never far from the surface of concerns in the midst of industrial urbanization. Engels had certainly noted it in his examination of Manchester in 1844, in his celebrated description of the different residential zones of consumption that reflected class relations in production. Urban proletariats had long formed significant captive markets to which capitalists catered, and the question of the importance of local effective demand as the basis of a vigorous export trade had long been broached. And then there were those cities, like Paris or London, that traditionally functioned as centers of conspicuous consumption, and where the volume and type of effective demand were critical in setting the tone and pace of local industrial activity.

The Keynesian city was not blind to questions of production either. But there was a shift of emphasis which was of sufficient proportions to warrant depiction as a major transformation of the urban process. Though the Great Depression was much more than a crisis of underconsumption, the fact that it appeared as such and that the capitalist class responded to it as such laid the groundwork for a totally new patterning of the urban process. Nor does it matter that urbanization as a whole cannot survive without some consideration of cities as workshops for production if the whole response to underconsumption problems is to strive to create a "post-industrial city" in which industrial development has no role. The production of the Keynesian city was a real response to the surface appearance of underconsumption as the root of capitalism's problems. That real response to a surface appearance created, of course, as many problems as it solved.

Demand-side urbanization produced a very different-looking city of low-density sprawl, distinctive spaces of consumption (ranging from produced rural bliss to intense in-town living separated by what increasingly appeared as the no man's land of the suburb), and strange significations of life-style and social status etched into a landscape of unrelieved consumerism. Production increasingly meant the production of space and of long-term investments, behind which stood powerful growth coalitions that managed the new-style urbanization of capital in ways symbiotic with their own interests. They needed new instrumentalities in the realms of finance capital and the state and strong powers of persuasion and ideological control to ensure that consumer sovereignty was sovereign in the right way, that it produced "rational consumption" in relation to accumulation through the expansion of certain key industrial sectors (autos, household equipment, oil, and so forth). The Keynesian city increasingly appeared, then, as a post-industrial city, as a consumption artifact nourished by service provision, information processing, and the support of command functions in government and finance.

The politics also changed. The class relations of production were partially masked by artificial marks of consumption while struggles over distributive shares and the control of social space generated a troublesome factionalism that had the fortunate side-effect of permitting the ruling-class alliance to divide and rule with relative ease. The basis of political legitimacy shifted from managing class relations toward distributive justice and a not necessarily compatible concern to satisfy consumer desire and sovereignty. Fights over the control of social space (some progressive and other reactionary) and the increasing cleavage between city and suburb produced new lines of geopolitical tension. The urban crises of the 1960s were built out of exactly such ingredients as these. There were fights over consumption (individual and collective) and distribution as well as struggles over command of social space and what it contained. And the whole style of thinking about urbanization followed suit. The literature of that era on the delivery of health care, education, transportation and welfare, and on the rational organization of space for accumulation as well as on the resolution of intercommunity conflict, reflected a style of urbanization in which questions of production and fundamental class relations were held in abeyance, a constant backdrop to a foreground of quite different political and economic concerns.

V. BALANCING SURPLUS PRODUCTION AND ABSORPTION: THE STRUGGLE FOR URBAN SURVIVAL IN THE POST-KEYNESIAN TRANSITION

The collapse of the Keynesian program changed all that. Each of the pinions of the postwar strategy for avoiding the dangers of underconsumption eroded during the late 1960s. The revival of world trade through international capital flow led to a proliferation of the overaccumulation problem. Competition from Western Europe and Japan sharpened as the capacity to absorb further investments profitably fell. Inflationary financing appeared to resolve the difficulty by provoking a wave of international lending that was to lie at the root of the subsequent monetary difficulties (the instability of the dollar as a reserve currency) and the international debt crisis of the 1980s. The same policies generated a spiraling flow of surplus capital and labor power mainly into the production of urban built environments (property investment, office construction, housing development) and to a lesser degree into expansions of the social wage (education and welfare). But when monetary policy was tightened in response to spiraling inflation in 1973, the boom of fictitious capital formation came to an abrupt end, the cost of borrowing rose, property markets collapsed, and local governments found themselves on the brink of, or in New York's case plunged into, the traumas of fiscal crisis (no mean affair when we consider that New York City's budget and borrowing were far greater than those of most nation states). Capital flows into the creation of physical and social infrastructures (the secondary and tertiary circuits of fig. 3) slowed at the same time as recession and fiercer competition put the efficiency and productivity of such investments firmly on the agenda. That there had been and were serious problems of overaccumulation of assets in the built environment and of obligations in the field of social expenditures became apparent for all to see. Much of the investment was producing a very low rate of return, if any at all. The problem was to try to rescue or trim as much of that investment as possible without massive devaluations of physical assets and destruction of services offered. The pressure to rationalize the urban process and render it more efficient and cost-effective was immense.

The running out of steam of demand-side urbanization was powerfully intermingled, therefore, with the grumbling economic problems of the 1970s and 1980s. And to the degree that urbanization had become part of the problem, so it had to be part of the solution. The result was a fundamental transformation of the urban process after 1973. It was, of course, a shift in emphasis rather than a total revolution (in spite of what supply-siders and neoconservatives proclaimed on both sides of the Atlantic). It had to transform the urban legacy of preceding eras and was strictly limited by the quantities, qualities, and configurations of those raw materials. It occurred in fits and starts, dancing uncertainly to the seemingly arbitrary shifts in monetary and fiscal policy and the strong surges of international and interurban competition within the social and spatial divisions of labor. It also had to move tentatively in the face of uncertain powers of popular resistance. And it was not clear how, exactly, the urbanization of capital should adapt to problems that were anything but underconsumption problems. The problems of stagflation could be resolved only through a closer equilibrium between the production of surpluses and their real as opposed to fictitious absorption. The question of the proper organization of production came back center stage after a generation or more of building an urban process around the theme of demand-led growth. How could urban regions blessed largely with a demand-side heritage adapt to a supply-side world?

Four different possibilities, none of them mutually exclusive and none of them costless or free of serious political and economic pitfalls, seemed possible. I consider each in turn. For the sake of clarity, I shall consider them from the standpoint of urban regions as competitive economic and geo-political units within a capitalist geography of seesawing uneven development (Smith 1984).

Competition within the Spatial Division of Labor

Urban regions can seek individually to improve their competitive positions with respect to the international division of labor. The aggregate effect is not necessarily beneficial. The transformation of the conditions of concrete labor within an urban region will, if replicated elsewhere, alter the meaning of abstract labor on the world market and so change the context in which different kinds of concrete labor are possible. Heightened competition between urban regions, like heightened competition between firms, does not necessarily lead capitalism back to some comfortable equilibrium but can spark movements that push the system farther away from it. Nevertheless, those urban regions that achieve a superior competitive position survive, at least in the short run, better than those that do not. There are, however, different paths to that end, the most important distinction being between raising the rate of exploitation of labor power (absolute surplus value) or seeking out superior technologies and organization (relative surplus value). I consider each in turn.

A shift to superior technology and organization helps particular industries within an urban region survive in the face of sharpening competition. But such a shift can just as easily eliminate jobs as create them. Growth of output and investment and decline in jobs is a familiar enough pattern (Massey and Meegan 1982). The search for superior organization can sometimes dictate radical changes in the scale of enterprise (thereby affecting the ability of firms to insert themselves into the matrix of urban possibilities, if only because of the different land needs). But it also carries over to considerations of the cost and efficiency of physical and social infrastructures. The ruling-class alliance within the urban region then has to pay much closer attention to the fine details of urban organization of cities as workshops for the production of relative surplus value. There are a number of ways it can go about that. Improved physical infrastructures and close attention to the productive forces embedded in the land (water, sewage, and so forth) improve the capacity to generate relative surplus value. But then so too do those investments in social infrastructures – education, science, and technology – that improve the urban climate as a center of innovation. Or costs to industry may be artificially reduced by subsidies. But that means redistributions of the social wage (absolute surplus value).

Sharpening interurban competition (of which there are abundant signs) poses problems. Continuous leapfrogging of technologies and organizational forms (including those provided through public investment) promotes ever fiercer competition to capture investment and jobs from highly mobile corporate capital. This has destabilizing effects and tends to accelerate the devaluation of assets and infrastructures associated with older technological mixes. Besides, accelerating technological change at the expense of growth (of output or employment) undermines the whole logic of accumulation and leads straight into the mire of global crises. Preoccupation with creating a "favorable business climate," as well as corporate handouts and other forms of subsidy to industry, can also spark popular resistance, particularly if it affects, as it usually does, the social wage. Urban politics is then in danger of reverting to class struggle rather than to more fragmented squabbles over distribution.

There are a number of checks to such immediate transitions. To begin with, the control of technology lies more within the corporation than within the innovative proclivities of the urban mix (though product innovation still retains some of its older urban base). Technology transfers between urban regions are, therefore, broadly a matter of corporate decisions. In this respect the social dominates over the spatial aspect of the division of labor. That sort of restraint, however, does not apply to infrastructure provision. Here we find the state acting as an entrepreneur (Goodman 1979) offering bait to corporate capital. And the latter is sensitive to the qualities and quantities of labor power and social infrastructures as well as to the physical resources developed within an urban region.

Raising the rate of exploitation of labor power forms another path to survival in the face of international competition in production. The classical Marxian account depicts this as a concerted attack upon labor's standard of living and an attempt to lower real wages through increased unemployment, job insecurity, the diminution of the social wage (particularly welfare provision), and the mobilization of a cheap industrial reserve army (immigrants, women, minorities, and so on). It also means an attack upon working-class institutions (such as trade unions) and the utility of skills and qualifications in employment. But this means an attack upon what may well be an important constituency of an urban-based class alliance. While we can see many an urban region moving down such a path – and in some cases urban administration has become the cutting edge for disciplining labor by wage cuts and rollbacks – there are other options that are less confrontational. The rate of exploitation is always relative, after all, to the qualities of labor power. The unique package of qualities that each urban labor market can offer, supported by selected infrastructures, can be alluring bait for mobile corporate capital. Interurban competition over quantities, qualities, and costs of labor power is, therefore, rather more nuanced than the simple version of the Marxian model would suggest. And the nuances permit a ruling-class alliance much greater flexibility to divide and rule a work force. Besides, the mobility of labor power between urban regions provides further checks to the repressive tactics through which absolute surplus value might otherwise be gained. Nevertheless, interurban competition on the labor market has a disciplining effect upon the labor force in times of faltering accumulation. The threat of job loss and of corporate flight and disinvestment, the clear need to exercise budgetary restraint in a competitive environment, point to a changing thrust of urban politics away from equity and social justice and toward efficiency, innovation, and rising real rates of exploitation.

Competition within the Spatial Division of Consumption

Urban regions can, as a second option, seek individually to improve their competitive position with respect to the spatial division of consumption. There is more to this than the redistributions achieved through tourism, important and extensive though these may be. For more than a generation, demand-side urbanization had focused heavily on life-style, the construction of community, and the organization of social space in terms of the signs and symbols of prestige, status, and power. It had also produced an ever-broadening basis for participation in such consumerism. While recession, unemployment, and the high cost of credit rendered that participation moot for important layers of the population, the game continued for the rest. Competition for their consumer dollars became more frenetic, while they, in turn, had the opportunity to become much more discriminating. The mass consumption of the 1960s was transformed into the less mass-based but more discriminating consumption of the 1970s and 1980s. Interurban competition for that consumption dollar can be fierce and costly. Investments that make for a "good living environment" and that enhance the so-called qualities of life do not come cheap. Investments seeking to establish new patterns of the spatial division of consumption are notoriously risky. Nevertheless, urban regions that successfully undertake them stand to appropriate surpluses from the circulation of revenues. And strong coalitions can be forged behind such strategies. Landlords and property owners, developers and financiers, and urban governments desperate to enhance their tax base can be joined by workers equally desperate for jobs in promoting new amusement options (of which Disney World is but a prototype), new consumer playgrounds (like Baltimore's Inner Harbor or London's docklands scheme), sports stadia and convention centers, marinas and hotels, exotic eating places and cultural facilities, and the like. The construction of totally new living environments (gentrification, retirement communities, integrated "villages in the city") fits into such a program.

But much more than physical investment is involved. The city has to appear as innovative, exciting, and creative in the realms of life-style, high culture, and fashion. Investment in support of cultural activities as well as in a wide range of urban services connects to this drive to capture surpluses from the circulation of revenues. The risks are considerable, but the pay-offs are correspondingly high. Fierce competition in this arena leads toward geo-political struggles in the realm of cultural imperialism. The survival of cities like New York, Los Angeles, London, Paris, and Rome depends in large degree on their relative positions within this international competition for cultural hegemony and for a cut from the global circulation of revenues.

Interurban competition with respect to the spatial division of consumption has important effects. It highlights the contrast between cities as workshops for production and technological innovation and cities as centers for con-spicuous consumption and cultural innovation. Serious conflicts can arise between the infrastructures necessary for these quite different functions. It also has profound implications for employment structures, emphasizing so-called services rather than blue-collar skills. And it calls for the formation of a particular kind of urban-based class alliance in which public-private co-operation in support of conspicuous consumption and cultural innovation has to play a vital role. Out of that comes a tendency, exacerbated by interurban competition, for the public subsidy of consumption by the rich at the expense of local support of the social wage of the poor. The polarizing effects of that are hard to keep in check. The argument that the only way to preserve jobs for an increasingly impoverished under class is to create consumer palaces for the rich with public subsidy has at some point to wear thin. So, too, does the ideology of a post-industrial city as the solution for capitalism's contra-dictions. That ideology has, however another base aside from the justification for pursuing urban survival through spatial competition for consumption. To this broader issue we now turn.

Competition for Command Functions

Urban areas can, as a third possibility, compete for those key control and command functions in high finance and government that tend, by their very nature, to be highly centralized while embodying immense power over all manner of activities and spaces. Cities can compete to become centers of finance capital, of information gathering and control, of government decision-making. Competition of this sort calls for a certain strategy of infrastructural provision. Efficiency and centrality within a worldwide network of transport and communications is vital, and that means heavy public investments in airports, rapid transit, communications systems, and the like. The provision of adequate office space and linkages depends upon a public-private coalition of property developers, financiers, and public interests capable of responding to and anticipating needs. Assembling a wide range of supporting services, particularly those that gather and process information rapidly, calls for other kinds of investments, while the specific skills requirements of such activities put a premium on urban centers with certain kinds of educational provision (business and law schools, computer training facilities, and so forth).

Competition in this realm is expensive and peculiarly tough because this is an arena characterized by monopoly power that is hard to break. The agglomeration of powerful functions in a city like New York naturally attracts other powerful functions to it. Yet, to be maximally effective command and control functions have to be hierarchically organized across space, thus imparting a powerful impulse toward hierarchical organization of the urban system as a whole (Cohen 1981). Shifts in relative spatial structures (particularly those wrought by new systems of communication) create abundant opportunities for shifts in the shape and form of the hierarchy, while new regional centers can emerge with shifts in the social and spatial divisions of labor and consumption. Indeed, command and control functions can be the cutting edge of regional readjustments and differential urban growth. And powerful advantages attach thereto. The very existence of monopolistic power permits the appropriation of surpluses produced elsewhere. And at times of economic difficulty, as Marx once observed, the financiers always tend to enrich themselves at the expense of the industrial interest simply because control over money and credit yields short-term control over the lifeblood of capitalism at a time of crisis. It is, therefore, no accident that interurban competition in the troubled years of the 1970s and 1980s focused heavily on the search to procure command and control functions at a time when there was rapid growth in such functions and multiple forces making for geographical readjustments (Friedmann and Wolff 1982).

The overall effect of such competition is to subsidize the location of command and control functions in the hope that the monopoly powers that reside therein will permit the subsidy to be recaptured through the appropriation of surplus value. That this does not necessarily help stabilize the capitalist system as a whole should be fairly self-evident. But it certainly offers a path toward individual urban survival in a world of heightened interurban competition. The effect, however, is to make it appear as if the city of the future is going to be a city of pure command and control functions, an informational city, a post-industrial city in which services lie at the heart of the urban economy.

Competition for Redistribution

Fourth, in an intricately organized society such as ours, there are many channels for direct redistribution of economic power with respect to which urban regions can and do compete. The private systems of redistribution — through organizations like the church, trade unions, professional associations, charitable organizations, and the like — are by no means negligible. Most overt interurban competition is targeted, however, on redistributions to be had from higher-order levels of government. Such expenditures grew rapidly during the Keynesian era and are still massive, though very much under attack to the degree that they were viewed by the bourgeoisie as the main culprit in inflationary deficit financing. The channels for such redistributions are, however, numerous, varied, and often hidden in obscure provisions in the tax code or in some curious executive order. The amounts that flow through these channels depend upon politics, the economy, and executive judgments. A shift in flows from one channel to another can devastate the economy of one urban region while enhancing that of another. For example, the switch from policies designed to support the social wage in the United States to deficit-financed defense expenditures after 1980 (a kind of defense-side Keynesianism) brought economic prosperity to many urban regions caught up in the defense industry. Those urban regions — located in a great arc sweeping from Connecticut and Long Island through North Carolina, Texas, and California to the state of Washington — were by no means antagonistic to the continuation of that kind of political mix.

Redistributions depend in part upon the sophistication of ruling-class alliances in procuring funds to which they might have some claim (grants for highways, sewers, education, mass transit, and so forth). But they also depend upon raw geopolitical power in relation to higher-order politics (the importance, say, of delivering the urban vote) and the threat of social unrest and political-economic disruption. The tactics of interurban competition are as varied as the modes of redistribution. The political attack on redistributive politics during the 1970s and 1980s should not be taken to mean, however, that this is no longer a viable strategy for urban survival. The city still preserves vast redistributive privileges and functions, but the mode of competition has changed quite radically since the breakdown of the Keynesian compromise.

The four options we have considered are not mutually exclusive. Happy the urban region that competes so well for the spatial division of consumption that it draws command and control functions whose high-paid personnel help capture tax redistributions for defense industries. Better still if there also exists a mix of highly skilled technocrats and a mass of recent immigrants willing to work at very low wages not only in services but also in basic production for an extensive local consumer market that forms the basis for a booming export trade. Los Angeles, for example, scored positively on all four options during the difficult years after 1973. Cities like Baltimore, Lille, and Liverpool, in contrast, scored low on most or all of them with the most dismal of results.

The coercive laws of interurban competition for the production, control, and realization of surplus value are compelling major shifts in the paths of the urbanization of capital. The forces brought to bear on urbanization are changing, but then so too is the meaning of the urban process for all aspects of economic, political, and social life. At such times of brutal and often seemingly incoherent transition, it is hard to assess that meaning, decode its complex messages, or even grasp intellectually and empirically how the variegated forces are meshing and with what consequences.

We have seen the grim headlines of capital flight, job loss, and corporate disinvestment in production against a background of rapid technological change, stuttering accumulation, a new international division of labor, a shaky international financial system, and crumbling worker power to prevent unemployment, wage cuts, and rollbacks of fringe benefits. The same headlines can be seen under the most diverse political circumstances: the United States, France, Britain, Sweden, Spain, Canada – the list is endless. Dissections of deindustrialization and programs for reindustrialization abound, as do speculations about the prospects for survival on the basis of so-called services and command functions.

The surface appearance of crisis, and therefore the focus of political and social concern, shifted dramatically between 1970 and 1980. Underconsumption no longer appeared as the central contradiction of capitalism, but stagflation did. The solutions to that looked quite different from those embedded in the broadly Keynesian response to the Great Depression. But behind the glamour of the high-tech industries, which are supposed to cure the problems of sagging productivity at the same time as they spawn a whole new round of product innovations, lies a reality of deep de-skilling and the routinization of boring and low-paid labor, much of it that of women. That reality was paralleled by many a journalistic exposé of the resurgence of sweatshop labor in New York, Los Angeles, London, and Paris – a different kind of solution that rested on a return to conditions of working (unregulated and tolerated) that many thought had long ago been abolished from a supposedly civilized and civilizing capitalist world. New systems of outwork, subcontracting, and home work (a wonderful way to save on direct fixed capital investment and capitalize on women's captive labor) entered upon the scene, facilitated by sophisticated systems of communication and external control. Centralization of command functions could be matchd by highly decentralized, even individualized production systems that make communication between workers difficult and so check collective consciousness and action. Behind the illusions of the post-industrial city lie the realities of a newly industrializing city. Hong Kong and Singapore are prototypes being forced back into the advanced capitalist world through interurban competititon within the spatial division of labor.

We have also witnessed the headlines of glimmering hope in even the most dismal of urban regions for an urban renaissance pinned together out of some mix of office development, entertainment centers, shopping malls, and investment in new living environments and gentrification of the old. Some cities present such a glamorous and dynamic face to the world that it is hard to credit some of the realities that lie within. In New York City, that amazing center of immensely centralized economic power, cultural imperialism, conspicuous consumption, and dramatic gentrification (Soho, the Upper West Side, even into Harlem), one in four households now ekes out a living on incomes below the poverty level, and one out of every two children is raised under similar conditions. The supply of affordable housing for an increasingly impoverished population in Baltimore is worse now than in the 1960s. Yet Baltimore is touted as a national, even an international model of urban renaissance built upon tourism and increasingly conspicuous consumption. Curiously, the headlines of housing deprivation, hunger, lack of access to medical care and education, injustices of distribution, and discrimination based on race, gender, and place have lost the primacy they had in the supposed urban crisis of the 1960s, even though the conditions now are worse than they were then. If the question of distribution is placed upon the political agenda at all, it is in terms of restructuring material incentives to the enterprising and diminishing the power of labor in order to confront a sagging ability to produce rather than realize surplus value. From that follows the savage attack in some advanced capitalist countries (principally Britain and the United States) upon the welfare state. But interurban competition, by concentrating on subsidies to corporations and upper-income consumption, feeds that process of polarization at the local level in powerful ways. Capitalist urbanization thereby drops its seemingly human mask. We turn back to a style of capitalist urbanization that the Keynesian social planners struggled so gamely to reverse after World War II. The rich now grow richer and the poor grow poorer, not necessarily because anyone wills it that way (though there are plainly those in power who do), but because it is the natural outcome of the coercive laws of competition. And within the many dimensions of the heightened competition, interurban competition has a powerful role to play.

VI. THE URBANIZATION OF CAPITAL

Henri Lefebvre has long argued, somewhat in the wilderness it must be admitted, that the urban process has more importance in the dynamics of capitalism that most analysts are ever prepared to contemplate. The studies I have undertaken these last few years on the history and theory of the urbanization of capital bear witness to the cogency of Lefebvre's message. They do so on a number of counts.

Urbanization has always been about the mobilization, production, appropriation, and absorption of economic surpluses. To the degree that capitalism is but a special version of that, we can reasonably argue that the urban process has more universal meaning than the specific analysis of any particular mode of production. This is, of course, the track that much comparative urban study has taken. But urbanization is used under capitalism in very specific ways. The surpluses sought, set in motion and absorbed are surpluses of the product of labor (appropriated as capital and usually expressed as concentrated money power) and surpluses of the capacity to labor (expressed as labor power in commodity form). The class character of capitalism dictates a certain manner of appropriation and a split of the surplus into the antagonistic and sometimes mutually irreconcilable forms of capital and labor. When the antagonism cannot be accommodated, capitalism has to add powers of devaluation and destruction of both capital and labor surpluses to its lexicon of possibilities. Powerfully creative in many ways – particularly with respect to technology, organization, and the ability to transform material nature into social wealth – the bourgeoisie also has to face up to the uncomfortable fact that it is, as Berman (1982, 100) puts it, "the most destructive ruling class in world history." It is the master of creative destruction. The class character of capitalism radically modifies the manner and meaning of the mobilization, production, appropriation, and absorption of economic surpluses. The meaning of urbanization is likewise radically redefined.

It is always tempting when faced with categories of this sort to turn them into "historical stages" of capitalist development. I have taken such a path in this chapter to some degree by pointing to the mobilization of surpluses in the mercantile city, the production of surpluses in the industrial city, and the absorption of surpluses in the Keynesian city as pegs on which to hang an abbreviated account of the history of capitalist urbanization. In truth, matters are somewhat more complicated and nuanced. Though the emphasis may vary, appropriation, mobilization, production and absorption are ever separate moments in an integrated process. How they hang together in space and time is what counts. A reconstruction of the temporal and spatial dynamics of capital circulation under the specific class relations of capitalism indicates the points of integration for a capitalist mode of production. But as we saw in the case of urbanization in the post-Keynesian era of transition, all kinds of mixes of strategies are possible, given the particular form of urban organization and economy in the context of its space relations.

While urbanization might reasonably be presented as an expression of all that, we have also to recognize that it is through urbanization that the surpluses are mobilized, produced, absorbed, and appropriated and that it is through urban decay and social degradation that the surpluses are devalued and destroyed. And like any means, urbanization has ways of determining ends and outcomes, of defining possibilities and constraints, and of modifying the prospects for capitalist development as well as for the transition to socialism. Capitalism has to urbanize in order to reproduce itself. But the urbanization of capital creates contradictions. The social and physical landscape of an urbanized capitalism is far more, therefore, than a mute testimony to the transforming powers of capitalist growth and technological change. Capitalist urbanization has its own distinctive logic and its own distinctive forms of contradiction.

The grounds for that can be established by a different path. There are, I submit, immense gains to be had from looking closely at the rich complexity and intricately woven textures of urban life as the crucible for much that is fundamental to human experience, consciousness formation, and political action. I take up such matters at much greater length in *Consciousness and the Urban Experience,* but I cannot let them pass without some commentary here. The study of urban life illuminates people in multiple roles – workers, bosses, homemakers, consumers, community residents, political activists, borrowers, lenders, and so forth. The roles do not necessarily harmonize. Individuals internalize all kinds of stresses and strains, and external signs of individual and collective conflict abound. But urbanization means a certain mode of human organization in space and time that can somehow embrace all of these conflicting forces, not necessarily so as to harmonize them, but to channel them into so many possibilities of both creative and destructive social transformation. There is plainly much more at stake here than mere class interest. Yet capitalist urbanization presupposes that the urban process can somehow be mobilized into configurations that contribute to the perpetuation of capitalism. How can that be? The short answer is quite simply that it is not necessarily so. The urban form of organization that capitalism implants does not necessarily adapt to every dictate of that mode of production any more than individual or collective consciousness boils down to simple and polarized class struggle.

Such dilemmas lurk in the various strategies for urban survival in the post-Keynesian transition. The search to produce surpluses in one place depends on the ability to realize and absorb them in another. The mobilization of surpluses via command functions presumes there is some production somewhere to command. The overall stability of capitalism depends on the coherence of such integrations. Yet urban-based class alliances (even when themselves coherently organized) do not form and strategize in relation to such global considerations of coordination. They compete to save their own asset base as best they can and to preserve their power of appropriation whatever way they can. To be sure, corporate and finance capital and, to a lesser degree, labor power are mobile across urban entities (thus rendering the urban-based class alliances permanently vulnerable). But this does not guarantee an urban evolution exactly geared to capitalism's requirements. It simply emphasizes the ever-present tension between the social and spatial divisions of production, consumption, and control.

Interurban competition is, then, one important determinant in capitalism's evolution and is fundamental, as I argued in Chapter 5, to its uneven geographical development. That competition could be viewed as potentially harmonious if Adam Smith was right that the hidden hand of the market invariably transforms individual selfishness, ambition, and short-sightedness into a global social outcome that benefits all. But Marx's devastating rebuttal of that thesis prevails here too. The more perfect the hidden hand of interurban competition, the more the inequality between capital and labor builds and the more unstable capitalism becomes. Heightened competition is a way into rather than out of capitalist crisis in the long run.

What, then, is the post-Keynesian transition a transition to? That is a question to which there is no automatic answer. The laws of motion of capitalism track the underlying contradictions that push capitalism to evolve, but they do not dictate the paths to take. Our historical geography is always ours to make. But the conditions under which we seek to make that historical geography are always highly structured and constrained. Viewed solely from the standpoint of interurban competition, for example – and I admit this is a drastic simplification that I shall not even try to justify – there is much to indicate spiraling temporal disequilibrium within a rapidly seesawing movement of uneven geographical development; sporadic place-specific devaluations coupled with even more sporadic bursts of place-specific accumulation. And there is more than a little evidence to support that. The Sun Belt cities in the United States that rode so high and secure on the energy boom after 1973 slip rapidly into depression with every drop in oil price – Houston, Dallas, and Denver, once boom towns, are now in deep trouble. High-tech centers like Silicon Valley turn rapidly sour, while New York City, which seemed on the point of total collapse in the early 1970s, suddenly adds command-type functions and even low-wage manufacturing jobs oriented to the local market. These are the kinds of rapid shifts in fortune that we would expect to see under conditions of heightened interurban competition for the mobilization, production, appropriation, and absorption of surpluses.

But are there any broader indicators? The emphasis on command and consumption in the United States puts the focus on appropriation rather than on production, and in the long run that spells acute geopolitical danger as more and more cities become centers of mercantilist endeavor in a world of shrinking profitable production possibilities. This was the kind of volatile mix that, at the nation state level, led straight into those lopsided patterns of uneven geographical development characteristic of the age of high imperialism. And that was the kind of tension that lay at the root of two world wars. Yet, the search for profitable production possibilities under conditions of heightened competition between firms, urban regions, and nations points to rapid transitions in the sociotechnical and organizational conditions of production and consumption. And that portends disruption of whatever structured coherence has been achieved within an urban economy, substantial devaluation of many of the physical and social infrastructural assets built up there, and instability within any ruling-class alliance. It also means destruction of many traditional skills within the labor force, the devaluation of labor power, and disruption of powerful cultures of social reproduction. Bringing the Third World back home is not an easy follow-up to Keynesian-style urbanization. Ironically, moving too rapidly down that path also dramatizes the crisis tendencies of capitalism as underconsumption problems once more.

What, then, of the possibilities of transition to some alternative mode of production and consumption? At a time when the struggle for survival within capitalism dominates political and economic practice and consciousness, it becomes doubly hard to think about a radical break and the construction of a socialist alternative. Yet the present insecurities and instabilities, to say nothing of the threat of massive devaluation and destruction through internal reorganization, geopolitical confrontation, and political-economic breakdown, make the question more vital than ever.

The alternative cannot, however, be constructed out of some unreal socialist blueprint. It has to be painfully wrought through a transformation of society, including its distinctive forms of urbanization, as we know it. A study of the urbanization of capital indicates the possibilities and the necessary constraints that face struggle toward that goal. The historical geography of capitalism has shaped physical and social landscapes in profound ways. These landscapes now form the humanly created resources and productive forces and mirror the social relations out of which socialist configurations will have to be carved. The uneven geographical development of capitalism can at best be slowly modified and the maintenance of existing spatial configurations – so essential to the reproduction of social life as we now know it – means the continued structuration and replication of spaces of domination and subservience, of advantage and disadvantage. How to break out of that without destroying social life is the quintessential question. The urbanization of capital imprisons us in myriad and powerful ways. Like any sculptor, we are necessarily limited by the nature of the raw material out of which we try to build new shapes and forms. And we have to recognize that the physical and social landscape of capitalism as structured through its distinctive form of urbanization contains all manner of hidden flaws, barriers, and prejudices inimical to the construction of any idealized socialism.

But capitalism is also destructive of all that, perpetually revolutionizing itself and always teetering on that knife-edge of preserving its own values and traditions and necessarily destroying them to open up fresh room for accumulation. What Henry James called "the reiterated sacrifice to pecuniary profit" makes the urbanization of capital a peculiarly open and dynamic affair. The urban is, consequently, as Lefebvre (1974) is fond of saying, "the place of the unexpected"; and out of that all manner of possibilities can flow. The problem is to understand the possibilities and create the political instrumentalities appropriate to their exploitation. The tactics of working-class struggle have to be as fluid and dynamic as capitalism itself. The shift, for example, toward a more corporatist style of urbanization in the United States in the period of the post-Keynesian transition opens a space into which movements toward municipal socialism can more readily be inserted to form the basis for broader political struggle. But for that opportunity to be seized requires a radical transition in American urban politics away from fragmented pluralism into a more class-conscious mode of politics. The barriers to that process, as I show in *Consciousness and the Urban Experience,* are profound indeed because they are deeply embedded in the structures of contemporary capitalism itself. The individualism of money, the consciousness of family and community, the chauvinism of state and local governments, compete with the experience of class relations on the job and create a cacophony of conflicting ideologies which all of us to some degree internalize.

But even presupposing that consciousness of class emerges supreme within the complex rivalries of urban social movements, there is another whole dimension to struggle that has to be confronted. It is noticeable, for example, that in those European countries in which municipal socialism has already won its laurels and where a more articulate class-based politics does indeed prevail, that the corporatist powers of the urban-based class alliance are whittled away and replaced by the powers of the nation state where the bourgeoisie can more easily retain its power. The allocation of powers between urban region, state, and multinational organs is itself an outcome of class struggle. The bourgeoisie will always seek to shift authority, powers, and functions away from the spaces it cannot control into the spaces within which its hegemony prevails. The tension between city and state that Braudel (1984) makes so much of in his description of the rise of capitalism is still with us. It deserves more careful scrutiny as part and parcel of the processes of class struggle around the survival of capitalism and the production of socialism. Capitalism has survived not only through the production of space, as Lefebvre insists, but also through superior command over space — and that truth prevails as much within urban regions as over the global space of capitalist endeavor.

The urbanization of capital is but a part of the total complex of problems that confronts us in the search for an alternative to capitalism. But it is a vital part. An understanding of how capital becomes urbanized and the consequences of that urbanization is a necessary condition for the articulation of any theory of the transition to socialism. In the final paragraph of *Social Justice and the City* I wrote these lines:

A genuinely humanizing urbanism has yet to be brought into being. It remains for revolutionary theory to chart a path from an urbanism based in exploitation to an urbanism appropriate for the human species. And it remains for revolutionary practice to accomplish such a transformation.

That aim still stands. But I would now want to put it in a broader perspective. Any movement toward socialism that does not confront the urbanization of capital and its consequences is bound to fail. The construction of a distinctively socialist form of urbanization is as necessary to the transition to socialism as the rise of the capitalist city was to the sustenance of capitalism. Thinking through the paths to socialist urbanization is to chart the way to the socialist alternative itself. And that is what revolutionary practice has to accomplish.

2

The Urban Process under Capitalism: A Framework for Analysis

My objective is to understand the urban process under capitalism. I confine myself to the capitalist forms of urbanization because I accept the idea that the "urban" has a specific meaning under the capitalist mode of production which cannot be carried over without a radical transformation of meaning (and of reality) into other social contexts.

Within the framework of capitalism, I hang my interpretation of the urban process on the twin themes of *accumulation* and *class struggle*. The two themes are integral to each other and have to be regarded as different sides of the same coin – different windows from which to view the totality of capitalist activity. The class character of capitalist society means the domination of labor by capital. Put more concretely, a class of capitalists is in command of the work process and organizes that process for the purposes of producing profit. The laborer, however, has command only over his or her labor power, which must be sold as a commodity on the market. The domination arises because the laborer must yield the capitalist a profit (surplus value) in return for a living wage. All of this is extremely simplistic, of course, and actual class relations (and relations between factions of classes) within an actual system of production (comprising production, services, necessary costs of circulation, distribution, exchange, etc.) are highly complex. The essential Marxian insight, however, is that profit arises out of the domination of labor by capital and that the capitalists as a class must, if they are to reproduce themselves, continuously expand the basis for profit. We thus arrive at a conception of a society founded on the principle of "accumulation for accumulation's sake, production for production's sake." The theory of accumulation which Marx constructs in *Capital* amounts to a careful enquiry into the dynamics of accumulation and an exploration of its contradictory character. This may sound rather economistic as a framework for analysis, but we have to recall that accumulation is the means whereby the capitalist class reproduces both itself and its domination over labor. Accumulation cannot, therefore, be isolated from class struggle.

I. THE CONTRADICTIONS OF CAPITALISM

We can spin a whole web of arguments concerning the urban process out of an analysis of the contradictions of capitalism. Let me set out the principal forms these contradictions take.

Consider, first, the contradiction that lies within the capitalist class itself. In the realm of exchange each capitalist operates in a world of individualism, freedom, and equality and can and must act spontaneously and creatively. Through competition, however, the inherent laws of capitalist production are asserted as "external coercive laws having power over every individual capitalist." A world of individuality and freedom on the surface conceals a world of conformity and coercion underneath. But the translation from individual action to behavior according to class norms is neither complete nor perfect — it never can be because the *process* of exchange under capitalist rules always presumes individuality, while the law of value always asserts itself in social terms. As a consequence, individual capitalists, each acting in his own immediate self-interest, can produce an aggregative result that is wholly antagonistic to the collective class interest. To take a rather dramatic example, competition may force each capitalist to so lengthen and intensify the work process that the capacity of the labor force to produce surplus value is seriously impaired. The collective effects of individual entrepreneurial activity can seriously endanger the social basis for future accumulation.

Consider, second, the implications of accumulation for the laborers. We know from the theory of surplus value that the exploitation of labor power is the source of capitalist profit. The capitalist form of accumulation therefore rests upon a certain violence that the capitalist class inflicts upon labor. Marx showed, however, that this appropriation could be worked out in such a way that it did not offend the rules of equality, individuality, and freedom as they must prevail in the realms of exchange. Laborers, like capitalists, "freely" trade the commodity they have for sale in the marketplace. But laborers are also in competition with each other for employment, while the work process is under the command of the capitalist. Under conditions of unbridled competition, the capitalists are forced willy-nilly into inflicting greater and greater violence upon those whom they employ. The individual laborer is powerless to resist this onslaught. The only solution is for the laborers to constitute themselves as a class and find collective means to resist the depredations of capital. The capitalist form of accumulation consequently calls into being overt and explicit class struggle between labor and capital. This contradiction between the classes explains much of the dynamic of capitalist history and is in many respects quite fundamental to understanding the accumulation process.

The two forms of contradiction are integral to each other. They express an underlying unity and are to be construed as different aspects of the same reality. Yet we can usefully separate them in certain respects. The internal contradiction within the capitalist class is rather different from the class confrontation between capital and labor, no matter how closely the two may be linked. In what follows I focus on the accumulation process in the absence of any overt response on the part of the working class to the violence that the capitalist class must necessarily inflict upon it. I then broaden the perspective and consider how the organization of the working class and its capacity to mount an overt class response affect the urban process under capitalism.

Various other forms of contradiction could enter in to supplement the analysis. For example, the capitalist production system often exists in an antagonistic relationship to non- or precapitalist sectors that may exist within (the domestic economy, peasant and artisan production sectors, etc.) or without it (precapitalist societies, socialist countries, etc.). We should also note the contradiction with "nature" which inevitably arises out of the relation between the dynamics of accumulation and the "natural" resource base as it is defined in capitalist terms. Such matters obviously have to be taken into account in any analysis of the history of urbanization under capitalism.

II. THE LAWS OF ACCUMULATION

I begin by sketching the structure of flows of capital within a system of production and realization of value. This I do with the aid of a series of diagrams which appear highly "functionalist" and perhaps unduly simple in structure, but which nevertheless help us to understand the basic logic of the accumulation process. We shall also see how problems arise because individual capitalists produce a result inconsistent with their class interest and consider some of the means whereby solutions to these problems might be found. In short, I attempt a summary of Marx's argument in *Capital* in the ridiculously short space of three or four pages.

The Primary Circuit of Capital

In volume one of *Capital*, Marx presents an analysis of the capitalist production process. The drive to create surplus value rests either on an increase in the length of the working day (absolute surplus value) or on the gains to be made from continuous revolutions in the "productive forces" through reorganizations of the work process which raise the productivity of labor power (relative surplus value). The capitalist captures relative surplus value from the organization of cooperation and division of labor within the work process or by the application of fixed capital (machinery). The motor for these continuous revolutions in the work process, for the rising productivity of labor, lies in capitalist competition as each capitalist seeks an excess profit by adopting a production technique superior to the social average.

The implications of all of this for labor are explored in a chapter entitled "The General Law of Capitalist Accumulation." Marx here examines alterations in the rate of exploitation and in the temporal rhythm of changes in the work process in relation to the supply conditions of labor power (in particular, the formation of an industrial reserve army), assuming all the while that a positive rate of accumulation must be sustained if the capitalist class is to reproduce itself. The analysis proceeds around a strictly circumscribed set of interactions, with all other problems assumed away or held constant. Figure 1 portrays the relations examined.

The second volume of *Capital* closes with a model of accumulation on an expanded scale. The problems of proportionality involved in the aggregative production of means of production and means of consumption are examined, with all other problems held constant (including technological change, investment in fixed capital, etc.). The objective here is to show the potential for crises of disproportionality within the production process. But Marx has now broadened the structure of relationships put under the microscope (fig. 2). Note, however, that in both cases Marx tacitly assumes that all commodities are produced and consumed within one time period. The structure of relations examined in figure 2 can be characterized as the *primary circuit of capital*.

Much of the analysis of the falling rate of profit and its countervailing tendencies in volume 3 similarly presupposes production and consumption within one time period, although there is some evidence that Marx intended to broaden the scope of this; however, he did not live to complete the work. But it is useful to consider the volume 3 analysis as a synthesis of the arguments presented in the first two volumes and as at the very least a cogent statement of the internal contradictions that exist within the primary circuit. Here we can clearly see the contradictions that arise out of the tendency for individual capitalists to act in a way that, when aggregated, runs counter to their own class interest. This contradiction produces a tendency toward *overaccumulation* – too much capital is produced in aggregate relative to the opportunities to employ that capital. This tendency is manifest in a variety of guises. We have:

1. Overproduction of commodities – a glut on the market.
2. Falling rates of profit (in pricing terms, to be distinguished from the falling rate of profit in value terms, which is a theoretical construct).

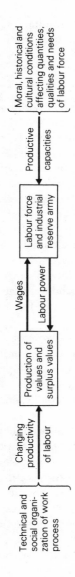

Fig. 1. The relations considered in Marx's "general law of accumulation."
(Source: Capital, Vol. 1.)

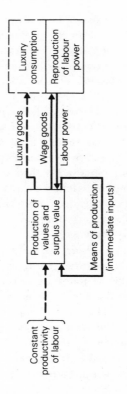

Fig. 2. The relations considered in Marx's representation of "reproduction on an expanded scale."
(Source: Capital, Vol. 2.)

3.   Surplus capital, which can be manifest either as idle productive capacity
     or as money capital lacking opportunities for profitable employment.
4.   Surplus labor and/or a rising rate of exploitation of labor power.

One or a combination of these manifestations may be present simultaneously.
We have here a preliminary framework for the analysis of capitalist crises (cf.
Harvey 1982, chap. 7).

The Secondary Circuit of Capital

I now drop the tacit assumption of production and consumption within one
time period and consider the problems posed by production and use of
commodities requiring different working periods, circulation periods, and
the like. This is an extraordinarily complex problem which Marx addresses to
some degree in volume 2 of *Capital* and in the *Grundrisse*. Here I confine
myself to some remarks regarding the formation of *fixed capital* and the
consumption fund. Fixed capital, Marx argues, requires special analysis because
of certain peculiarities that attach to its mode of production and realization.
These peculiarities arise because fixed capital items can be produced in the
normal course of capitalist commodity production, but they are used as aids
to the production process rather than as direct raw material inputs. They are
also used over a relatively long time period. We can also usefully distinguish
between fixed capital enclosed within the production process and fixed capital
that functions as a physical framework for production. The latter I call the
built environment for production.

On the consumption side, we have a parallel structure. A *consumption fund*
is formed out of commodities that function as aids rather than as direct inputs
to consumption. Some items are directly enclosed within the consumption
process (consumer durables such as stoves, washing machines, etc.), while
others act as a physical framework for consumption (houses, sidewalks, etc.) –
the latter I call the *built environment for consumption*.

We should note that some items in the built environment function jointly
for both production and consumption – the transport network, for example –
and that items can be transferred from one category to another by changes in
use. Also, fixed capital in the built environment is immobile in space in the
sense that the value incorporated in it cannot be moved without being
destroyed. Investment in the built environment therefore entails the creation
of a whole physical landscape for purposes of production, circulation,
exchange, and consumption.

I call the capital flows into fixed asset and consumption fund formation the
secondary circuit of capital. Consider, now, the manner in which such flows can
occur. There must obviously be a "surplus" of both capital and labor in
relation to current production and consumption needs in order to facilitate
the movement of capital into the formation of long-term assets, particularly

those constituting the built environment. The tendency toward overaccumulation produces such conditions within the primary circuit on a periodic basis. One feasible if *temporary* solution to this overaccumulation problem would therefore be to switch capital flows into the secondary circuit.

Individual capitalists will often find it difficult to bring about such a switch in flows for a variety of reasons. The barriers to individual switching of capital are particularly acute with respect to the built environment, where investments tend to be large-scale and long-lasting, often difficult to price in the ordinary way, and in many cases open to collective use by all individual capitalists. Indeed, individual capitalists left to themselves will tend to undersupply their own collective needs for production precisely because of such barriers. Individual capitalists tend to overaccumulate in the primary circuit and to underinvest in the secondary circuit; they have considerable difficulty in organizing a balanced flow of capital between the primary and secondary circuits.

A general condition for the flow of capital into the secondary circuit is, therefore, the existence of a functioning capital market and, perhaps, a state willing to finance and guarantee long-term, large-scale projects with respect to the creation of the built environment. At times of overaccumulation, a switch of flows from the primary to the secondary circuit can be accomplished only if the various manifestations of overaccumulation can be transformed into money capital that can move freely and unhindered into these forms of investment. This switch of resources cannot be accomplished without a money supply and credit system that creates "fictitious capital" *in advance* of actual production and consumption. This applies as much to the consumption fund (hence the importance of consumer credit, housing mortgages, municipal debt) as it does to fixed capital. Since the production of money and credit is a relatively autonomous process, we have to conceive of the financial and state institutions controlling the process as a kind of collective nerve center governing and *mediating* the relations between the primary and secondary circuits of capital. The nature and form of these financial and state institutions and the policies they adopt can play important roles in checking or enhancing flows of capital into the secondary circuit of capital or into certain specific aspects of it (such as transportation, housing, public facilities, and so on). An alteration in these mediating structures can therefore affect both the volume and the direction of capital flows by constricting movement down some channels and opening up new conduits elsewhere.

The Tertiary Circuit of Capital

In order to complete the picture of the circulation of capital in general, we have to conceive of a *tertiary circuit of capital* which comprises, first, investment in science and technology (the purpose of which is to harness science to production and thereby to contribute to the processes that continuously revolutionize the productive forces in society) and second, a wide range of social expenditures that relate primarily to the processes of reproduction of labor power. The latter can usefully be divided into investments directed toward the qualitative improvement of labor power from the standpoint of capital (investment in education and health by means of which the capacity of the laborers to engage in the work process will be enhanced) and investments in cooptation, integration, and repression of the labor force by ideological, military, and other means.

Individual capitalists find it hard to make such investments as individuals, no matter how desirable they may regard them. Once again, the capitalists are forced to some degree to constitute themselves as a class — usually through the agency of the state — and thereby to find ways to channel investment into research and development and into the quantitative and qualitative improvement of labor power. We should recognize that capitalists often *need* to make such investments in order to fashion an adequate social basis for further accumulation. But with regard to social expenditures, the investment flows are very strongly affected by the state of class struggle. The amount of investment in repression and in ideological control is directly related to the threat of organized working-class resistance to the depredations of capital. And the need to coopt labor arises only when the working class has accumulated sufficient power to require cooptation. Since the state can become a field of active class struggle, the mediations that are accomplished by no means fit exactly with the requirements of the capitalist class. The role of the state requires careful theoretical and historical elaboration in relation to the organization of capital flows into the tertiary circuit.

III. THE CIRCULATION OF CAPITAL AS A WHOLE AND ITS CONTRADICTIONS

Figure 3 portrays the overall structure of relations constituting the circulation of capital amongst the three circuits. The diagram looks very structuralist-functionalist because of the method of presentation. I can conceive of no other way to communicate clearly the various dimensions of capital flow. We now have to consider the contradictions embodied within these relations. I shall do so initially as if there were no overt class struggle between capital and labor. In this way we shall be able to see that the contradiction between the individual capitalist and capital in general is itself a source of major instability within the accumulation process.

We have already seen how the contradictions internal to the capitalist class generate a tendency toward overaccumulation within the primary circuit of capital. And I have argued that this tendency can be overcome, temporarily at

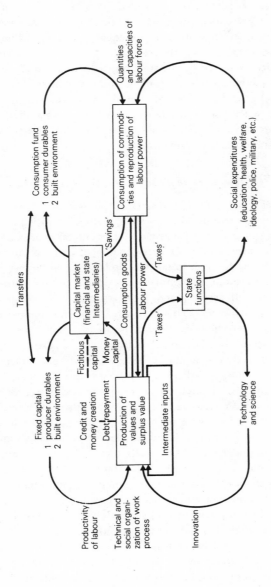

Fig. 3. The structure of relations between the primary, secondary, and tertiary circuits of capital

least, by switching capital into the secondary or tertiary circuits. Capital has, therefore, a variety of investment options open to it — fixed capital or consumption fund formation, investment in science and technology, investment in "human capital, as labor is usually called in bourgeois literature," or outright repression. At particular historical conjunctures capitalists may not be capable of taking up all of these options with equal vigor, depending upon the degree of their own organization, the institutions they have created, and the objective possibilities dictated by the state of production and the state of class struggle. I shall assume away such problems for the moment in order to concentrate on how the tendency toward overaccumulation, which I have identified so far only with respect to the primary circuit, manifests itself within the overall structure of circulation of capital. To do this I first need to specify the concept of productivity of investment.

On the Productivity of Investments in the Secondary and Tertiary Circuits

I choose the concept of "productivity" rather than "profitability" for a variety of reasons. First of all, the rate of profit as Marx treats of it in volume 3 of *Capital* is measured in value rather than pricing terms and takes no account of the distribution of the surplus value into its component parts of interest on money capital, profit on productive capital, rent on land, profit on merchants' capital, etc. The rate of profit is regarded as a social average earned by individual capitalists in all sectors, and it is assumed that competition effectively ensures its equalization. This is hardly a suitable conception for examining the flows between the three circuits of capital. To begin with, the formation of fixed capital in the built environment — particularly the collective means of production — cannot be understood without understanding the formation of a capital market and the distribution of part of the surplus in the form of interest. Second, many of the commodities produced in relation to the secondary and tertiary circuits cannot be priced in the ordinary way, while collective action by way of the state cannot be examined in terms of the normal criteria of profitability. Third, the rate of profit which holds is perfectly appropriate for understanding the behaviors of individual capitalists in competition but cannot be translated into a concept suitable for examining the behavior of capitalists as a class without some major assumptions (treating the total profit as equal to the total surplus value, for example).

The concept of productivity helps us to by-pass some of these problems if we specify it carefully enough. For the fact is that capitalists as a class — often through the agency of the state — do invest in the production of conditions that they hope will be favorable to accumulation, to their own reproduction as a class, and to their continuing domination over labor. This leads us immediately to a definition of a productive investment as one that directly or indirectly expands the basis for the production of surplus value. Plainly, investments in the secondary and tertiary circuits have the *potential* under certain conditions to do this. The problem – which besets the capitalists as much as it confuses us – is to identify the conditions and means that will allow this potential to be realized.

Investment in new machinery is the easiest case to consider. The new machinery is directly productive if it expands the basis for producing surplus value and unproductive if these benefits fail to materialize. Similarly, investment in science and technology may or may not produce new forms of scientific knowledge which can be applied to expand accumulation. But what of investment in roads, housing, health care and education, police forces and the military, and so on? If workers are being recalcitrant in the workplace, then judicious investment by the capitalist class in a police force to intimidate the workers and to break their collective power may indeed be productive indirectly of surplus value for the capitalists. If, however, the police are employed to protect the bourgeoisie in the conspicuous consumption of their revenues in callous disregard of the poverty and misery that surrounds them, then the police are not acting to facilitate accumulation. The distinction may be fine but it demonstrates the dilemma. How can the capitalist class identify, with reasonable precision, the opportunities for indirect and direct productive investment in the secondary and tertiary circuits of capital?

The main thrust of the modern commitment to planning (whether at the state or corporate level) rests on the idea that certain forms of investment in the secondary and tertiary circuits are potentially productive. The whole apparatus of cost-benefit analysis, of programming and budgeting, and of analysis of social benefits, as well as notions regarding investment in human capital, expresses this commitment and testifies to the complexity of the problem. And at the back of all of this is the difficulty of determining an appropriate basis for decision-making in the absence of clear and unequivocal profit signals. Yet the cost of bad investment decisions – investments that do not contribute directly or indirectly to accumulation of capital – must emerge somewhere. It must, as Marx would put it, come to the surface and thereby indicate the errors that lie beneath. We can begin to grapple with this question by considering the origins of crises within the capitalist mode of production.

On the Forms of Crisis under Capitalism

Crises are the real manifestation of the underlying contradictions within the capitalist process of accumulation. The argument that Marx puts forward throughout much of *Capital* is that there is always the potential within capitalism to achieve "balanced growth," but that this potential can never be realized because of the structure of the social relations prevailing in a capitalist society. This structure leads individual capitalists to produce results collectively that are antagonistic to their own class interest and leads them also to inflict an insupportable violence upon the working class which is bound to elicit its own response in the field of overt class struggle.

We have already seen how the capitalists tend to generate states of overaccumulation within the primary circuit of capital and have considered the various manifestations that result. As the pressure builds, either the accumulation process grinds to a halt or new investment opportunities are found as capital flows down various channels into the secondary and tertiary circuits. This movement may start as a trickle and become a flood as the potential for expanding the production of surplus value by such means becomes apparent. But the tendency toward overaccumulation is not eliminated. It is transformed, rather, into a pervasive tendency toward overinvestment in the secondary and tertiary circuits. This overinvestment is in relation solely to the needs of capital and has nothing to do with the real needs of people, which inevitably remain unfulfilled. Manifestations of crisis thus appear in both the secondary and tertiary circuits of capital.

As regards fixed capital and the consumption fund, the crisis takes the form of a crisis in the valuation of assets. Chronic overproduction results in the devaluation of fixed capital and consumption fund items – a process that affects the built environment as well as producer and consumer durables. We can likewise observe crisis formation at other points within the diagram of capital flows – crises in social expenditures (health, education, military repression, and the like), in consumption-fund formation (housing), and in technology and science. In each case the crisis occurs because the potential for productive investment within each of these spheres is exhausted. Further flows of capital do not expand the basis for the production of surplus value. We should also note that a crisis of any magnitude in any of these spheres is automatically registered as a crisis within the financial and state structures, while the latter, because of the relative autonomy that attaches to them, can be an independent source of crisis (we can thus speak of financial, credit, and monetary crises, the fiscal crises of the state, and so on).

Crises are the "irrational rationalizers" within the capitalist mode of production. They are indicators of imbalance and force a rationalization (which may be painful for certain sectors of the capitalist class as well as for labor) of the processes of production, exchange, distribution, and consumption. They may also force a rationalization of institutional structures (financial and state institutions in particular). From the standpoint of the total structure of relationships I have portrayed, we can distinguish different kinds of crises:

1. *Partial crises,* which affect a particular sector, geographical region, or set of mediating institutions. These can arise for any number of reasons but are

potentially capable of being resolved within that sector, region, or set of institutions. We can witness autonomously forming monetary crises, for example, which can be resolved by institutional reforms, crises in the formation of the built environment which can be resolved by reorganization of production for that sector, etc.

2. *Switching crises,* which involve a major reorganization and restructuring of capital flows and/or a major restructuring of mediating institutions in order to open up new channels for productive investments. It is useful to distinguish between two kinds of switching crises:

a. *Sectoral switching crises,* which entail switching the allocation of capital from one sphere (e.g. fixed capital formation) to another (e.g. education);

b. *Geographical switching crises,* which involve switching the flows of capital from one place to another. We note here that this form of crisis is particularly important in relation to investment in the built environment because the latter is immobile in space and requires interregional or international flows of money capital to facilitate its production.

3. *Global crises,* which affect, to a greater or lesser degree, all sectors, spheres, and regions within the capitalist production system. We will thus see devaluations of fixed capital and the consumption fund, a crisis in science and technology, a fiscal crisis in state expenditures, and a crisis in the pro-ductivity of labor, all manifest at the same time across all or most regions within the capitalist system. I note, in passing, that there have been only two global crises within the totality of the capitalist system – the first during the 1930s and its World War II, aftermath; the second, that which became most evident after 1973 but which had been steadily building throughout the 1960s.

A complete theory of capitalist crises should show how these various forms and manifestations relate in both space and time (see Harvey 1982). Such a task is beyond the scope of this chapter, but I can shed some light by returning to my fundamental theme – that of understanding the urban process under capitalism.

IV. ACCUMULATION AND THE URBAN PROCESS

The understanding I have to offer of the urban process under capitalism comes from seeing it in relation to the theory of accumulation. We must first establish the general points of contact between what seem, at first sight, two rather different ways of looking at the world.

Whatever else it may entail, the urban process implies the creation of a material physical infrastructure for production, circulation, exchange, and consumption. The first point of contact, then, is to consider the manner in which this built environment is produced and the way it serves as a resource system – a complex of use values – for the production of value and surplus value. We have, secondly, to consider the consumption aspect. Here we can usefully distinguish between the consumption of revenues by the bourgeoisie and the need to reproduce labor power. The former has a considerable impact upon the urban process, but I shall exclude it from the analysis because consideration of it would lead me into a lengthy discourse on the question of bourgeois culture and its complex significations without revealing very much directly about the specifically capitalist form of the urban process. Bourgeois consumption is, as it were, the icing on top of a cake that has as its prime ingredients capital and labor in dynamic relation to each other. The reproduction of labor power is essential and requires certain kinds of social expenditures and the creation of a consumption fund. The flows we have sketched, insofar as they portray capital movements into the built environment (for both production and consumption) and the laying out of social expenditures for the reproduction of labor power, provide us, then, with the structural links we need to understand the urban process under capitalism.

It may be objected, quite correctly, that these points of integration ignore the "rural-urban dialectic" and that the reduction of the urban process as we usually conceive of it to questions of built environment formation and reproduction of labor power is misleading if not downright erroneous. I would defend the reduction on a number of counts. First, as a practical matter, the mass of the capital flowing into the built environment and a large proportion of certain kinds of social expenditures are absorbed in areas that we usually classify as "urban." From this standpoint the reduction is a useful approximation. Second, I can discuss most of the questions that normally arise in urban research in terms of the categories of the built environment and social expenditures related to the reproduction of labor power with the added advantage that the links with the theory of accumulation can be clearly seen. Third, there are serious grounds for challenging the adequacy of the urban-rural dichotomy even when expressed as a dialetical unity, as a primary form of contradiction within the capitalist mode of production. In other words, and put quite bluntly, if the usual conception of the urban process appears to be violated by the reduction I am here proposing, then it is the usual conception of the urban process which is at fault.

The urban-rural dichotomy, for example, is regarded by Marx as an expression of the division of labor in society. In this, the division of labor is the fundamental concept and not the rural-urban dichotomy, which is just a particular form of its expression. Focusing on this dichotomy may be useful in seeking to understand social formations that arise in the transition to capitalism – such as those in which we find an urban industrial sector opposed to a rural peasant sector which is only formally subsumed within a system of commodity production and exchange. But in a purely capitalist mode of production – in which industrial and agricultural workers are all under the real domination of capital – this form of expression of the division of labor loses much of its particular significance. It disappears within a general concern for geographical specialization in the division of labor. And the other aspect of the urban process – the geographical concentration of labor power and use values for production and reproduction – also disappears quite naturally within an analysis of the rational spatial organization of physical and social infrastructures. In the context of advanced capitalist countries as well as in the analysis of the capitalist mode of production, the urban-rural distinction has lost its real economic basis, although it lingers, of course, within the realms of ideology with some important results. But to regard it as a fundamental conceptual tool for analysis is in fact to dwell upon a lost distinction that was in any case but a surface manifestation of the division of labor.

Overaccumulation and Long Cycles in Investment in the Built Environment

The acid test of any set of theoretical propositions comes when we seek to relate them to the experience of history and to the practices of politics. In the space of a chapter I cannot hope to demonstrate the relations between the theory of accumulation and its contradictions, on the one hand, and the urban process, on the other, in the kind of detail which would be convincing. I shall therefore confine myself to illustrating some of the more important themes that can be identified. I will focus first, exclusively on the processes governing investment in the built environment.

The system of production which capital established was founded on a physical separation between a place of work and a place of residence. The growth of the factory system, which created this separation, rested on the organization of cooperation, division of labor, and economies of scale in the work process as well as on the application of machinery. The system also promoted an increasing division of labor between enterprises and collective economies of scale through the agglomeration of activities in large urban centers. All of this meant the creation of a built environment to serve as a physical infrastructure for production, including an appropriate system for the transport of commodities. There are abundant opportunities for the productive employment of capital through the creation of a built environment for production. The same conclusion applies to investment in the built environment for consumption. The problem is, then, to discover how capital flows into the construction of this built environment and to establish the contradictions inherent in this process.

I should first say something about the concept of the built environment and consider some of its salient attributes. It is a complex composite commodity comprising innumerable different elements – roads, canals, docks and harbors, factories, warehouses, sewers, public offices, schools and hospitals, houses, offices, shops, etc. – each of which is produced under different conditions and according to quite different rules. The "built environment" is, then, a gross simplification, a concept that requires disaggregation as soon as we probe deeply into the processes of its production and use. Yet we also know that these components have to function as an ensemble in relation to the aggregative processes of production, exchange, and consumption. For purposes of exposition I can afford to remain at this level of generality. We also know that the built environment is long-lived, difficult to alter, spatially immobile, and often absorbent of large, lumpy investments. A proportion of it will be used in common by capitalists and consumers, and even those elements that can be privately appropriated (houses, factories, shops, etc.) are used in a context in which the externality effects of private uses are pervasive and often quite strong. All of these characteristics have implications for the investment process.

The analysis of fixed capital formation and the consumption fund in the context of accumulation suggests that investment in the built environment is likely to proceed according to a certain logic. Presume, for the moment, that the state does not take a leading role in promoting vast public works programs ahead of the demand for them. Individual capitalists, when left to their own devices, tend to underinvest in the built environment relative to their own individual and collective needs at the same time as they tend to overaccumulate. The theory then suggests that the overaccumulation can be siphoned off – via financial and state institutions and the creation of fictitious capital within the credit system – and put to work to make up the slack in investment in the built environment. This switch from the primary to the secondary circuit may occur in the course of a crisis or be accomplished relatively smoothly depending upon the efficiency of the mediating institutions. But the theory indicates that there is a limit to such a process and that at some point investments will become unproductive. At such a time the exchange value being put into the built environment has to be written down, diminished, or even totally lost. The fictitious capital contained within the credit system is seen to be just that, and financial and state institutions may find themselves in serious financial difficulty. The devaluation of capital in the built environment does not necessarily destroy the use value – the physical resource – constituted by the built environment. This physical resource can now be used as "devalued capital," and as such it functions as a free good that can help to reestablish the basis for renewed accumulation. From this we can see the logic of Marx's statement that periodic devaluations of fixed capital provide "one of the means immanent in capitalist production

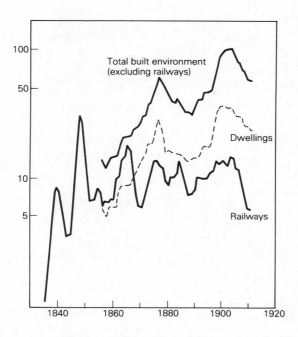

Fig. 4.   Investment in selected components of the built environment in Britain, 1835–1914 (million £ at current prices)

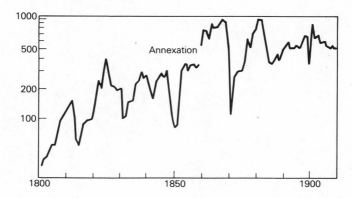

Fig. 5.   Construction activity in Paris — entries of construction materials into the city, 1800–1910 (millions of cubic meters). (After Rougerie, 1968.)

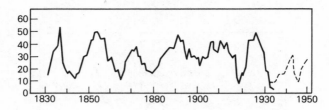

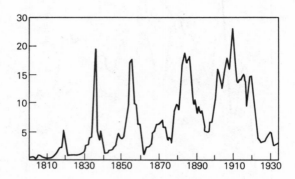

Fig. 6.   *Construction cycles in the United States, 1810–1950.* Top: *Building activity per capita in the United States (1913 dollars per capita). (After B. Thomas, 1972.)* Bottom: *Sale of public lands in the United States (millions of acres of original land entries). (U.S. Department of Agriculture data.)*

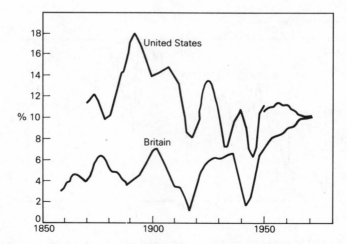

Fig. 7.   *Different rhythms of investment in the built environment in relation to GNP (U.S.A.) and GDP (Britain), 1860–1970 (five-year moving averages)*

to check the fall of the rate of profit and hasten accumulation of capital-value through formation of new capital."

Since the impulses deriving from the tendency to overaccumulate and to underinvest are rhythmic rather than constant, we can construct a cyclical model of investment in the built environment. The rhythm is dictated in part by the rhythms of capital accumulation and in part by the physical and economic lifetime of the elements within the built environment – the latter means that change is bound to be relatively slow. The most useful thing we can do at this juncture is to point to the historical evidence for "long waves" in investment in the built environment. Somewhere in between the short-run movements of the business cycle – the "Juglar cycles" of approximately ten years' length – and the very long "Kondratieff cycles," we can identify movements of an intermediate length (sometimes called "Kuznets cycles"), which are strongly associated with waves of investment in the built environment. Gottlieb's recent investigation[1] of building cycles in thirty urban areas located in eight countries showed a periodicity clustering between fifteen and twenty-five years. While his methods and framework for analysis leave much to be desired, there is enough evidence accumulated by a variety of researchers to indicate that this is a reasonable sort of first-shot generalization. Figures 4, 5, and 6 illustrate the phenomenon. The historical evidence is at least consistent with my argument, taking into account, of course, the material characteristics of the built environment itself and in particular its long life, which means that instant throwaway cities are hardly feasible no matter how hard the folk in Los Angeles try.

The immobility in space also poses its own problematic with, again, its own appropriate mode of response. The historical evidence is, once more, illuminating. In the "Atlantic economy" of the nineteenth century, for example, the long waves in investment in the built environment moved inversely to each other in Britain and the United States (see figs. 7 and 8). The two movements were not independent of each other but were tied via migrations of capital and labor within the framework of the international economy at that time. The commercial crises of the nineteenth century switched British capital from home investment to overseas investment or vice versa. The capitalist "whole" managed, thereby, to achieve a roughly balanced growth through counterbalancing oscillations of the parts all encompassed within a global process of geographical expansion.[2] Uneven spatial development of the built environment was a crucial element in the achievement of relative global stability under the aegis of the *Pax Britannica*

---

[1] Gottlieb (1976) provides an extensive bibliography on the subject as well as his own statistical analysis. The question of long waves of various kinds has recently been brought back into the Marxist literature by Mandel (1975) and Day (1976).

[2] The main source of information is Brinley Thomas, *Migration and Economic Growth* (1972 edition), which has an extensive bibliography and massive compilations of data.

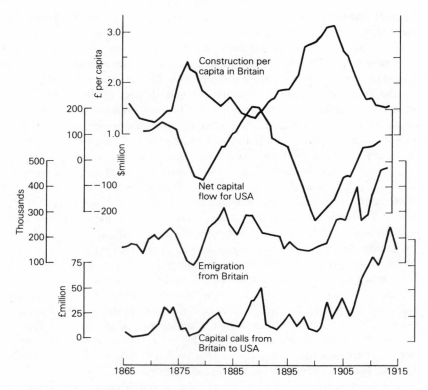

Fig. 8.   Uneven development in the Atlantic economy, 1865–1914 – Britain and the United States. (After B. Thomas, 1972.)

of the nineteenth century. The crises of this period were either of the partial or of the switching variety, and we can spot both forms of the latter – geographical and sectoral – if we look carefully enough.

The global crises of the 1930s and the 1970s can in part be explained by the breakdown of the mechanisms for exploiting uneven development in this way. Investment in the built environment takes on a different meaning at such conjunctures. Each of the global crises of capitalism was in fact preceded by the massive movement of capital into long-term investment in the built environment as a kind of last-ditch hope for finding productive uses for rapidly overaccumulating capital. The extraordinary property boom in many advanced capitalist countries from 1969 to 1973, the collapse of which at the end of 1973 triggered (but did not cause) the onset of the current crisis, is a splendid example (see fig. 9).

While I am not attempting in any strict sense to verify the theory by

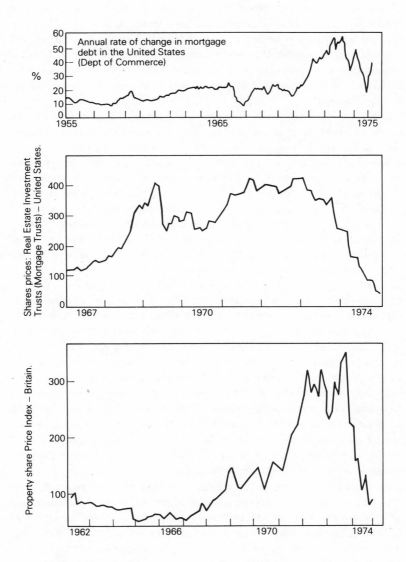

Fig. 9. Some indices of the property boom in Britain and the United States, 1955–1975.
Top: *Annual rate of change in mortgage debt in the United States. (Department of Commerce data.)* Middle: *Share prices of real estate investment trusts in the United States.*
(Source: Fortune Magazine.)
Bottom: *Property share price index in Britain.*
(Source: Investors Chronicle.)

appeal to the historical record, the latter most certainly is not incompatible with the broad outlines of the theory I have sketched. Bringing the theory to bear on the history is in fact an extraordinarily difficult task far beyond the scope of a short chapter. But rather than make no argument at all I shall try to illustrate how the connections can be made. I shall therefore look a little more closely at the two aspects of the theory which are crucial — overaccumulation and devaluation.

The flow of investment into the built environment depends upon the existence of surpluses of capital and labor and upon mechanisms for pooling the former and putting it to use. The history of this process is extremely interesting. The eighteenth century in Britain was characterized, for example, by a capital surplus, much of which went into the built environment because it had nowhere else to go. Investment in the built environment took place primarily for financial rather than use-value reasons — investors were looking for a steady and secure rate of return on their capital. Investment in property (much of it for conspicuous consumption by the bourgeoisie) and in turnpikes, canals, and rents (agricultural improvement) as well as in state obligations was about the only option open to rentiers. The various speculative crises that beset investment in the turnpikes and canals as well as urban property markets indicated very early that returns were by no means certain and that investments had to be productive if they were to succeed.[3]

It would be difficult to argue that during this period the surplus of capital arose out of the tendency to overaccumulate as I have specified it. The latter is, strictly speaking, a phenomenon that arises only in the context of the capitalist mode of production or in capitalist social formations that are relatively well developed. The long cycles of investment in the built environment predate the emergence of industrial capitalism and can be clearly identified throughout the transition from feudalism.[4] We can see, however, a strong relationship between these long cycles and fluctuations in the money supply and in the structure of capital markets. Perhaps the most spectacular example is that of the United States (see fig. 6) — when Andrew Jackson curbed land deals in paper currency and insisted on specie payment in 1836, the whole land development process came to a halt and the financial reverberations were felt everywhere, particularly by those investing in the built environment. The role of "fictitious" capital (see Harvey 1982, chaps. 9 and 10) and the credit and money supply system has always been fundamental

---

[3] The whole question of the capital surplus in the eighteenth century was first raised by Postan (1935) and subsequently elaborated on by Deane and Cole (1967). Recent studies on the financing of turnpikes and of canals in Britain by Albert (1972) and Ward (1974) provide some more detailed information.

[4] The best study is that by Parry Lewis (1965).

in relationship to the various waves of speculative investment in the built environment.

When, precisely, the tendency toward overaccumulation became the main agent producing surplus capital and when the long waves became explicitly tied to overaccumulation is a moot point. The evidence suggests that by the 1840s the connections had been strongly forged in Britain at least. By then, the functioning of the capital market was strongly bound to the rhythms imposed by the development of industrial capitalism. The "nerve center" that controls and mediates the relations between the primary and secondary circuits of capital increasingly functioned after 1830 or so according to a pure capitalist logic that affected both government and private activity. It is perhaps symptomatic that the fall of the July Monarchy in France in 1848 was directly related to the indebtedness of that regime incurred in the course of promoting a vast program of public works (many of which were not very productive). When the financial crisis, which had its origins in England and the extraordinary speculation in railroad construction, struck home in late 1846 and 1847, even the state debt of France could not withstand the shock.[5] For good reason, this crisis can perhaps be regarded as the first really solid and all-pervasive crisis in the capitalist world.

And what of the devaluation that inevitably results? If the devaluation is to function effectively, according to our theory, then it must leave behind a use value that can be used as the basis for further development. When many of the American states defaulted on their debts in the early 1840s, they failed to meet their obligations on the British capital market but kept the canals and other improvements that they had built. This was, in effect, expropriation without compensation – a prospect that the United States government treats with great moral indignation when some Third-World country threatens it today. The great railroad booms of the nineteenth century typically devalued capital while littering the landscape with physical assets that could usually be put to some use. When the urban mass transit systems went bankrupt at the turn of the century because of chronic overcapitalization, the mass transit systems were left behind as physical assets. Somebody had to pay for the devaluation, of course. There were the inevitable attempts to foist the costs onto the working class (often through municipal expenditures) or onto small investors. But big capital was not immune either, and the problems of the property companies in Britain or the real estate investment trusts in the United States in the years 1973–6 were exactly of this sort (although the involvement of pension funds and insurance companies affects individuals). The office space is still there, however, even though the building that houses it has been devalued and is now judged a nonearning asset. The history of

[5] See Girard (1952) and *The Urbanization of Consciousness*, chap. 3.

devaluations in the built environment is spectacular enough and fits, in general, with the theoretical argument.

The Contradictory Character of Investments in the Built Environment

I have so far treated the process of investment in the built environment as a mere reflection of the forces emanating from the primary circuit of capital. There are, however, a whole series of problems which arise because of the specific characteristics of the built environment itself. I shall consider these briefly.

Marx's extensive analysis of fixed capital in relation to accumulation reveals a central contradiction. On the one hand, fixed capital enhances the productivity of labor and thereby contributes to the accumulation of capital. But, on the other hand, it functions as a use value and requires the conversion of exchange values into a physical asset that has certain attributes. The exchange value locked up in this physical use value can be recouped only by keeping the use value fully employed over its lifetime, which for simplicity's sake I shall call its "amortization time." As a use value the fixed capital cannot easily be altered, and so it tends to freeze productivity at a certain level until the end of the amortization time. If new and more productive fixed capital comes into being before the old is amortized, then the exchange value still tied up in the old is devalued (Harvey 1982, chap. 8). Resistance to this devaluation checks the rise in productivity and, thus, restricts accumulation. The pursuit of new and more productive forms of fixed capital, however – dictated by the quest for relative surplus value – accelerates devaluations of the old.

We can identify exactly these same contradictory tendencies in relation to investment in the built environment, although they are even more exaggerated here because of the generally long amortization time involved, the fixity in space of the asset, and the composite nature of the commodity involved. I can demonstrate the argument most easily using the case of investment in transportation.

The cost, speed, and capacity of the transport system relate directly to accumulation because of the impacts these have on the turnover time of capital. Investment and innovation in transport are therefore potentially productive for capital in general. Under capitalism, consequently, we see a tendency to "drive beyond all spatial barriers" and to "annihilate space with time" (to use Marx's own expressions – see Chap. 2). This process is, of course, characterized typically by long cycles of the sort that we have already identified, uneven development in space, and periodic massive devaluations of capital.[6]

[6] See Isard (1942) for some interesting material.

I am here concerned, however, with the contradictions implicit in the process of transport development itself. Exchange values are committed to create "efficient" and "rational" configurations for spatial movement at a particular historical moment. There is, as it were, a certain striving toward spatial equilibrium, spatial harmony. In contrast, accumulation for accumulation's sake spawns continuous revolutions in transportation technology as well as a perpetual striving to overcome spatial barriers — all of which is disruptive of any existing spatial configuration.

We thus arrive at a paradox. In order to overcome spatial barriers and to annihilate space with time, spatial structures are created that themselves act as barriers to further accumulation. These spatial structures are expressed in the form of immobile transport facilities and ancillary facilities implanted in the landscape. We can in fact extend this conception to encompass the formation of the built environment as a whole. Capital represents itself in the form of a physical landscape created in its own image, created as use values to enhance the progressive accumulation of capital. The geographical landscape that results is the crowning glory of past capitalist development. But at the same time it expresses the power of dead labor over living labor, and as such it imprisons and inhibits the accumulation process within a set of specific physical constraints. And these can be removed only slowly unless there is a substantial devaluation of the exchange value locked up in the creation of these physical assets.

Capitalist development has therefore to negotiate a knife-edge path between preserving the exchange values of past capital investments in the built environment and destroying the value of these investments in order to open up fresh room for accumulation. Under capitalism there is, then, a perpetual struggle in which capital builds a physical landscape appropriate to its own condition at a particular moment in time, only to have to destroy it, usually in the course of a crisis, at a subsequent point in time. The temporal and geographical ebb and flow of investment in the built environment can be understood only in terms of such a process. The effects of the internal contradictions of capitalism, when projected into the specific context of fixed and immobile investment in the built environment, are thus writ large in the historical geography of the landscape that results.

V. CLASS STRUGGLE, ACCUMULATION, AND THE
URBAN PROCESS UNDER CAPITALISM

What, then, of overt class struggle — the resistance that the working class collectively offers to the violence that the capitalist form of accumulation inevitably inflicts upon it? This resistance, once it becomes more than merely nominal, must surely affect the urban process under capitalism in definite ways. We must, therefore, seek to incorporate some understanding of it into any analysis of the urban process under capitalism. By switching our window on the world – from the contradictory laws of accumulation to the overt class struggle of the working class against the effects of those laws – we can see rather different aspects of the same process with greater clarity. In the space that follows I shall try to illustrate the complementarity of the two viewpoints.

In one sense, class struggle is very easy to write about because there is no theory of it, only concrete social practices in specific social settings. But this immediately places upon us the obligation to understand history if we are to understand how class struggle has entered into the urban process. Plainly I cannot write this history in a few pages, so I shall confine myself to a consideration of the contextual conditions of class struggle and the nature of the bourgeois responses. The latter are governed by the laws of accumulation because accumulation always remains the means whereby the capitalist class reproduces itself as well as its domination over labor.

The central point of tension between capital and labor lies in the workplace and is expressed in struggles over the work process and the wage rate. These struggles take place in a context. The nature of the demands, the capacity of workers to organize, and the resolution with which the struggles are waged depend a great deal upon the contextual conditions. The law (property rights, contract, combination and association, etc.), together with the power of the capitalist class to enforce its will through the use of state power, is obviously fundamental, as any casual reading of labor history will abundantly illustrate. What specifically interests me here, however, is the process of reproduction of labor power in relation to class struggle in the workplace.

Consider, first, the quantitative aspects of labor power in relation to the needs of capitalist accumulation. The greater the labor surplus and the more rapid its rate of expansion, the easier it is for capital to control the struggle in the workplace. The principle of the industrial reserve army under capitalism is one of Marx's most telling insights. Migrations of labor and capital as well as the various mobilization processes by means of which "unused" elements in the population are drawn into the workforce are manifestations of this basic need for a relative surplus population. But we also have to consider the costs of reproduction of labor power at a standard of living which reflects a whole host of cultural, historical, moral, and environmental considerations. A change in these costs or in the definition of the standard of living has obvious implications for real-wage demands and for the total wage bill of the capitalist class. The size of the internal market formed by the purchasing power of the working class is not irrelevant to accumulation either. Consequently, the consumption habits of the workers are of considerable direct and indirect interest to the capitalist class.

But we should also consider a whole host of qualitative aspects of labor power encompassing not only skills and training but attitudes of mind, levels of compliance, the pervasiveness of the work ethic and of "possessive individualism," and the variety of fragmentations within the labor force which derive from the division of labor and occupational roles, as well as from older fragmentations along racial, religious, and ethnic lines. The ability and urge of workers to organize along class lines depends upon the creation and maintenance of a sense of class consciousness and class solidarity in spite of these fragmentations. The struggle to overcome these fragmentations in the face of divide-and-conquer tactics often adopted by the capitalists is fundamental to understanding the dynamics of class struggle in the workplace.

This leads us to the notion of *displaced* class struggle, by which I mean class struggle that has its origin in the work process but that ramifies and reverberates throughout all aspects of the system of relations which capitalism establishes. We can trace these reverberations to every corner of the social totality and certainly see them at work in the flows of capital between the different circuits. For example, if productivity fails to rise in the workplace, then, perhaps judicious investment in human capital (education), in co-optation (homeownership for the working class), in integration (industrial democracy), in persuasion (ideological indoctrination), or in repression might yield better results in the long run. Consider, as an example, the struggles around public education. In *Hard Times,* Dickens constructs a brilliant satirical counterpoint between the factory system and the educational, philanthropic, and religious institutions designed to cultivate habits of mind amongst the working class conducive to the workings of the factory system, while elsewhere he has that archetypal bourgeois, Mr. Dombey, remark that public education is a most excellent thing provided it teaches the common people their proper place in the world. Public education as a right has long been a basic working-class demand. The bourgeoisie at some point grasped that public education could be mobilized against the interests of the working class. The struggle over social services in general is not merely over their provision but over the very nature of what is provided. A national health care system that defines ill health as inability to go to work (to produce surplus value) is very different indeed from one dedicated to the total mental and physical well-being of the individual in a given physical and social context.

The socialization and training of labor – the management of human capital – cannot be left to chance. Capital therefore reaches out to dominate the living process – the reproduction of labor power – and it does so because it must. The links and relations here are intricate and difficult to unravel. Next I consider various facets of activity within the dwelling place as examples of displaced class struggle.

Some Remarks on the Housing Question

The demand for adequate shelter is clearly high on the list of priorities from the standpoint of the working class. Capital is also interested in commodity production for the consumption fund, provided this presents sufficient opportunities for accumulation. The broad lines of class struggle around the housing question have had a major impact upon the urban process. We can trace some of the links back to the workplace directly. The agglomeration and concentration of production posed an immediate quantitative problem for housing workers in the right locations – a problem that the capitalist initially sought to resolve by the production of company housing but that thereafter was left to the market system. The cost of shelter is an important item in the cost of labor power. The more workers have the capacity to press home wage demands, the more capital becomes concerned about the cost of shelter. But housing is more than just shelter. To begin with, the whole structure of consumption in general relates to the form that housing provision takes. The dilemmas of potential overaccumulation which faced the United States in 1945 were in part resolved by the creation of a whole new life style through the rapid proliferation of the suburbanization process. Furthermore, the social unrest of the 1930s pushed the bourgeoisie to adopt a policy of individual homeownership for the more affluent workers as a means to ensure social stability. This solution had the added advantage of opening up the housing sector as a means for rapid accumulation through commodity production. So successful was this solution that the housing sector became a Keynesian "contra-cyclical" regulator of the accumulation process as a whole, at least until the *débâcle* of 1973. The lines of class struggle in France were markedly different (see Houdeville 1969). With a peasant sector to ensure social stability in the form of small-scale private property ownership, the housing problem was seen politically mainly in terms of costs. The rent control of the interwar years reduced housing costs but curtailed housing as a field for commodity production with all kinds of subsequent effects on the scarcity and quality of housing provision. Only after 1958 did the housing sector open up as a field for investment and accumulation – and this under government stimulus. Much of what has happened in the housing field and the shape of the "urban" that has resulted can be explained only in terms of these various forms of class struggle.

The "Moral Influence" of Suburbanization as an Antidote to Class Struggle

My second example is even more complex. Consider, in its broad outlines, the history of the bourgeois response to acute threats of civil strife, which are often associated with marked concentrations of the working class and the unemployed in space. The revolutions of 1848 across Europe, the Paris Commune of 1871, the urban violence that accompanied the great railroad strikes of 1877 in the United States and the Haymarket incident of 1886 in Chicago, clearly demonstrated the revolutionary dangers associated with the high concentration of the "dangerous classes" in certain areas. The bourgeois response was in part characterized by a policy of dispersal so that the poor and the working class could be subjected to what nineteenth-century urban reformers on both sides of the Atlantic called the "moral influence" of the suburbs. Cheap suburban land, housing, and transportation were all a part of this solution entailing, as a consequence, a certain form and volume of investment in the built environment on the part of the bourgeoisie. To the degree that this policy was necessary, it had an important impact upon the shape of both British and American cities. And what was the bourgeois response to the urban riots of the 1960s in the ghettos of the United States? Open up the suburbs, promote low-income and black homeownership, improve access via the transport system . . . the parallels are remarkable.

The Doctrine of "Community Improvement" and Its Contradictions

The alternative to dispersal lies in the application of doctrines of community improvement. As early as 1812, the Reverend Thomas Chalmers proposed to mobilize the "spirit of community" as an antidote to the class consciousness and its associated threat of revolutionary violence then engulfing the rapidly growing proletariat in British cities. In Chalmers's hands this mainly meant the use of the church and other community institutions as weapons of ideological control, searching to promote a doctrine of community harmony in the face of the realities of class struggle. But in the hands of the civic, urban, and "moral" reformers of the late nineteenth century (in countries as diverse as Britain, France, and the United States) it meant a real effort to improve the qualities of life for at least the respectable working class if not for the urban poor. In the hands of sociologists like Le Play and the founders of the Chicago School, the religious imperative was subtly buried within seemingly neutral principles of scientific enquiry that also suggested modes of social action to counter the threat of social unrest. From the urban reformers like Joseph Chamberlain of Birmingham and the "progressives" of the United States, to the architects of the "great society" programs in the 1960s in the United States, we find a continuous thread of bourgeois response to a structural problem that just will not disappear.

But the "principle of community" is not a bourgeois invention. It also has its authentic working-class counterpart as a defensive and even an offensive weapon in class struggle. The conditions of life in the community are of great import to the working class, and they can therefore become a focus of struggle which can assume a certain relative autonomy from that waged in the factory. The institutions of community can be captured and put to work for working-class ends. The church in the early years of the industrial revolution was on occasion mobilized at the local level in the interests of the working class much as it also became a focus for the black liberation movement in the United States in the 1960s and is a mobilization point for class struggle in the Basque country of Spain. The principle of community can then become a springboard for class action rather than an antidote to class struggle. Indeed, we can argue that the definition of community as well as the command of its institutions is one of the stakes in class struggle in capitalist society. This struggle can break open into innumerable dimensions of conflict, pitting one element within the bourgeoisie against another and various fragments of the working class against others as the principles of "turf" and "community autonomy" become an essential part of life in capitalist society. The bourgeoisie has frequently sought to divide and rule but just as frequently has found itself caught in the harvest of contradictions it has helped to sow. We find bourgeois sub-urbanites resisting the further accumulation of capital in the built environment, and individual communities in competition for development producing a grossly inefficient and irrational spatial order even from the standpoint of capital at the same time as they incur levels of indebtedness which threaten financial stability (the dramatic fiscal difficulties of New York City, 1973–75, is typical of the historical experience of the United States). We find also civil disorder within the urban process escalating out of control as ethnic, religious, and racial tensions take on their own dynamic in partial response to bourgeois promptings (the use of ethnic and racial differences by the bourgeoisie to split organization in the workplace has a long and ignoble history in the United States in particular).

Working-Class Resistance and the Circulation of Capital

The strategies of dispersal, community improvement, and community competition, arising as they do out of the bourgeois response to class antagonisms, are fundamental to understanding the material history of the urban process under capitalism. And they are not without their implications for the circulation of capital either. The direct victories and concessions won by the working class have their impacts. But at this point we come back to the principles of accumulation, because if the capitalist class is to reproduce itself and its domination over labor it must effectively render whatever concessions labor wins from it consistent with the rules governing the productivity of investments under capitalist accumulation. Investments may switch from one sphere to another in response to class struggle to the degree that the rules for the accumulation of capital are observed. Investment in working-class housing or in a national health service can thus be transformed into a vehicle for accumulation via commodity production for these sectors. Class struggle can, then, provoke switching crises, the outcome of which can change the structure of investment flows to the advantage of the working class. But those demands that lie within the economic possibilities of accumulation as a whole can in the end be conceded by the capitalist class without loss. Only when class struggle pushes the system beyond its own internal potentialities are the accumulation of capital and the reproduction of the capitalist class called into question. How the bourgeoisie responds to such a situation depends on the possibilities open to it. For example, if capital can switch geographically to pastures where the working class is more compliant, then it may seek to escape the consequences of heightened class struggle in this way. Otherwise it must invest in economic, political, and physical repression or simply fall before the working-class onslaught.

Class struggle thus plays its part in shaping the flows of capital between spheres and regions. The timing of investments in the built environment of Paris, for example, is characterized by deep troughs in the years of revolutionary violence – 1830, 1848, 1871 (see fig. 5). At first sight the rhythm appears to be dictated by purely political events, yet the typical fifteen- to twenty-five-year rhythm works just as well here as it does in other countries where political agitation was much less remarkable. The dynamics of class struggle are not immune to influences stemming from the rhythms of capitalist accumulation, of course, but it would be too simplistic to interpret the political events in Paris solely in these terms (see *The Urbanization of Consciousness*, chap. 3). What seems so extraordinary is that the overall rhythms of accumulation remain broadly intact in spite of the variations in the intensity of working-class struggle.

But if we think it through, this is not, after all, so extraordinary. We still live in a capitalist society. And if that society has survived, then it must have done so by imposing those laws of accumulation whereby it reproduces itself. To put it this way is not to diminish working-class resistance but to show that a struggle to abolish the wages system and the domination of capital over labor must necessarily look to the day when the capitalist laws of accumulation are themselves relegated to the history books. And until that day, the capitalist laws of accumulation, replete with all of their internal contradictions, must necessarily remain the guiding force in our history.

3

Land Rent under Capitalism

Rent is that theoretical concept through which political economy (of whatever stripe) traditionally confronts the problem of spatial organization and the value to users of naturally occurring or humanly created differentials in fertility. Under the private property arrangements of capitalism, the actual appropriation of land rent by owners forms the basis for various forms of social control over the spatial organization and geographical development of capitalism.

But the social interpretation to be put upon land rent still remains a matter of controversy in the Marxist literature. Marx himself left the topic in a good deal of theoretical confusion. In incomplete and for the most part posthumously published writings, he posed as many conundrums as he solved. The central theoretical difficulty is to explain a payment made to the owners of land (as opposed to improvements embedded by human labor on the land) on the basis of a theory of value in which human labor is key. How can raw land, not itself a product of human labor, have a price (the appearance if not the reality of value)? Marx gives seemingly diametrically opposed answers to this fundamental question. On the one hand he characterizes the value of land as a totally irrational expression that can have no meaning under pure capitalist social relations; on the other he also characterizes ground rent as that "form in which property in land . . . produces value" (*Capital* 3:830–35, 618). In *Theories of Surplus Value* (pt. 2:152) he asserts that if the dominant class relation is between capital and labor then "the circumstances under which the capitalist in turn has to share a part of the . . . surplus value which he has captured with a third, non-working person, are only of secondary importance," whereas in *Capital* (3:618) he discusses how "wage labourers, industrial capitalists, and landowners" together constitute "in their mutual opposition, the framework of modern society" (in itself a startling jump, since landlords suddenly appear as a third "major class" right at the end of an analysis that rests on a two-class interpretation of capitalism).

Any solution to the theoretical conundrum that Marx left behind must be

robust enough to handle a wide diversity of practical and material circumstances. Marx himself observed that land can variously function as an *element,*
a *means,* or a *condition* of production, or simply be a *reservoir* of other use values
(such as mineral resources). Exactly how these different functions acquire
political-economic significance depends upon the kind of society we are
dealing with and the kinds of activities set in motion. In agriculture, for
example, the land becomes a *means* of production in the sense that a
production process literally flows through the soil itself. Under capitalism
this means that the soil becomes a conduit for the flow of capital through
production, therefore a form of fixed capital (or "land capital" as Marx
sometimes called it). When factories and houses are placed on the land, then
that land functions as a *condition* of production (space), though for the
building industry that puts them there in the first place land appears as an
element of production. Land "demands its tribute" (as Marx puts it) in all of
these different senses, but we must also bear in mind that the form and social
meaning of rent vary according to these diverse kinds of use. Furthermore,
the theory of rent must also encompass a wide diversity of payments – from
land-hungry peasants to landlords, from oil-rich potentates seeking pres-
tigious penthouses in the world's capital cities, from industrialists seeking
adequate sites for production, from builders seeking land for development,
from migrants seeking room and board in the city, from boutique owners
seeking access to upper-income clients, and the like. And the landowners are
themselves likely to be a motley bunch – wealthy families with large
holdings, workers with savings in a small land plot, land companies,
churches, insurance companies, banks and mortgage companies, multinational corporations, and the like. The "tribute" that flows on the basis of
landownership evidently moves in a multiplicity of directions.

Yet somehow we have to make sense of all this. We desperately need a
"scientific analysis of ground-rent," of the "independent and specific form of
landed property on the basis of the capitalist mode of production" in its "pure
form free of all distorting and obfuscating irrelevancies" (*Capital* 3:624). In
what follows I shall attempt such a scientific analysis on the basis of results
achieved elsewhere (Harvey 1982, chap. 11). To reduce the levels of
confusion, I shall begin with an analysis of land rent appropriated from the
circulation of capital in production before proceeding to an analysis of land
rent in relation to the circulation of revenues. I shall end with an analysis of
land rent in relation to those transitional conditions that typically arise before
capitalism is fully implanted as the dominant economic form within a social
formation. This permits me to address the problem of so-called "feudal
residuals" and the role of land rent in the transition to capitalism. I hope by
these steps to arrive at a clearer understanding of the role of land rent in the
historical geography of capitalist development.

I. RENT AND THE CIRCULATION OF CAPITAL

The monopoly of private property in land is, Marx asserts, both a "historical premise" and a "continuing basis" for the capitalist mode of production (*Capital* 3:617). Our task is to show how, why, and in what sense this assertion is true. To this end I shall begin with a strong set of simplifying assumptions. First, that all transitional features (feudal residuals) have been eliminated and that we are dealing with a purely capitalist mode of production. Second, that the rent on land can be clearly distinguished from all payments for commodities embodied in the land (land improvements, buildings, etc., which are the product of human labor and which have not yet been fully amortized). Third, that the circulation of *capital* can be clearly distinguished from the circulation of *revenues* (I take up the latter topic in the next section). And, finally, that land has a use value as an element, means, or condition of production (rather than of consumption; note also that I leave aside the concept of land as a reservoir of use values such as mineral resources as a special case). We are then in a position to analyze land rent directly in relation to the circulation of capital.

The best synoptic statement Marx provides of the continuing basis for land rent under capitalism is the following:

Landed property has nothing to do with the actual process of production. Its role is confined to transferring a portion of the produced surplus value from the pockets of capital to its own. However, the landlord plays a role in the capitalist process of production not merely through the pressure he exerts upon capital, nor merely because large landed property is a prerequisite and condition of capitalist production since it is a prerequisite and condition of the expropriation of the labourer from the means of production, but particularly because he appears as the personification of one of the most essential conditions of production. (*Capital* 3:821)

From this we can distinguish three distinctive roles. The expropriation of the laborer from the land was vital in the stage of primitive accumulation precisely because the land can always be used as a means of production. If labor is to be kept as wage labor then the laborer has to be denied free access to the land. From this standpoint we can see the barrier that landed property puts between labor and the land as socially necessary for the perpetuation of capitalism. This function could just as well be performed, however, if the land becomes state property, "the common property of the bourgeois class, of capital." The problem here is that many members of the bourgeoisie (including capitalists) are landowners, while "an attack upon one form of property . . . might cast considerable doubt on the other form" (*Theories of Surplus Value*, pt. 2:44, 104). From this standpoint, rent can be regarded as a side-payment allowed to landowners to preserve the sanctity and inviolability of private property in general and private ownership of the means of production in particular. This ideological, juridical, and political aspect of landed property is exceedingly important but not in itself sufficient to explain the capitalist forms of rent. The third role of landed property, which turns out to be the most difficult to pin down firmly, is crucial, therefore, to the social interpretation of land rent under capitalism.

The key to the interpretation of the role of landed property under capitalism lies in the pressure it asserts upon the capitalist. The nature of the pressure varies according to the kind of rent extracted. Monopoly and absolute rents interfere with accumulation and arise only to the degree that landed property acts as a barrier to the free flow of capital. Absolute rent, Marx asserts, must eventually disappear (*Capital* 3:765; *Theories of Surplus Value*, pt. 2:244, 393). And monopoly rents, to some degree unavoidable, particularly in urban areas and on land of special qualities (including location), must be kept to a minimum. But absolute and monopoly rents are not the important categories. This conclusion runs counter to Marx's often-quoted assertions concerning the importance of absolute rent (see *Selected Correspondence,* 134) but is consistent with the brief treatments he accords these concepts in *Capital* and *Theories of Surplus Value* compared to the page after page given over to wrestling with the nature of differential rents. I therefore follow Fine (1979) in thinking that Marx's views on differential rent, particularly those partially worked out in *Capital,* are quite distinct from those of Ricardo and provide the clue to the true interpretation to be put upon land rent in relation to the circulation of capital.

Marx follows Ricardo in distinguishing two kinds of differential rent but innovates by analyzing how the two forms of rent relate and "serve simultaneously as limits for one another" (*Capital* 3:737). Marx's insights are hard to recover from chapters full of convoluted argument and elaborate arithmetic calculations. I shall simply summarize the most important features.

Differential rent of the first type (DR-1) arises because producers on superior soils or in superior locations receive excess profits relative to production costs on the worst land in the worst locations. Superior soils and locations, like superior technology, are indeed sources of relative surplus value to individual producers (which explains why all of them can appear as "productive of value"). But unlike superior technology, superior locations and soils can form relatively permanent sources of excess profits. If the latter are taxed away as rent, the profit rate is equalized across different soils and locations. Capitalists can then compete with each other only through adoption of superior techniques – which pushes the capitalist system back onto its central track of looking to revolutions in the productive forces as the means to its salvation. The extraction of DR-1 has a vital social function in relation to the dynamics of capital accumulation. Without it, some producers could sit complacently on the excess profits conferred by "natural" or "locational" advantages and fail in their mission to revolutionize the productive forces on the land.

This conception of DR-1, essentially no different from that of Ricardo, has to be modified in three important respects. First, trade-offs can exist between fertility and location so that the worst land has to be understood as a combination of characteristics. Second, both fertility and location are social appraisals and subject to modification either directly (through soil exhaustion or improvement, changing transport facilities, etc.) or indirectly (through changing techniques of production which have different land or locational requirements). The excess profits from superior soils or locations are permanent only in relation to changing appraisals. Third, DR-1 depends upon a "normal" flow of capital into production on the land. And when we switch to consider what constitutes that normal flow of capital onto the land, we immediately encounter the problem of the second kind of differential rent (DR-2). The immediate implication is that DR-1 depends crucially on capital flows that automatically generate DR-2.

Imagine a situation in which no advantages due to location or fertility existed. Differentials in productivity on the land would then be caused solely by the different quantities of capital invested (assuming some pattern of returns to scale). Excess profits in this case are entirely due to the investment of capital. Conversion of these excess profits into DR-2 will simply check the flow of capital onto the land except under two particular conditions. First, if the investments embed relatively permanent productive forces in the land, then the flow of capital leaves behind a residue of improvements which form the basis for the appropriation of DR-1. Such residues (drained and cleared land and other forms of land improvement) are widespread and of great importance. Second, the direct appropriation of DR-2 can, under the right circumstances, prevent the flow of capital down channels that might be productive of profit for the individual capitalist but that would have a negative impact upon the aggregate growth in surplus value production. We here encounter a classic situation in which individuals, left to their own devices and coerced by competition, would engage in investment strategies that would undermine the conditions for the reproduction of the capitalist class as a whole. Under such conditions the external discipline imposed by landowners, like the external discipline exercised through the credit system, has a potentially positive effect in relation to the stabilization of accumulation. The emphasis, however, has to be upon the "potentiality" of this result, because what Marx's tedious arithmetic examples appear to show is that the appropriation of DR-2 can exercise a negative, neutral, or positive pressure upon the accumulation of capital depending upon the circumstances. Furthermore, the flow of capital onto the land also depends upon general conditions of accumulation – a plethora of capital in general or particular conditions prevailing within the credit system have direct implications for the flow of capital onto the land (*Capital* 3:770, 676).

Now combine the interpretations of DR-1 and DR-2. We will be seriously in error, as Fine (1979) points out, if we treat the two forms of rent as separate and additive. Insofar as DR-1 depends on a social appraisal of "natural and locational advantage," it depends upon capital flows that often modify nature in crucial ways. The appropriation of DR-2, for its part, could not occur without DR-1 as its basis. The two forms of differential rent in effect merge to the point where the distinction between what is due to land (with the aim of equalizing the rate of profit and keeping the impulsion to revolutionize the productive forces engaged) and what is due to capital (with the aim of keeping the flow of capital into revolutionizing the productive forces on the land at a level consistent with sustained accumulation) is rendered opaque. In other words, the appropriation of rent internalizes contradictory functions. The permanent tension between landowners and capitalists within a purely capitalistic mode of production is a reflection of this contradiction. Furthermore, to the degree that rental appropriation can have negative, neutral, or positive effects in relation to accumulation, the social relations that arise in response to this contradiction can have a powerful effect upon the allocation of capital to land, the whole structure of spatial organization, and, hence, the overall dynamic of accumulation. In order to explore these contradictions and their effects, however, we must first establish the form that private property in land must assume if it is to be integrated within a purely capitalist mode of production.

The conclusion to which Marx points, without full explication, is that land must be treated as a pure financial asset and that land has to become a form of "fictitious capital." This conclusion calls for some explanation (Harvey 1982, chaps. 9 and 11). "Fictitious capital" amounts to a property right over some future revenue. Stocks and shares, for example, can be sold before any actual production takes place. The buyers trade their money in return for a share of the fruits of future labor. Insofar as the money is used to set labor in motion (or create conditions, such as physical infrastructures, to enhance the productivity of social labor), then the fictitious capital stands to be realized. Even under the best conditions, fictitious capital entails speculation; and under the worst, it provides abundant opportunity for fraud and devaluation. Capitalism could not function, however, without the large-scale creation and movement of fictitious forms of capital via the credit system and capital markets. Only in this way can capital be shifted rapidly from unprofitable to profitable sectors and regions, new lines of activity be opened up, centralization of capitals be achieved, etc. The credit system (capital markets in particular) becomes the central nervous system for the coordination of accumulation. It also becomes the central locus of all of capitalism's internal contradictions. Crises always appear, in the first instance, therefore, as financial and monetary crises.

Once the significance of fictitious forms of capital is established, we can see how property rights over any form of future revenue might be bought and traded. Government debt (a right to a share of future taxes) and mortgages on land (a right to future rents) and property (a right to amortization payments) all stand to be freely traded. In the case of land, what is bought and sold is the title to the ground rent yielded by it. That ground rent, when capitalized at the going rate of interest, yields the land price. Hence arises an intimate relationship between rent and interest. The money laid out by the buyer of land is equivalent to an interest-bearing investment, a claim upon the future fruits of labor. Title to land becomes a form of fictitious capital, in principle no different from stocks and shares, government bonds, etc. (although it has certain qualities of security, illiquidity, etc.). Land, in short, can be regarded as a pure financial asset. This is the condition, I argue, that dictates the pure form of landed property under capitalism.

The theory of ground rent tells us that landowners should ruthlessly appropriate all excess profits due to relatively permanent advantages of fertility or location (no matter whether the product of capital or not). Anticipated future excess profits (due to future capital flows and future labor) affect the price of land in the present insofar as land becomes a pure financial asset, a form of fictitious capital. Marx excluded such speculative activity from his purview (except in a few rare instances, e.g., *Capital* 3:774–76) and was therefore content to view landownership as an entirely passive function. But land markets, like capital markets, play a vital coordinating role in the allocation of future capital and labor to the land. Landowners leave behind their passive stances and can play an active role in the creation of conditions that permit enhanced future rents to be appropriated. In so doing, of course, they condemn future labor to ever-increasing levels of exploitation in the name of the land itself. But they also play a vital role in relation to accumulation.

Landowners can coerce or cooperate with capital to ensure the creation of enhanced ground rents in the future. By perpetually striving to put the land under its "highest and best use," they create a sorting device that sifts land uses and forces allocations of capital and labor that might not otherwise occur. They also inject a fluidity and dynamism into the use of land which would otherwise be hard to generate and so adjust the use of land to social requirements. They thereby shape the geographical structure of production, exchange, and consumption, the technical and social division of labor in space, and the socioeconomic spaces of reproduction, and invariably exert a powerful influence over investment in physical infrastructures (particularly transportation). They typically compete for that particular pattern of development, that particular bundle of investments and activities, which has the best prospect for enhancing future rents. In this way, as Marx puts it, "rent, instead of binding man to Nature, merely bound the exploitation of the land to competition" (*Poverty of Philosophy*, 159).

We can now bring the argument full circle. Not only is the appropriation of rent socially necessary under capitalism by virtue of the key coordinating functions it performs, but landowners must also treat the land as a pure financial asset, a form of fictitious capital, and seek, thereby, an active role in coordinating the flow of capital onto and through the land. The effect is to free up the land to the circulation of interest-bearing capital and to tie land markets, land uses, and spatial organization into the general circulation process of capital.

But by the same token, the more open the land market is, the more recklessly can surplus money capital build pyramids of debt claims and seek to realize these claims through the pillaging and destruction of the land itself. Investment in appropriation, so necessary if the land market is to perform its vital coordinating functions, simultaneously opens up the land to "all manner of insane forms" let loose within the credit system in general. What appears as a sane and sober device for coordinating the use of land to surplus value production and realization can all too easily dissolve into a nightmare of incoherence and periodic orgies of speculation. Here, as elsewhere, the only ultimate form of rationality to which capitalism responds is the irrationality of crisis.

I can, at this point, rest my case. There is a form of landownership and land rent which fully integrates with the circulation of capital. Land markets, like capital markets, do not produce value in the primary sense, but they play a vital role in coordinating the application of social labor. Capitalism simply would not work without them. And land markets could not exist without land rent, the appropriation of excess profit from capital. The crisis-prone character of capitalism is, of course, carried over and even heightened within the credit system as well as within land markets. The detailed study of the specific form these internal contradictions take within land markets is an urgent matter.

Yet all of this requires that land be treated as a pure financial asset, a form of fictitious capital. This requires that the power of any distinct class of landowners be broken, that ownership of land become from all standpoints (including psychological) simply a matter of choosing what kinds of assets to include in a general portfolio of investments. And this, of course, is increasingly how pension funds, insurance companies, and even private

individuals tend to view land investment. This is not to say that in practice
all traditional forms of landownership have disappeared in the advanced
capitalist world. But it is interesting to note that land has long been
dominantly viewed as a pure financial asset in the United States (the country
least hindered by "feudal residuals") and that the direction of the transition in
countries such as Britain has been very much toward the acceptance of land as a
form of fictitious capital. The point, of course, is that these forms of
landownership (and the social attitudes they generate) are entirely consistent
with the circulation of capital, at the same time as they are fully expressive of
the internal contradictions within that circulation process.

II. RENT AND THE CIRCULATION OF REVENUES

Within a purely capitalist mode of production, all forms of revenue – wages,
profit of enterprise, interest, taxes, rent, etc. – have their origin in the
production of value and surplus value. But, once distributed, revenues are
free to circulate, thereby creating opportunities for various secondary forms of
exploitation. Rents can, therefore, just as easily be appropriated from the
circulation of revenues as from the circulation of capital. Landlords are
presumably indifferent to the immediate origin of the rental payment. They
are satisfied as long as the rent keeps rolling in. But the theoretical
distinctions are of interest because circumstances often arise, particularly
though not exclusively in urban areas, where it is impossible to understand
the social meaning of rental payments without explicit consideration of the
circulation of revenues.

The intricacy of the circulation of revenues bears some initial elaboration.
The total wage bill, for example, is split among different factions of the
proletariat according to their reproduction costs and their gains through class
struggle. Capitalists, furthermore, do not normally discriminate as to
individual needs of their workers and simply pay the going rate for a job. But
individual worker wants and needs vary enormously depending upon family
status, age, health, and, of course, tastes and fancies. On a given day,
therefore, some workers will possess money surpluses while others will be
unable to meet their needs. The stage is set for the circulation of wage
revenues within the working class. First, payments may be made for services
rendered (baby-sitting, washing, mending, cooking, etc.). Second, workers
may borrow and lend to one another, sometimes at a rate of interest. The
early benefit societies, savings and loan associations, and so forth, were
simply attempts to institutionalize such activity. The extent of this circulation of revenue varies, but it can be quite massive. The social security
system, for example, is a transfer from those now working to those now
retired, in return for a claim on a share of future wages.

Various factions of the bourgeoisie can also circulate revenues amongst and between one another, either by trading services or through intricate patterns of lending (read any tale by Balzac or Dickens to get some sense of the importance, socially, of this form of the circulation of revenues). Revenues can also circulate between the social classes. The bourgeoisie frequently hires workers at a going rate to render the kinds of services that taste, fashion, custom, fancy, and income dictate. The cook, the valet, the prostitute, the gardener, are all paid out of the circulation of revenues and not directly out of the circulation of capital. Workers may likewise pay, or be forced to pay, for services rendered them by the bourgeoisie (legal, administrative, etc.).

The circulation of revenues is, evidently, both intricate in its detail and massive in scale. Much of the detail of what happens in bourgeois society, including the appropriation of rent, has to be understood in relation to it. We will be seriously in error if we seek to explain that detail by direct reference to categories Marx designed to cope with the dynamics of capital circulation. Yet the circulation of revenues necessarily integrates with the circulation of capital at well-defined points. In a purely capitalist mode of production, all revenues have their origin in value and surplus value production and ultimately return to the circulation of capital through the purchase of commodities. If this aggregate relation does not hold, then the circulation of capital breaks down. Furthermore, to the degree that circulation time is vital to capital, time lost through the circulation of revenues is a drag upon accumulation. But we here encounter situations in which an appropriate circulation of revenues can play a positive role in relation to accumulation. If, for example, houses had to be bought for cash and individuals had to save the full cash amount to buy them, then vast sums of money would have to be hoarded. The circulation of money as capital and the demand for housing (an important field for accumulation) would both be held in check. Renting or a credit system through which individuals with surplus savings can lend to those in need overcomes the blockage. Hoards are reduced and the free circulation of capital maximized. An inadequate structure for the circulation of revenues can therefore act as a barrier to the circulation of capital. State policy, particularly in its welfare aspects, has often been dedicated to achieving more efficient structures for the circulation of revenues in relation to the circulation of capital. There is, in this, a certain convenience because social unrest can often be coopted by reforms that appear to satisfy worker needs by rationalizing the circulation of revenues while leaving the circulation of capital if anything enhanced rather than diminished. The reforms of the American New Deal were very much of this sort.

The problem, of course, is that once revenues begin to circulate, then there is nothing to guarantee that they will do so in ways appropriate to the circulation of capital. While lending to cover the purchase of a house may appear perfectly rational from the standpoint of accumulation, the passing of

IOU's to cover spiraling gambling debts does not. All kinds of opportunities exist, also, for secondary forms of exploitation – usurious lending or rack-renting practices, for example. And to cap it all, the distinction between the circulation of capital and the circulation of revenues is also hard to sustain in the diverse money transactions that characterize daily life. If workers lend to other workers at a rate of interest, then why can't they lend also to capitalists, particularly if the rate of interest is higher? And if workers borrow, then what is to stop the rise of usurious practices within the working class (the hated pawnshop) or the penetration of capitalist lending to control and stimulate working-class consumption? The problem arises here because the distinction between workers and capitalists is obscured within the credit system where the primary relation is between lenders and borrowers, debtors and creditors, of whatever sort. All kinds of cross-currents then arise inconsistent with the primary forms of exploitation that Marx dwells upon at such length and so exclusively.

Consider, now, how this relates to the social interpretation to be put upon the rental payment. The monopoly power conferred by private property in land always remains the basis. But we now see that rent is not only appropriated from capitalists as a straight deduction out of the surplus value produced under their command. Rent is also levied from workers, other members of the bourgeoisie (financiers, professionals, retired businessmen, other landlords, etc.), the state, and cultural, religious, and educational organizations. Rent can be appropriated from the circulation of revenues of *all* sorts. We can hardly use Marx's categories (which deal solely with the circulation of capital) to explain the rent paid by company executives for penthouses in Paris or London, the rent paid by rich retirees in Florida or unemployed blacks in Baltimore's ghetto. Furthermore, to the degree that land has been reduced to a pure form of fictitious capital, a pure financial asset, anyone who saves can invest in it, appropriate rent, and speculate in land price. If workers own small plots of land and the property thereon, they can just as well play this game as anyone else. Indeed, petty land and property trading and renting (even a room) has been a prime means for upward mobility within the working class and the petite bourgeoisie for centuries. The destruction of the singular power of any coherent landlord class, a concomitant of the rise of the purely capitalist form of ground rent (see Massey and Catalano 1978), opens up the possibility to anyone who has savings to invest them in land and so acquire the power to appropriate rent.

Is there any way to see through this crazy patchwork quilt of social relations and say something coherent about the social meaning of the rental payment? I think Marx's analysis, suitably modified, remains helpful.

To begin with, we can situate the appropriation of rent as a moment within the circulation of revenues in general and then invoke the necessary relation between the latter and the circulation of capital in order to explore the limits of the total capacity for rental appropriation. If all surplus value is appropriated and held as rent, then there would be no place for the accumulation of capital or, for that matter, any other form of revenue circulation. I quote the *reductio* case to pose this question: how much rental appropriation is appropriate to sustain the accumulation of capital? We have already argued that rental appropriation from production has an important function to play in allocating land to uses and in shaping spatial organization to capitalism's requirements. We now see that exactly the same consideration holds for the "rational" allocation of consumption uses across space. The flow of fictitious capital through the land therefore has the positive attribute that it can forge "rational" spatial configurations of both production and consumption in relationship to aggregate accumulation. Capitalism stands to benefit from the persistence of private property and land rent. The problem, of course, is that there is nothing to prevent the rise of all manner of insane speculative and monopolistic practices within the field of rental appropriation or the transmission of speculative impulses from within the credit system. The dual consequence of excessive appropriation of rent in relation to the circulation of capital and gross distortions of spatial structure leads to strong demands to eliminate or control the power to appropriate rent through state interference. The positive, neutral, or negative effects of rental appropriation in relation to accumulation remain perpetually with us, part and parcel of the equilibrating and disequilibrating tendencies within the capitalist mode of production.

The interior details of the appropriation of rent in relation to the circulation of revenues are also open to closer scrutiny, in part by analogy to the basic Marxian categories. Consider, for example, the rent appropriated from the working class. A secondary form of exploitation, as both Marx (in passing) and Engels (1935) argued, the rent extracted from the worker can affect the value of labor power and so diminish surplus value to the capitalist. On this basis Engels attacked those who sought any solution to the housing question in the absence of any attack upon the wages question. While correct in substance, this does not absolve us from the need to analyze the economic, social, and ideological consequences of the rental payment. Analysis of such questions reveals some interesting insights. For example, if workers receive a uniform wage, then those who live close to work will incur lower transport costs and therefore lower costs of social reproduction. Properly structured rents on working-class housing would then have the effect of equalizing the real wage to workers at different locations. The analogy with differential rent on capital is exact. The problem, of course, is that there is nothing in the power relations between landowners and workers to ensure that rents are "properly" structured in the first place. Furthermore, workers also compete for living space against capitalist producers and bourgeois consumers. The level of appropriation of rent from one kind of revenue cannot be understood independently of the others. The relations between land and property rent, transport availability, employment opportunities, and housing, as well as other consumer functions, all in the context of shifting geographical patterns in the circulation of both capital and revenues, then define the nexus of forces shaping the spatial configuration of land uses.

It is into such a situation that those who use land as an *element* of production – the developers and builders – insert themselves as the prime movers creating new spatial configurations of the built environment and new opportunities for rental appropriation. The analogy is with DR-2, but in this case the investment of capital yields its return through an enhanced capacity to tap the circulation of revenues. This is as true for the builders of back-to-back housing as it is for the developers of expensive condominiums for the haute bourgeoisie. Fictitious capital in land makes its claim upon future labor indirectly (as in the case of housing purchase with the aid of a mortgage) through the future circulation of wages and other forms of revenue.

But the combination of the monopoly privileges inherent in any form of private property in land and the active processes of production of particular spatial configurations generates many an opportunity to garner monopoly rents. This tendency, as Marx observed, is particularly strong in urban areas. Specific sites can command a premium land rent precisely because of their privileged location relative to previous investments. Indeed, whole islands of privilege can be constructed within which all landowners acquire the collective power to garner monopoly rent – be it landlords within the confines of the ghetto or developers peddling loft space to affluent young professionals in New York's Soho district (Zukin 1982). Situations arise, therefore, in which the concept of "class-monopoly rent" makes eminent sense. We do not have to appeal here to the idea of any inherent class power on the part of all landholders nor even depart from the concept of land as a pure financial asset, a form of fictitious capital. We simply have to recognize that within the complex matrix of urban development, situations arise in which space can be collectively monopolized and a given pattern of the circulation of revenues trapped within its confines. Even the concept of "housing class" makes sense when projected and understood against such a background.

The full theory of such relationships remains to be worked out. Marx's theory of rent is partial because it deals solely with the circulation of capital and excludes any direct analysis of the circulation of revenues. We cannot, therefore, simply take Marx's categories and make them work for us in the actual analysis of the total complex of land and property markets (particularly in urban areas). Something more is involved, even presuming a purely capitalist mode of production. And that something more is the circulation of revenues, albeit always related back to the circulation of capital that necessarily lies at its basis. A closer look at how rent is appropriated from the circulation of both capital and revenues will generate more precise understandings of the surface appearance of the functioning of land markets without abandoning the deep structural insights that Marx generated.

III. RENT IN TRANSITIONAL SOCIAL FORMATIONS

The social interpretation to be put on rent varies from society to society and undergoes a fundamental alteration with the transition from one mode of production to another. "In each historical epoch," Marx writes, "property has developed differently and under a set of entirely different social relations" (*Poverty of Philosophy*, 154). We will be grossly in error if we interpret feudal rents, or rents in the transitional phase when landed capital held sway, directly by reference to the role of rent in advanced capitalist society. Yet a knowledge of the latter is indispensable to an interpretation of the former. Furthermore, it is in the nature of the transition to merge two often quite antagonistic roles so they become indistinguishable. The difficulty is, then, to keep the social interpretations distinct from each other while simultaneously understanding how they can coexist within the same money payment for the use of land. Only in this way can we understand how one form of rent is gradually converted into the other through a material historical process.

Marx considered that money rent on land and its corollary, the formation of land markets, were preconditions for the rise of capitalism. Like merchants' capital and usury, landed capital precedes the modern standard form of capital. The latter ultimately subjugates these earlier forms and converts them to its own requirements. The actual history of this process is strewn with complexities generated out of the cross-currents of class struggle and the diversity of initial conditions of land tenure and ownership. Marx's general version of this history, based on the Western European experience, can be divided into two phases. In the first, feudal labor rents (the source of a surplus product) are transformed into rent in kind and finally into a money payment, while land is increasingly released from those constraints that prevent it from being freely traded as a commodity. Furthermore, the conversion to money payments implies either a voluntary or a forcible integration of land users (particularly agricultural producers) into some kind of general system of commodity production and exchange.

None of this ensures, however, that rent assumes its modern, purely capitalistic form, thoroughly integrated into the circulation of capital (and revenues). All kinds of intermediate forms can arise. In a stimulating and provocative work, Pierre-Philippe Rey (1973) proposes that these be viewed as "complex articulations" of different modes of production, one upon the other. Rey goes on to show how material conditions and class configurations and alliances can freeze the transition in a half-way state between precapitalist and capitalist modes of production for extended periods (as often appears to be the case in Third World peasant societies). What Marx viewed as an inevitable though lengthy transition can, in Rey's view, be all too easily blocked. Unfortunately, Rey goes on to argue that rent has no real basis within a capitalist mode of production and that it can be interpreted only as a relation of distribution which reflects a relation of production of precapitalist modes of production (e.g., feudalism) with which capitalism is "articulated." We have already seen how that conclusion can be refuted and a real social basis uncovered for the appropriation of rent within a purely capitalist mode of production. But for the moment we shall follow Rey's perceptive line of argument as it applies to the transitional phase.

Under transitional conditions, landlords can play a direct and active role in the exploitation of labor (as opposed to the backseat, passive role that Marx [incorrectly] assigned them under capitalism). This is as true for slave economies (the American South prior to the Civil War) as it is for landlord-peasant systems of agricultural production in the present era. There is a direct incentive for the landlord to extract the maximum of rent (whether in kind or in money does not immediately concern us), not only because this maximizes the landlord's revenues, but also because the peasant is forced to work harder and harder and produce more and more commodities for the market at ever lower prices (given the increase in supply). The massive exploitation of a rural peasantry by a landlord class is, from this standpoint, perfectly consistent with industrial capitalism as long as it provides cheap food for workers and cheap raw materials for industry. And even if the peasants nominally own their own land (there is no overt landlord class), indebtedness at usurious interest rates and the obligation to pay taxes to the state can have the same effect. It is not hard to see how a powerful alliance of classes comprising landowners, industrial bourgeoisie, and money lenders, backed by the state, can form and block any full transition to capitalist social relations on the land.

But such a form of exploitation, like absolute surplus value (of which it is a bastard form), has negative social consequences and inherent limits. First, the extraction of a fixed money payment from basically subsistence producers may diminish the supply of commodities when prices rise because producers have to sell less to reach a fixed money goal. Prices continue to rise as a consequence. When prices go down, however, peasants have to sell more and so increase the supply in the face of falling prices. Price movements and commodity supplies do not, under such conditions, integrate at all well with the general dynamic of accumulation. That dynamic, second, invariably requires an expansion of output which, with a fixed technology of peasant production, means increasing rates of exploitation. And as exploitation increases, so do the conditions for revolutionary movements ripen. Even in the absence of such resistance, there is an absolute limit to this kind of absolute exploitation. At some point the productive forces on the land have to be revolutionized to accommodate the expanding demands of capitalism. We then discover that the transitional forms of organization inhibit "the development of the social productive forces of labour, social forms of labour, social concentration of capital . . . and the progressive application of science" (*Capital* 3:807). New productive forces have to be deployed, and that means opening up the land to the free flow of capital.

This brings us to the second phase of Marx's version of the transition to capitalist forms of rental appropriation. Capital and labor must confront each other on the land free from any direct interference of the landlord class. The landlord must be reduced to a purely passive figure. The class alliance between an industrial bourgeoisie and a landlord class breaks down, and antagonistic relations arise between them until such time as the latter class entirely disappears as a coherent force in society. And all of this must happen because this is the only way, under capitalism, for productive forces to be revolutionized on the land itself.

We can understand this transition from the standpoint of the landlord in the following way. The landlord can dominate a peasantry tied to the land and has everything to gain from maximizing the extraction of rent. But the landlord cannot similarly compel the capitalist to invest, and therefore has much to lose from maximizing the extraction of rent from the capitalist. The power of landed property then acts as a barrier to the free flow of capital onto the land and inhibits the development of the productive forces. The possibility exists, however, for a terrain of compromise between landowner and capitalist. The use value of land to the capitalist is as an element, means, or condition of production which, when worked on by labor, produces surplus value. The capitalist is concerned with rent in relation to surplus value produced. The landlord, in contrast, is concerned with the rent per acre. Under conditions of strong capital flow onto the land the rent per acre can rise while the rent as a portion of surplus value produced declines (cf. *Capital* 3:683). Under these conditions, the landlord has everything to gain by minimizing the barrier that landed property places to the flow of capital. This was, of course, the basis of the compromise that existed in England during the period of "high farming," 1850–73.

The relationship between capital and landed property is not reduced thereby to one of perpetual harmony. It is often hard to distinguish, for example, between peasant producers and small-scale capitalist producers, while landlords may not be sophisticated enough to appreciate the long-term gain to them of the shift from rack-renting peasants to seducing capitalists to invest. Also, to the degree that the expansion of social labor "stimulates the demand for land itself," landed property acquires "the capacity of capturing an ever-increasing portion" of surplus value (*Capital* 3:637–39). Blessed with such an opportunity, what landlord could resist exploiting it? The landlord is perpetually caught between the evident foolishness of extracting too little from capital and the penalties that accrue from trying to take too much. And there are, in addition, all kinds of institutional problems relating to permanent improvements, tenancy conditions, leasing arrangements, and the like, which are the focus of interminable struggles between capitalist and landlord. Like contractual issues that arise between capital and labor these institutional arrangements are ultimate regulated through the state.

Marx evidently did not feel too secure in his rendition of how the capitalist form of private property came to be. He was later to claim that he had merely sought to "trace the path by which, in Western Europe, the capitalist economic system emerged from the womb of the feudal economic system," and he attacked those who transformed his "historical sketch of the genesis of capitalism into an historico-philosophical theory of the general path of development prescribed by fate to all nations, whatever the historical circumstances in which they find themselves" (*Selected Correspondence*, 312–13). His studies of the evolution of landed property in the colonies and the United States, as well as in Russia, convinced him that the transition was not unilinear. Even in Western Europe considerable variation existed, in part because of residual features "dragged over into modern times from the natural economy of the Middle Ages," but also because of the uneven penetration of capitalist relations under historical circumstances showing "infinite variations and gradations in appearance" which demand careful empirical study (*Capital* 3:787–93). Under such conditions even the neatness of the two-phase transition breaks down. We almost certainly will find radically different forms of rental appropriation side by side.

Properly used, Marx's framework can provide many insights. For example, in a careful reconstruction of the historical record of rental appropriation in the Soissonais district of France, Postel-Vinay (1974) shows that over the last two centuries large-scale farmers working the better land have consistently paid about half the rent per acre extracted from small peasant proprietors working inferior soils. In Rey's eyes this makes a mockery of both Marxian and neoclassical views of differential rent (supposedly extracted from lands with superior productivity) and confirms his view that rent can be understood only as a feudal relation of production perpetuated as a capitalist relation of distribution. Rey is only partly right. If my reading of Marx is correct, then the superior rent paid by small peasant proprietors is a reflection of a landlord-labor relation as opposed to the landlord-capital relation found on the better lands. Two different social relationships have coexisted within the same region for two centuries. Yet rent is still paid by the capitalists according to a logic that has nothing to do with the articulation of feudal and capitalist modes of production. Rey's depiction of conditions during the transition (including blocked transitions that freeze social relations into the landlord-laborer pattern) may be quite appropriate. But he is way off target when he asserts that this is the only form that rent can take under capitalism.

The possibility that radically different social relations may coexist within a given region over extended periods must give us pause. It alerts us to the danger of assuming that the same social interpretation can be put upon the rental payment even within seemingly coherent capitalist social formations. This is not to make any strong claim for the persistence of "feudal residuals" under capitalism. It simply means that the owners of any important means of production (land, productive capacity, money) have the habit of trying to appropriate as much surplus value as they can by virtue of that ownership and that circumstances have to be very special to reduce them to that "passive" state that Marx depicted. Furthermore, as I initially argued, there is an active role for rental appropriation even under the purest form of capitalism.

IV. CONCLUSION

Rent is, I repeat, simply a money payment for the use of land and its appurtenances. This simple money payment can conceal a host of possible social significations that can be unraveled only through careful sociohistorical investigation. The task of theory under such circumstances is to establish the underlying forces that give social meaning to and fix the level of the rental payment. Under a purely capitalist mode of production, these forces merit disaggregation into those that attach to the circulation of capital and those that relate to the circulation of revenues (while recognizing that the two circulation processes are dependent upon each other). Additional complications arise because it is not always easy to distinguish between interest on capital fixed in land (interest on buildings and permanent improvements) and rent on land pure and simple. Furthermore, the different uses of land as a means, condition, or element of production, or as a reservoir of present or potential use values, means that the significance of land to users varies from sector to sector. Project all of these complexities into the framework of land use competition in which land is just one of several different forms of fictitious capital (stocks and bonds, government debt, etc.) competing for investment, and we are forced to conclude that there is nothing simple about that simple money payment even under conditions of a purely capitalist mode of production.

But the notion of a purely capitalist mode of production is at best a convenient fiction, more or less useful depending upon historical circumstance. And many situations indeed arise in which the dominant forces underlying the rental payment can best be understood in terms of the articulation of quite different modes of production, one upon the other. To the degree that different modes of production have specific forms of distribution and revenue circulation associated with them, all of the complexity of a purely capitalist mode of production becomes compounded many times over.

I do not regard the rich complexity of these theoretical determinations as anything other than an exciting challenge to bring the theory of rent out from the depths of underlying simplicity (where some Marxists seek to confine it in perpetuity) step by step toward the surface appearance of everyday life. The framework outlined here can have as much to say about the role of private property in land and the appropriation of rent in the social transformation of Kinshasa as it can be used to look at landlordism in Baltimore, loft-living and gentrification in New York, landed property in the Soissonais, and corporate farming in Iowa. The theory does not tell us the answers, but it does help us pose the right questions. It might also help us get back to some basic issues about class structures and alliances, different modes of appropriation and exploitation, and the role of landownership as a form of social power in the shaping of spatial configurations of land uses. And all of this can be done, I would submit, without refuting or "going beyond" supposedly outdated Marxian formulations but simply through the proper application of Marx's own methods to a question that he never himself resolved to his own satisfaction.

4

Class Structure and the Theory of Residential Differentiation

The theory of residential differentiation is desperately in need of revision. Sociological explanations of residential differentiation (see the review by Timms 1971) have never progressed much beyond elaborations on the rather simplistic theme that similar people like to, or just do, live close to each other. The seeming complexity of sociological accounts derives from the difficulty of defining "similar" and the difficulty of showing whether people are similar because they live close to each other or live close to each other because they are similar. The explanations constructed out of neoclassical economic theory are no less simplistic in that they rely upon consumer sovereignty and utility-maximizing behavior on the part of individuals which, when expressed in the market context, produces residential differentiation. Complexity in this case arises because it is not easy to give concrete meaning to the utility concept and because it is possible to envisage a wide variety of conditions under which individuals might express their market choices.

Most thoughtful commentators on the matter have concluded that the problem lies in specifying the *necessary* relationships between social structure in general and residential differentiation in particular. For example, Hawley and Duncan (1957, 342) remark that "one searches in vain for a statement explaining why residential areas would differ from one another or be internally homogeneous. The elaborate discussion of social trends accompanying urbanization is nowhere shown to be relevant to this problem." Most attempts to integrate social theory and the theory of residential differentiation have produced, in fact, "not a single integrated theory, connecting residential differentiation with societal development, but, rather, two quite distinct theories which are accidentally articulated to the extent that they happen to share the same operational methods."

The problem here lies in part in the realm of methodology. Plainly, it is inappropriate to speak of residential differentiation causing or being caused by changes in the total social structure, while a functionalist language, although somewhat more appropriate, is so dominated by the notion of harmonious equilibrium that it cannot deal with the complex dynamics and evolutionary character of a capitalist society. Yet most analysts have been trapped into the use of an inappropriate causal or functionalist language when they have dared to venture beyond statistical descriptions. All of this has produced an enormous amount of material on a variety of facets of the residential differentiation process, but no clue is provided as to how this material might be integrated into general social theory.

The Marxian method, however, founded in the philosophy of internal relations (Ollman 1971), is fashioned precisely to provide a coherent methodology for relating parts to wholes and wholes to parts. Indeed, the central conception in Marx's version of the dialectic was to view things relationally in order that the integrity of the relationship between the whole and the part should always be maintained. Consequently, Marx criticized the categories of bourgeois social science on the grounds that they are abstractly fashioned without reference to the "relations which link these abstractions to the totality" (Ollman 1973, 495). Marx's abstractions are of a different kind, for they focus on such things as social relations. Relatively simple structures might be isolated from the whole for purposes of analysis, but "what is decisive is whether this process of isolation is a means towards understanding the whole and whether it is integrated within the context it presupposes and requires, or whether the abstract knowledge of an isolated fragment retains its 'autonomy' and becomes an end in itself" (Lukács 1968, 8).

The theory of residential differentiation has rarely been subjected to an analysis from a Marxian standpoint, and it is predictable, therefore, that the "theory" consists of an incoherent mass of autonomous bits and pieces of information, arrived at by means of studies each conceived of as an end in itself and each conceived in terms of relationships specified in a causal, functional, or empiricist language (with all the limitations that each of these imposes). And it is predictable that attempts to integrate this material into some general social theory would meet with little or no success. In this chapter I shall therefore attempt an outline of the relation between residential differentiation and social structure. Such an investigation is bound to be preliminary and sketchy at this stage. But I hope to show where the key relations lie and thereby indicate where we have to look for a revision of the theory of residential differentiation that will make sense. I shall begin with an analysis of the forces creating class structure in advanced capitalist society.

I. CLASS AND CLASS STRUCTURE

Theories of class and class structure abound. Marx and Weber laid the basis, and a host of contemporary interpreters have added insights, glosses, reinterpretations, and, it must be added, mystifications. Rather than attempt a synthesis of this work, I shall sketch in a theory of class which derives primarily from a reading of Marx and secondarily from adapting materials from Giddens (1973) and Poulantzas (1973).

A central tenet of Marx's historical and materialist method is that a concept such as "class" can take on a meaning only in relation to the historical context in which it is to be applied. "Class" has a contingent meaning depending upon whether we are considering feudal, capitalist, or socialist modes of production. Class theory is not therefore, a matter of identifying a fixed set of categories which are supposed to apply for all times and places. The relational view of class which Marx espouses focuses our attention on the forces of "class structuration" (as Giddens 1973 calls them) which shape actual class configurations. In the context of the capitalist mode of production, however, "class" has a more specific meaning that relates to the basic social relationships pertaining in capitalist society. The forces of class structuration under capitalism are identical to those contained in the dynamics of capitalism; hence arises a necessary relation between the evolution of capitalist societies and the evolution of social configurations.

Marx argues that the basic social relationship within capitalism is a power relation between capital and labor. This power relation is expressed directly through a market mode of economic integration. Thus, the proportion of national product set aside for wages and profits (which includes rents and interest) is determined by the outcome of a class struggle between the representatives of labor (now usually the unions) and capital (usually the employers). Marx also argues that the power relation between the two great classes in society can be understood only in terms of the particular historical conditions achieved with the emergence of the capitalist order. Thus, labor power has to assume a commodity character, which means that it can be "freely" bought and sold in the market and that the laborer has legal rights over the disposition of his or her labor. Ownership and control over the means of production gives capital its power over labor, since the laborer has to work in order to live and the employer holds control over the means of work. A relatively stable power relation between capital and labor requires for its maintenance a wide variety of institutional, legal, coercive, and ideological supports, most of which are either provided or managed through state institutions.

The power relation between capital and labor may be regarded as the primary force of class structuration in capitalist society. However, this force does not necessarily generate a dichotomous class structure. The two-class model that Marx presents in volume 1 of *Capital* is an assumed relation through which he seeks to lay bare the exploitative character of capitalist production – it is not meant as a description of an actual class structure (*Capital* 1:167–70 and 508–10; 2:421). Marx also distinguishes between the roles of capital and labor and the personifications of those roles – the capitalist, although functioning as a mere personification of capital much of the time, is still a human being. The concepts of "class" and "class role" function in *Capital* are analytic constructs. Yet Marx often used the dichotomous model of class structure as if it had an empirical content, and in his more programmatic writings he insists that socialism will be achieved only through a class struggle that pits the capitalist class against the proletariat.

The reason for this stance is not hard to find. Marx attributed the exploitative character of capitalist society to the capital-labor relation, and he also traced the innumerable manifestations of alienation back to this one fundamental source. These negative aspects of capitalist society could be transcended in Marx's view only by transcending the power relation that permitted the domination of labor by capital. The analytic constructs of *Capital* consequently become normative (ought-to-be) constructs in his programmatic writings. And if actual class struggle crystallized around the capital-labor relation, then both the analytic and the normative constructs would come to take on an empirical validity as descriptions of actual social configurations.

But social configurations could crystallize along quite different lines in an actual situation. In *The Eighteenth Brumaire of Louis Bonaparte,* for example, Marx analyzes conflict in the France of 1848–51 in terms of the class interests of lumpenproletariat, industrial proletariat, petite bourgeoisie, industrialists, financiers, a landed aristocracy, and a peasantry. In using this more complex model of a social configuration, Marx was plainly not saying that France was not capitalist at that time. He was suggesting, rather, that capitalism had evolved at that particular time and in that particular place to a stage in which class interests (often of a myopic and nonrevolutionary sort) could and did crystallize around forces other than the fundamental power relation between capital and labor.

It is convenient to designate these forces as "secondary forces of class structuration" and to divide them into two groups. The first I shall call "residual," for they stem either from some historically prior mode of production or from the geographical contact between a dominant and a subordinate mode of production. In the early years of capitalism, residuals from the feudal order – a landed aristocracy and a peasantry, for example – were very important. Moreover, there is evidence that these residual features can be very persistent and last for centuries after the initial penetration of capitalist social relationships. The geographical expansion of capitalism into a global system has also created residuals. The patterns of dominance and subservience associated with colonialism and neocolonialism are products of an intersection between the forces of class structuration in a dominant capitalist society and forms of social differentiation in subordinate traditional societies. Residual elements may disappear with time or be so transformed that they become almost unrecognizable. But they can also persist. And insofar as transformed residuals become incorporated into the social structure of advanced capitalist societies, they help to explain the existence of transitional classes. Landlordism, preserved in a capitalist form, or a group subjected to neocolonial domination and transformed into a relatively permanent underclass (blacks, Puerto Ricans, and Chicanos in the United States, for example) are the kinds of features in a social configuration that have to be explained in terms of the residual forces of class structuration.

The other forces of class structuration derive from the dynamics of capitalist society. These "derivative forces," as I shall designate them, arise because of the necessities generated by the need to preserve the processes of capital accumulation through technological innovation and shifts in social organization, consumption, and the like. We can identify five such forces (following Giddens 1973), and we shall consider them briefly in turn.

The Division of Labor and Specialization of Function

The expansion of production requires improvements in labor productivity and in the forms of industrial organization, communication, exchange, and distribution. These improvements usually mean an increasing division of labor and specialization of function. As the technical and organizational basis of society changes, so there must be concomitant shifts in social relationships which create the potential for social differentiation. The distinction between manual and intellectual work, for example, may be reflected in the social distinction between blue-collar and white-collar workers. At the same time the growing complexity of economic organization may require the emergence of specialized financial intermediaries in the economy (banking and other financial institutions), which may be reflected in distinctions between financiers and industrialists within the capitalist class as a whole. The division of labor and specialization of function may fragment the proletariat and the capitalist class into distinctive strata. Social conflict may take place between strata and thus replace class struggle in the Marxian sense as the guiding principle of social differentiation.

Consumption Classes or Distributive Groupings

The progress of capitalist accumulation may be inhibited by the lack of an effective demand for its material products. If we leave aside the growth of demand inherent in demographic growth and tapping export markets, effective demand depends upon the creation of an internal market to absorb the increasing quantities of material products. Marx (*Grundrisse*, 401–23) argues that the creation of new modes of consumption and of new social wants and needs is essential to the survival of capitalism – otherwise capital accumulation faces an inpenetrable barrier of fixed demand, which means overproduction and crisis. Underconsumption, though not the fundamental underlying cause of capitalist crises (see Harvey 1982), is often a pervasive manifestation of crisis and, as such, has to be confronted directly as a key political and economic problem. Malthus (1951, 398–413), in first propos- ing a version of the Keynesian theory of effective demand, had argued that the existence of a class of "conspicuous consumers" (primarily the landed aristocracy in his time) was a necessity if sufficient effective demand were to be sustained to permit the accumulation of capital. Malthus's perspective is an interesting one. Not only does he suggest that specific mechanisms have to be employed to stimulate consumption, but that certain consumption classes have to exist to ensure sustained consumption. If this is the case, then social differentiation arises in the sphere of consumption. Distinctive consumption classes or distributive groupings are therefore bound to emerge in the course of capitalist history (Giddens 1973, 108–10). Since it is empirically observable that life-style and consumption habits vary across different strata in the population, and since this is an important differentiating feature in modern society, we may conclude that the emergence of distinctive consump- tion classes is inherent in the dynamics of capitalist society. Social differen- tiation can be structured, therefore, according to distribution and consump- tion criteria (*Grundrisse*, 402).

Authority Relations

The nonmarket institutions in society must be so ordered that they sustain the power relation between capital and labor and serve to organize produc- tion, circulation, and distribution. Marx (*Capital* 1:330–33) argues, for example, that cooperative activity in production requires a "directing authority" and that as capitalist production becomes more elaborate, so a specialized group of workers – administrators, managers, foremen, and the like – must assume an authority role in the direction of production. For the economy as a whole these management functions lie largely in the sphere of state activity – understood as the collective amalgam of legal, administrative, bureaucratic, military and political functions (Miliband 1969). Within this sphere, and within the corporate enterprise, authority relations are the basis for social relationships. In general, the structure of authority relations is coherent with the necessities imposed by the dynamics of accumulation within a social system organized along capitalist lines. But the authority relations appear independent of the relation between capital and labor and indeed are, to a certain degree, autonomous in their functioning (Poulantzas 1973). The structure of authority relations can, therefore, provide a basis for social differentiation within the population. Marx (*Theories of Surplus Value,* pt. 2:573) thus writes about the significance of "the constantly growing number of the middle classes [who] stand between the workman on the one hand and the capitalist and landlord on the other."

Class-Consciousness and Ideology

Marx argues that a class will become an observable aggregate of individuals only when that aggregate buries all the differences within it and becomes conscious of its class identity in the struggle between capital and labor. Since capitalism has evolved and survived, then presumably it has in part done so by an active intervention in those processes whereby class-consciousness in the Marxian sense is created. There is, as it were, a struggle for the mind of labor between, on the one hand, a political class-consciousness directed toward the transcendence of the capital-labor relation and, on the other hand, states of social awareness which allow of social differentiations consistent with the accumulation of capital and the perpetuation of the capital-labor relation. The struggle for the mind of labor is a political and ideological struggle. Marx considered that, in general, the ruling ideas in society are ever the ideas of the ruling class. Mass literacy and mass education have the effect of exposing the masses to a dominant bourgeois ideology, which seeks to produce states of consciousness consistent with the perpetuation of the capitalist order. Mass culture, or what Marcuse (1968) calls "affirmative culture," has the function of depoliticizing the masses rather than enlightening them as to the real source of alienation in society (see *Consciousness and the Urban Experience,* chap. 5).

Certain parallel processes can be observed in the political sphere. The survival of capitalism necessitates an increasing state interventionism, which, far from being neutral, actively sustains the power relation of capital over labor. In a given instance the state may throw its weight to the side of labor in order to restore some kind of balance between profits and wages, but state intervention is never geared to the transcendence of the capital-labor relation. Yet the state *appears* to be neutral. In part this appearance is real, for state institutions frequently arbitrate between factions of the ruling class (between financiers and industrialists, for example) and between strata of the working population. The separation between the economic and political-administrative spheres, which typically arises under capitalism, also permits the state to appear as a neutral party in economic conflict. At the same time the prospects for legal and political equality held out in the political sphere tend to divert attention from the inevitable subordination of labor to capital in the marketplace. This separation between economy and polity has been, as Giddens (1973, 202–7) points out, a fundamental mediating influence on the production of class-consciousness and social awareness in capitalist society. It typically feeds trade-union consciousness on the part of labor and a distinctive kind of middle-class awareness on the part of intermediate groups in the authority structure which focuses on civil and political liberties to the exclusion of questions of economic control.

Political and ideological struggles, and the manipulation of both, have great significance for understanding the states of consciousness of various strata within the population. Only in terms of such consciousness can we explain how and why a particular problem (say, unemployment) will elicit as a response conflict between capital and labor rather than conflict within labor. The second type of conflict might be between, say, the regularly employed and a largely unemployed underclass, that may also be a racial or ethnic minority. The first kind of conflict poses a threat to the capitalist order, whereas the latter kind of conflict does not. It is obviously in the interest of capitalism to transform conflict of the first sort into conflict of the latter variety. Consequently, bourgeois ideology and politics typically seek to forge a consciousness favorable to the perpetuation of the capitalist order and actively seek out ways to draw social distinctions along lines other than that between capital and labor. I take up these questions in detail in *Consciousness and the Urban Experience*.

Mobility Chances

The accelerating pace of change in the organization of production, exchange, communication, and consumption necessitates considerable adaptability in the population. Individuals must be prepared to alter their skills, geographical locations, consumption habits, and the like. This means that mobility chances must always be present within the population. Yet a completely open society as far as mobility is concerned would undoubtedly create considerable instability. In order to give social stability to a society in which social change is necessary, some systematic way has to be found for organizing mobility chances. This entails the structuring of mobility chances in certain important ways.

In capitalist society, mobility is organized so that most movement takes place between one stratum within the division of labor and another (from, say, the manual to the white-collar category). The mechanisms for achieving this controlled kind of mobility appear to lie in part in the differential distribution (both socially and geographically) of opportunities to acquire what Giddens (1973, 103) calls "market capacity" – that bundle of skills and attributes which permits individuals to market their labor power within certain occupation categories or to operate in certain functional roles. Restrictions and barriers to mobility chances give rise to social differentiations. Insofar as professional groups, for example, have better access to the acquisition of market capacity for their children, a professional "class" may become self-perpetuating. Once intergenerational mobility is limited, social distinctions become relatively fixed features in the social landscape and provide the possibility for the crystallization of social differentiation within the population as a whole.

The argument so far suggests that we can identify three kinds of forces making for social differentiation within the population:

1. A primary force arising out of the power relation between capital and labor
2. A variety of secondary forces arising out of the contradictory and evolutionary character of capitalism which encourage social differentiation along lines defined by (a) the division of labor and specialization of function, (b) consumption patterns and life-style, (c) authority relations, (d) manipulated projections of ideological and political consciousness, and (e) barriers to mobility chances
3. Residual forces reflecting the social relations established in a preceding or geographically separate but subordinate mode of production

In general we can see a perpetual struggle amongst these forces between those that create class configurations antagonistic to the perpetuation of the capitalist order and those that create social differentiations favorable to the replication of capitalist society.

II. RESIDENTIAL DIFFERENTIATION AND THE SOCIAL ORDER

The accumulation of capital on a progressively increasing scale has set in motion a distinctive and rapidly accelerating urbanization process. The distinctive features of this process need not delay us here (see Harvey 1973; Castells 1972; Lefebvre 1970, 1972). For the purpose at hand it is sufficient to note the progressive concentration of the population in large urban centers. There has been a parallel fragmentation of social structure as the primary, residual, and derivative forces of social differentiation have interacted over a century or more. Let us now locate these processes of progressive concentration and social fragmentation in the built environment we call the city and fashion some basic hypotheses to connect residential differentiation with social structure. Four hypotheses can be stated:

1. Residential differentiation is to be interpreted in terms of the reproduction of the social relations within capitalist society
2. Residential areas (neighborhoods, communities) provide distinctive milieus for social interaction from which individuals to a considerable degree derive their values, expectations, consumption habits, market capacities, and states of consciousness
3. The fragmentation of large concentrations of population into distinctive communities serves to fragment class-consciousness in the Marxian sense and thereby frustrates the transformation from capitalism to socialism through class struggle, but
4. Patterns of residential differentiation reflect and incorporate many of the contradictions in capitalist society; the processes creating and sustaining them are consequently the locus of instability and contradiction

These hypotheses, when fleshed out and if proven, provide a necessary link between residential differentiation and the social order. In the short space of this chapter, I can only sketch in a very general argument in support of them.

Residential differentiation in the capitalist city means differential access to the scarce resources required to acquire market capacity (Giddens 1973; Harvey 1973, chap. 2). For example, differential access to educational opportunity — understood in broad terms as those experiences derived from family, geographical neighborhood and community, classroom, and the mass media — facilitates the intergenerational transference of market capacity and typically leads to the restriction of mobility chances. Opportunities may be so structured that a white-collar labor force is reproduced in a white-collar neighborhood, a blue-collar labor force is reproduced in a blue-collar neighborhood, and so on. The community is the place of reproduction in which labor power suitable for the place of production is reproduced. This is a tendency only, of course, and there are many forces modifying or even offsetting it. And the relationships are by no means simple. Market capacity, defined in terms of the ability to undertake certain kinds of functions within the division of labor, comprises a whole set of attitudes, values, and expectations as well as distinctive skills. The relationship between function and the acquisition of market capacity can sometimes be quite tight — thus, miners are for the most part reproduced in mining communities. But in other cases the relationship may be much looser — a white-collar grouping, for example, comprises a wide range of occupational categories but is still differentiable, both socially and spatially, from other groupings.

Residential groupings that reproduce labor power to meet the needs of an existing division of labor may also form a distinctive grouping from the standpoint of consumption. Such a coalescence gives residential differentiation a much more homogeneous character. One thread of necessity as opposed to contingency in this relationship lies in the consumption of education, which unifies a consumption class with a grouping based in the division of labor. This thread is too slender to hang a proof on (although in the United States the connections between residential differentiation and the quality of education are very strong and a constant source of conflict and social tension). The full story rests on showing how attitudes generated out of the work experience imply certain parallel attitudes in the consumption sphere. To trace this connection is difficult, but it appears reasonable to suppose that the quality of the work experience and the attitudes necessary to perform that work under specific social conditions must be reflected, somehow or other, by attitudes and behaviors in the place of residence.

The relationships between values, consciousness, ideology, and life experiences are crucial – and they are the most profoundly difficult to unravel. From the standpoint of the creation of residential differentiation, it is plain that individuals do make choices and do express preferences. To sustain the argument, therefore, I have to show that the preferences and value systems, and perhaps even the choices themselves, are produced by forces external to the individual's will. The idea of an autonomously and spontaneously arising consumer sovereignty as the explanation of residential differentiation could be fairly easily disposed of (even though it is the prevalent myth that underlies conventional theories of residential differentiation). But it is more difficult to know what exactly to put in its place. And it is far too glib to attribute everything to the blandishments of the "ad-men," however important they may be.

If we ask, however, where peoples' values come from and what is it that creates them, then it is plain that the community provides a social milieu out of which distinctive value systems, aspirations, and expectations may be drawn. The neighborhood is, as it were, the primary source of socialization experiences (Newson and Newson 1970). Insofar as residential differentiation produces distinctive communities, we can expect a disaggregation of this process. Working-class neighborhoods, for example, typically produce individuals with values conducive to being in the working class; and these values, deeply embedded as they are in the cognitive, linguistic, and moral codes of the community, become an integral part of the conceptual equipment that individuals use to deal with the world (Giglioli 1972). The stability of such neighborhoods and of the value systems that characterize the people in them have been remarkable considering the dynamics of change in most capitalist cities. The reproduction of such value systems facilitates the reproduction of consumption classes as well as groupings with respect to the division of labor while it also functions to restrict mobility chances. Values and attitudes toward education, for example, vary greatly and affect the consumption of education – one of the main means of obtaining mobility chances (Robson

1969). The homogenization of life experiences which this restriction produces reinforces the tendency for relatively permanent social groupings to emerge within a relatively permanent structure of residential differentiation. Once this is translated into a social awareness that has the neighborhood or community as the focus, and once this form of social awareness becomes the basis for political action, then community-consciousness replaces class-consciousness (of the Marxian sort) as the springboard for action and the locus of social conflict.

Once such groupings form, it is relatively easy to understand how they may be perpetuated. But we also have to understand the history of such groupings because contemporary social differentiations have been arrived at by successive transformations and fragmentations of preceding social configurations. The reciprocity exhibited in working-class neighborhoods is to a large degree a defensive device constructed out of the transformation under capitalism of a well-tried and ancient mode of economic integration (Harvey 1973, chap. 6). In the United States, immigrant waves at particular periods in the evolution of the capitalist division of labor gave a strong ethnic flavor to certain occupational categories as well as to certain residential neighborhoods; both persist to the present day. The continued domination of blacks following the transformation of slavery, and the more modern neocolonial domination of Puerto Ricans and Chicanos, have produced the ghetto as a Third World colony in the heart of the American city, and it is broadly true that the underclass in American society is identified with neocolonial repression based in racism (Blaut 1974). The historical roots of social and residential differentiation are important. But then so also are the processes of social transformation that produce new social groupings within a social configuration.

Consider, for example, the emergence of a distinctive middle class, literate and skilled in mental labor, possessed of the dominant bourgeois ideology that McPherson (1962) felicitously calls "possessive individualism," attached as a consequence to certain distinctive modes of consumption, imbued with a political view that focuses on civil and political liberties, and instilled with the notion that economic advancement is solely a matter of individual ability, dedication, and personal ambition (as if everyone could become a successful doctor, lawyer, manager, and the like, if only they tried hard enough). The emergence of such a middle class over the past century or so has become etched into the city by the creation of distinctive middle-class neighborhoods with distinctive opportunities to acquire market capacity. In more recent times, affluent workers and white-collar employees have been encouraged to copy the middle-class life-style. And in the American city this process has been associated since the 1930s in particular with a strong suburbanization process. How do we explain the way in which the emergence of such social groupings relates to the process of residential differentiation?

The answer to this question depends in part upon an understanding of the processes whereby residential differentiation is produced by the organization of forces external to the individual or even to the collective will of the particular social grouping. These processes stretch back over a relatively long time period, and it is probably the case that residential differentiation in the contemporary sense was well established in most major cities in both the United States and Britain by 1850. In certain basic respects the processes have not changed, however, for we still have to turn to the examination of the activities of speculator-developers, speculator-landlords, and real estate brokers, backed by the power of financial and governmental institutions, for an explanation of how the built environment and residential neighborhoods are actually produced. I have attempted a full description of this process in the American city elsewhere, and so I shall merely offer a summary of it here.

Financial and governmental institutions are hierarchically ordered by authority relations broadly consistent with the support of the capitalist order. They function to coordinate "national needs" (understood in terms of the reproduction of capitalist society and the accumulation of capital) with local activities and decisions — in this manner, micro- and macro-aspects of housing market behavior are coordinated. These institutions regulate the dynamic of the urbanization process (usually in the interest of accumulation and economic crisis management) and also wield their influence in such a way that certain broad patterns in residential differentiation are produced. The creation of distinctive housing submarkets (largely through the mortgage market) improves the efficiency with which institutions can manage the urbanization process. But at the same time it limits the ability of individuals to make choices. Further, it creates a structure that individuals can potentially choose from but that they cannot influence the production of.

If residential differentiation is in large degree produced, then individuals have to adapt their preferences. The market mechanism curtails the range of choice (with the poorest having no choice, since they can take only what is left over after more affluent groups have chosen). The shaping of preferences of more affluent groups poses a more serious problem. The ad-man plays an important role, and considerations of status and prestige are likewise important. Consider, also, a white-collar worker forced to suburbanize (by a process I have elsewhere dubbed "blow out" — Harvey 1973, chap. 5) because of deteriorating conditions in the inner city; the preference in this case may be a somewhat shallow post-hoc rationalization of a "choice" that really was no choice. Dissatisfaction within such a group can easily surface. For example, a suburbanite angered by the prospect of gasoline shortages and recollecting the convenience of inner-city living complains that "we have all been had" because in order "to mold into the lifestyle dictated by builders, developers, and county planners, I have no choice but to provide my family with two automobiles" – one to get to work and the other to operate a household (*Baltimore Sun*, February 11, 1974). The consumption values attached to suburban living are plainly not open to choice once the location decision is made, and that decision may itself not be the outcome of a real choice.

Indeed, a strong argument can be made that suburbanization is a creation of the capitalist mode of production in very specific ways. First, suburbanization is actively produced because it sustains an effective demand for products and thereby facilitates the accumulation of capital. Second, the changing division of labor in capitalist society has created a distinctive group of white-collar workers who, largely by virtue of their literacy and their work conditions, are imbued with the ideology of competitive and possessive individualism, all of which appears uniquely appropriate for the production of a mode of consumption which we typically dub "suburban." It is intriguing to note that since the 1930s the United States has experienced the most sustained rate of economic growth (capital accumulation), the greatest growth in the white-collar sector, and the most rapid rate of suburbanization of all the advanced capitalist nations. These phenomena are not unconnected.

We can, thus, interpret the preference for suburban living as a created myth, arising out of possessive individualism, nurtured by the ad-man and forced by the logic of capitalist accumulation. But like all such myths, once established it takes on a certain autonomy out of which strong contradictions may emerge. The American suburb, formed as an economic and social response to problems internal to capitalist accumulation, now forms an entrenched barrier to social and economic change. The political power of the suburbs is used conservatively, to defend the life-style and the privileges and to exclude unwanted growth. In the process a deep irrationality emerges in the geography of the capitalist production system (residential and job opportunities may become spatially separated from each other, for example). The exclusion of further growth creates a further problem, for if a "no-growth" movement gathers momentum, then how can effective demand and capital accumulation be sustained? A phenomenon created to sustain the capitalist order can in the long run work to exacerbate its internal tensions.

This conclusion can possibly be extended to all aspects of social and residential differentiation. The social differentiations reproduced within the capitalist order are so structured as to facilitate the reproduction of the social relations of capitalism. As a result community-consciousness rather than class-consciousness in the Marxian sense is dominant in the capitalist city. In this fashion the danger of an emergent class-consciousness in the large concentrations of population to be found in urban areas has been averted by the fragmentation of class-consciousness through residential differentiation.

But community-consciousness with all of its parochialisms, once created, becomes deeply embedded, and it becomes just as difficult to piece it together in a configuration appropriate to the national interest (as perceived from the standpoint of capital accumulation) as it is to transform it into a class-consciousness antagonistic to the perpetuation of the capitalist order. In order, therefore, to maintain its own dynamic, capitalism is forced to disrupt and destroy what it initially created as part of its own strategy for self-preservation. Communities have to be disrupted by speculative activity, growth must occur, and whole residential neighborhoods must be transformed to meet the needs of capital accumulation. Herein lie both the contradictions and the potentials for social transformation in the urbanization sphere at this stage in our history.

Residential differentiation is produced, in its broad lineaments at least, by forces emanating from the capitalist production process, and it is not to be construed as the product of the autonomously and spontaneously arising preferences of people. Yet people are constantly searching to express themselves and to realize their potentialities in their day-to-day life-experiences in the workplace, the community, and the home. Much of the micro-variation in the urban fabric testifies to these ever-present impulses. But there is a scale of action at which the individual loses control of the social conditions of existence in the face of forces mobilized through the capitalist production process (in the community this means the congeries of interests represented by speculators, developers, financial institutions, big government, and the like). It is at this boundary that individuals come to sense their own helplessness in the face of forces that do not appear amenable, under given institutions, even to collective political mechanisms of control. As we cross this boundary, we move from a situation in which individuals can express their individuality and relate in human terms to each other to one in which individuals have no choice but to conform and in which social relations between people become replaced by market relations between things.

Residential differentiation on this latter scale plays a vital role in the perpetuation and reproduction of the alienating social relationships of capitalist society. Yet in the process of seeking stratagems for self-perpetuation, the forces of capitalist accumulation create value systems, consumption habits, states of awareness and political consciousness, and even whole built environments, which, with the passage of time, inhibit the expansion of the capitalist order. The permanently revolutionary character of capitalist society perpetually tears down the barriers it has erected to protect itself. The constant reshaping of urban environments and of the structures of residential differentiation are testimony to this never-ending process. Instead, therefore, of regarding residential differentiation as the passive product of a preference system based in social relationships, we have to see it as an integral mediating influence in the processes whereby class relationships and social differentiations are produced and sustained. It is clear, even at this preliminary stage in the analysis, that the theory of residential differentiation has much to offer as well as to gain from a thoroughgoing integration with general social theory.

5

The Place of Urban Politics in the Geography of Uneven Capitalist Development

There is an emerging consensus, as dangerous as it is unfounded, that the fluid movement of urban and regional politics cannot be incorporated into any rigorous statement of the Marxist theory of capital accumulation. The breadth of the consensus is quite surprising. It includes not only critics like Saunders (1981) who naturally tend to view any version of the Marxist theory with jaundiced eye but also a number of past sympathizers and current practitioners within the Marxist tradition. Mollenkopf (1983), for example, says quite firmly that an adequate theory of politics cannot be built upon Marxist propositions and that politics and government have to be viewed as "independent guiding forces" overriding economic considerations. More serious has been Castells's apparent defection from the Marxist fold. In *The City and the Grassroots* (1983, 296–300), he confesses that his "intellectual matrix" in the Marxist tradition "was of little help from the moment we entered the uncertain ground of urban social movements." The problem, he asserts, lies "deep in the core of the Marxist theory of social change," which has never overcome a duality between the logic of capital accumulation and historical processes of class struggle. Conceding the "intelligence" of Saunders's critique, Castells firmly rejects the idea that the city and space can be understood in terms of the logic of capital. He even doubts the relevance of class concepts and class struggle to understanding urban social movements. He seeks to build a more complicated reading of history, cities, and society out of "the glorious ruins of the Marxist tradition."

Defections of this magnitude testify to the depth of frustration which many feel as they try to bring the generalities of Marxian theory to bear on specific local and conjunctural events. In this chapter I try to confront this malaise directly. I try to show how, why, and within what limits a "relatively autonomous" urban politics can arise and how that "relative autonomy" is not only compatible with but also necessary to the processes of capital accumulation. In so doing, I accept that the problems posed by defectors and critics alike are real and not imagined. I also accept that the general theory of accumulation has not always been specified in a way that makes it easy to address urban processes and that there is a good deal of intellectual baggage (to say nothing of dogmatism) within the Marxist tradition which hinders rather than helps in the search for penetrating analyses and viable alternatives.

I cannot, in a single chapter, address all the problems that need to be addressed. I shall therefore rest content with the construction of a relatively simple line of argument which derives its strength, I think, from depicting accumulation as a spatiotemporal process at the very outset. I begin with the observation that the exchange of labor power is always spatially constrained. A fundamental defining attribute of an urban area is the geographical labor market within which daily substitutions of labor power against job opportunities are possible. After consideration of how capitalists act in the context of localized labor markets, I shall go on to show how unstable class alliances form within a loosely defined urban region. These alliances parallel the tendency for an urban economy to achieve what I call a "structured coherence" defined around a dominant technology of both production and consumption and a dominant set of class relations. The alliances, like the structured coherence they reflect, are unstable because competition, accumulation and technological change disrupt on the one hand what they tend to produce on the other. Here lies a political space within which a relatively autonomous urban politics can arise. That relative autonomy fits only too well into the geographical dynamics of accumulation and class struggle. In fact, it becomes a major means of bringing together the logic of capital accumulation with the history of class struggle. To the degree that different urban regions compete with each other – and Robert Goodman (1979) is not alone in regarding state and local governments as the "last entrepreneurs" – so they set the stage for the uneven geographical development of capitalism. Urban regions compete for employment, investment, new technologies, and the like by offering unique packages of physical and social infrastructures, qualities and quantities of labor power, input costs, life-styles, tax systems, environmental qualities, and the like. The effect of competition is, of course, to discipline any urban-based class alliance to common capitalist requirements.

But there is another side to all this. Capitalism is a continuously revolutionary mode of production. Speculative innovation in production processes is one of its hallmarks. But innovation in production requires parallel innovation in consumption. It also requires innovation in social and physical infrastructures, spatial forms, and broad social processes of reproduction. Innovation must extend to life-styles, organizational forms (political, cultural, and ideological as well as bureaucratic, commercial, and administrative) and spatial configurations. The ferment of urban politics and the diverse social movements contained therein is an important part of such an innovative process. It is as speculative, innovative, and unpredictable in its details as are capitalist processes of product innovation and technological and locational change. Furthermore, such behavior presupposes a wide range of individual liberties so that individuals, organizations, and social groups can probe in all manner of different directions. The more open the society, the more innovative it will likely be in all these different respects. But successful innovation and successful probing under capitalism mean profitable probing. Here the crude logic of capitalist rationality comes back into play. Cities, like entrepreneurs, can lose out to their competition, go bankrupt, or simply be left behind in the race for economic advantage. Urban politics then appear as the powerful and often innovative but in the end disciplining arm of uneven accumulation and uneven class struggle in geographic space. The discipline sparks conflict, of course, since the liberties conceded allow directions to be explored that are incompatible with or even antagonistic to capitalism. Cities may become hearths of revolution. But as the Paris Commune proved once and for all, there are then only two possible immediate outcomes. Either the revolution spreads and engulfs the whole of society, or the forces of reaction reoccupy the city and forcibly bring its politics under control.

I have long argued that urbanization should be understood as a process rather than as a thing. That process necessarily has no fixed spatial boundaries, though it is always being manifested within and across a particular space. When I speak of urban politics, then, it is in the broad sense of political processes at work within a fluidly defined but nevertheless explicit space. I do not mean the mayor and city council, though they are one important form of expression of urban politics. Nor do I necessarily refer to an exclusively defined urban region, because metropolitan regions overlap and interpenetrate when it comes to the important processes at work there. The urban space with which I propose to work is fixed only to the degree that the key processes I shall identify are confined within fixed spaces. To the degree that the processes are restlessly in motion, so the urban space is itself perpetually in flux.

I. THE URBAN LABOR MARKET

The working day, Marx long ago emphasized, is an important unit of analysis. It defines a normal time frame within which employers can seek to substitute one laborer for another and laborers can likewise seek to substitute one job opportunity for another. I therefore propose to view the "urban" in the first instance as a geographically contiguous labor market within which daily exchanges and substitutions of labor power are possible. Plainly, the geographical extent of that urban labor market depends upon the commuting range, itself historically determined by social and technological conditions. Furthermore, labor markets can overlap in space (fig. 10) and tend in any case to fade out over space rather than end at some discrete boundary. The urban labor market is better thought of as a complex drainage basin with firmer delineations at its center than on its periphery (Coing 1982). Nevertheless, a prima facie argument of considerable plausibility can be advanced which sees the urban-regional labor market as a unit of primary importance in the analysis of the accumulation of capital in space.

On a given day, the potential quantities and qualities of labor power available within this market area are fixed. This is a short-run inelasticity of supply to which capitalists may have to adapt. Whether or not they do so depends on a wide range of conditions, such as the gap between potential labor supply and that used (the labor surplus), the time horizon of capital investments, the ease of capital mobility, and the like. These are the questions I take up in section 2.

Urban labor markets exhibit all manner of peculiarities and imperfections. Labor power, Marx emphasized, is a peculiar commodity, unlike others in several important respects. To begin with, it is not produced under the control of capitalists but within a family or household unit. There also enters into the determination of its exchange value a whole host of moral, environmental, and political considerations. And finally, the use value of that labor power to the capitalist is hard to quantify exactly because of the fluidity of inherently creative labor processes. Storper and Walker (1984, 22–23) thus conclude that "labor differs fundamentally from real commodities because it is embodied in living, conscious human beings and because human activity (work) is the irreducible essence of social production and social life." The leveling and standardization achieved in other arenas of exchange can never be fully achieved in labor markets. Labor qualities always remain "idiosyncratic and place-bound." Each urban labor market, it then follows, is unique (Storper and Walker 1983, 1984).

The imperfections are likewise peculiar. Segmentations may exist in which certain kinds of jobs are reserved for certain kinds of workers (white males, women, racial minorities, recent immigrants, ethnic groups, etc.), while the geographical coherence may also be broken if certain kinds of workers (such as blacks in inner cities or women in the suburbs) are trapped by lack of transportation in geographically distinct submarkets or if different social groups have (by virtue of their incomes) differential access to different transportation modes. The principle of substitution is also modified by the nature of skill distributions in relation to the mix of labor processes within the urban region. There is, finally, the question of the available labor surplus

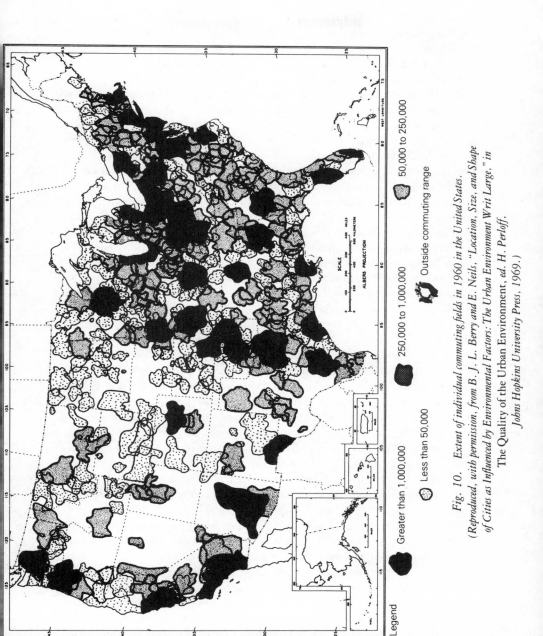

Legend

Greater than 1,000,000

250,000 to 1,000,000

50,000 to 250,000

Less than 50,000

Outside commuting range

SCALE

ALBERS PROJECTION

Fig. 10.   Extent of individual commuting fields in 1960 in the United States.
(Reproduced, with permission, from B. J. L. Berry and E. Neils, "Location, Size, and Shape
of Cities as Influenced by Environmental Factors: The Urban Environment Writ Large," in
The Quality of the Urban Environment, *ed. H. Perloff.*
Johns Hopkins University Press, 1969.)

of unemployed, underemployed, or potentially employable people. Such reserves are usually stored in urban labor markets, though their mobilization sometimes poses peculiar problems. In all of these respects, the short-run rigidity of supply within the urban labor market to which capitalists must adapt is a *structured* rigidity.

The rigidities stand to be relaxed as we shift the time-horizon. Migration (occasional, periodic, permanent) releases the supply of labor power from the constraint of a daily commuting range. Supply is then contingent upon conditions in a "migration field" which, though usually to some degree geographically constrained, has the whole world as its possible outer limit. The supply of labor power within the urban labor market fluctuates on a weekly, monthly, or annual basis depending upon the balance of in- and out-migration. Minor adjustments of quantity and quality can quickly be achieved, but major flows pose more serious problems, again because of the peculiar qualities of labor power as a commodity. The bearer of that labor power, the living laborer, has to be fed, housed, and cared for somehow, and that means social costs and the provision of commodities to meet the laborer's daily needs. Even temporary or migrant workers require some level of provision, however dismal. Labor supply is harder to import than most other commodities and, once brought in, has a relatively permanent presence (except in the cases of special guest worker programs, temporary contract labor, and the like). Population growth also loosens long-run supply constraints, but again, adjustments are slow and hard to reverse. Shifts in labor qualities depend largely upon long-term processes of education (formal and informal) and cultural change (for example, the acquisition of appropriate work habits, the internalization of a "Protestant ethic," etc.). Internal adjustments in patterns of segmentation (the tightening or relaxation of discriminatory barriers between the races and sexes), together with changing social pressures toward the mobilization of latent labor reserves (the participation of women in the work force, the imposition of workfare provisions by the state, etc.), can also give greater flexibility to urban labor markets. In the long run, therefore, the supply of both quantities and qualities of labor power stands to be reasonably elastic, though constrained by social costs, long time-horizons for certain kinds of adjustment, and important irreversibilities.

Given such a condition, how, then, does an urban labor market work? First, consider matters solely from the point of view of capital accumulation. This means accelerating either quantitative expansion in the work force or qualitative change in response to organizational and technological revolutions in methods of production. How are the surpluses of labor power or untapped reserves of labor qualities (i.e., appropriate attitudes and particular skills) produced and maintained? Marx's "general law of capitalist accumulation" provides one kind of answer. The paths of accumulation and technological change intersect to produce a labor surplus (an industrial reserve army), no matter what the pace of population growth or in-migration. Technologically induced unemployment allows capitalists to operate on the supply as well as the demand end of the labor market, thus controlling wage levels, unemployment, and the like (Harvey 1982, chap. 6). The condition of the labor reserve then depends upon traditions of welfare arising out of socioeconomic and political evolution. The ability to switch into new technologies and organizational forms, however, depends on the adaptability of labor qualities. While the "general law" is useful as a first approximation, it requires much more elaboration if we are to understand the dynamics of urban labor markets.

Now consider the importance of economies of scale in the geographical space of an urban labor market. Those capitalists who operate in a line of production with low barriers to entry or easy capacity for expansion (which implies no large discrete increments in employment numbers due to "lumpiness" of other investments) are drawn to large urban labor markets because a small relative labor surplus in a large labor pool provides them individually with abundant reserves for start-up and expansion. Daily rigidities of labor supply can be more easily by-passed there. The counter-effect, however, is to draw such capitalists to agglomerate in large urban labor markets and so to push against the ceiling of total labor supply. In the absence of strong in-migration or population growth, this pushes up wage rates and tends to stimulate labor-saving innovations. And that implies a shift in demand for particular labor qualities. But a large urban labor market also gives individual capitalists abundant opportunities for substitution, thus reemphasizing the advantages of agglomeration. While the need for particular skills may be diminished for all but a small elite within the labor force, other qualities such as discipline, work attitudes, respect for authority, loyalty, and cooperation may become even more important and just as difficult to ensure. De-skilling in the narrow sense does not mean, as some suppose, that the question of labor qualities evaporates. Flexibility of labor qualities is, therefore, an important attribute of urban labor markets. The broad sense of "qualities" I am here invoking connects those attributes to the sociopsychological and cultural evolution of the labor force. While industries with large production units and lumpiness of investment lie outside these imperatives to some degree, the same tendency toward geographical concentration is given, this time within the form of industrial organization itself, while the long-term investments involved put a premium on stable quantities and qualities of labor supply (Storper and Walker 1983, 1984).

Now consider matters from the standpoint of the laborers. Marx relies in theory, as the capitalist does in practice, upon the "laborers' instincts for self-preservation" to ensure the daily and long-term reproduction of labor power.

Behind that blanket phrase lie complex processes of household formation, gender, family and kinship relations, personal networks, community solidarity, individual ambition, and the like. Such conditions are outside the direct control of the capitalists (or others), though there are innumerable indirect paths (religion, education, state programs, etc.) through which capitalists can influence them. The practices of labor reproduction are diverse, and the particular mix arrived at has profound implications for the qualities and quantities of labor supply within an urban region.

The "instincts for self-preservation" can take on individual or collective manifestations and are, in any case, open to a variety of social or psychological interpretations. While some workers may view individual migration as a means to personal economic advancement, others may choose to stay in place, organize, and fight collectively for improvements within the urban region. In between lies a range of other possibilities, perhaps best captured by the concept of distinctive working-class cultures that combine elements of individualism with certain habits of collectivism and common attitudes toward work, living, consumption, and "social progress." Furthermore, rising wage rates and expanding job opportunities are not the only motivations for migration. The psychosocial motivation to move to a large urban labor market may be just as important. The peculiar mix of freedoms and alienations, of hopes and risks which a large urban labor market offers are powerful incentives. Though the streets of Birmingham or Chicago may not be paved with gold, there is enough gold in circulation there that any one individual might reasonably hope for a piece of it. In the same way that capitalists are attracted to large urban labor markets out of economies of scale, so individual laborers are drawn for analogous reasons; the range of choice and possibilities for substitution are that much greater. The effect, however, is that individual laborers, acting in their own self-interest, tend to produce a surplus of labor power in a particular urban labor market and so undermine their own class interest. To the degree that individual capitalists engage in the same type of behavior, so considerable pressure builds toward increasing the scale of economic activity within an urban region. Nevertheless, pressures also exist for class-conscious labor organizations to seek ways to limit inmigration in order to preserve wage levels and conditions of working and living. They may do so by monopolizing certain kinds of jobs or simply by giving an unfriendly reception to new immigrants. Here, too, is a condition where differences of race, religion, ethnicity, and gender can be used as means of control or of selective integration of new labor supplies into an existing urban labor market. I make that point in order to show that labor market segmentations arise as much out of the laborers' desire to control the supply of labor power as they do out of employers' search to divide and rule.

The question of labor qualities deserves closer scrutiny. How do the laborers' instincts for self-preservation affect these? We are dealing here, as Storper and Walker (1984) emphasize, not only with the particular mix of skills and capacities to cope with this or that labor process but also with the whole sociology and psychology of work. Work habits, respect for authority, attitudes toward others, initiative and individualism, pride, and loyalty are some of the qualities that affect the productivity of labor power as well as its capacity to engage in struggle against capitalist domination. These qualities are not uniformly present within an urban labor market and are often highly differentiated, tending to produce their own kinds of structured rigidities. The product of a long history of sociopolitical development, they are often relatively inelastic in the medium and perhaps even in the long term. The qualities tend to be modified, as does their distribution within a given population by complex interactions of class-bound processes. Laborers can educate themselves, raise their own consciousness, struggle to bring whatever benefits they acquire to others through active political militancy, or try to monopolize certain skills, thus segmenting qualities in ways advantageous to subgroups (such as an aristocracy of labor, a layer of foreman-managers, or a particular job-skill structure). The motivations and ambitions of individual laborers, taken together with their collective endeavors, play a crucial role in the transformation of labor qualities independent of the capitalists' own motivations. The drive to self- and collective improvement is something to which the capitalist must often adapt, rather than something that the capitalist deliberately sets in motion.

Capitalists can also launch or support programs for the modification of labor qualities in ways that appear amenable to them. Other groups within the bourgeoisie (religious, educational, bureaucratic) have their own agendas and can enter into strategic alliances with either capitalists or laborers to press home private or state efforts to improve labor skills and qualities. The evolution of labor skills does not proceed, therefore, in ways narrowly functional for employers. Of course, evolutions in the labor process set a context within which such drives unfold and in some cases dictate the general paths down which the evolution of labor qualities must march. They can likewise create conditions that force laborers to adjust and adapt their own capacities and attitudes. But there is always an interaction, mediated by the laborers' instincts for self-preservation and advancement.

Labor qualities, once acquired, do not, unlike many other forms of investment, necessarily run down over time. The productivity of labor (like that of the soil, to use an analogy that Marx invokes to great effect) can build up over time, provided proper care is taken. The effect is to make each labor market even more unique, because the long processes of sociopolitical development within an urban region can build up unique mixes of qualities. The plundering of those qualities through de-skilling, overworking, bad labor relations, unemployment, and so forth can, however, lead, like soil mining, to the rapid depletion of a prime productive force. Attitudes of cooperation can be turned overnight into attitudes of violent confrontation; technical skills can be by-passed and lost; attitudes toward race and gender can be turned around to flare into conflicts within the labor market as well as within the workplace. The problem, of course, is that the coercive laws of competition tend to force individual capitalists into strategies of plundering, even when that undermines their own class interest. Whether or not such a result comes to pass depends upon the internal conditions of labor demand and supply, the possibilities of replenishment of labor reserves through migration either of labor power or of capital, and the capacity of capitalists to put a floor under their own competition by agreeing to some kind of regulation of the labor market.

But once the surpluses of labor power within an urban labor market are exhausted, capitalists have no options except to move elsewhere, seek out labor-saving innovations in order to create an industrial reserve where there was none before, force changes in the conditions of labor power utilization (reduce the social and legal restraints on the length of the working day, raise the rate of exploitation of women, children, and the aged), or simply mobilize the wholesale importation of labor surpluses from elsewhere. In practice, capitalists (or at least a faction of them) engage in all of these strategies well before the point of total absorption of the labor surplus is reached. Even minor increases in labor costs or minor threats of labor organization can lead to major switches in individual strategies of accumulation. But those strategies spark resistance and struggle, since by definition they threaten the security of labor.

The value of labor power (understood as the physical standard of living of labor) and of other important magnitudes in social life, such as the length of the working day, have to be viewed as an outcome not only of class-bound processes but also of active class struggle. The evidence for that is so overwhelming that it scarcely needs demonstration. What does need elucidation is the way in which those processes operate within the confines of geographically specific labor markets so as to emphasize rather than diminish the unique qualities of each. There are plenty of nineteenth-century studies, of which Engels's *Condition of the Working Class in England in 1844* (1971) is one of the most outstanding examples, which depict labor struggles as unfolding in specific urban and regional contexts. John Foster's (1974) comparative study of class structure, struggle, and labor process evolution in Oldham, Northampton, and South Shields is an interesting example of this genre of labor history. Divergence between urban labor markets during this period appears just as important as any trend toward uniformity. Yet even at this period we can spot a problem. The state is a unit of regulation which casts its net over a far vaster space than that of the urban labor market. Though the pressure for state regulation may arise within particular labor markets, the effect is to impose a surface veneer of uniformity across all labor markets. Class struggle through the nation state tends to downgrade urban labor markets to acceptable variations around some national norm. The differences between nations become greater than those within nations.

There is considerable evidence, therefore, that the geography of labor markets has evolved in the twentieth century into a more coherent hierarchy of international, national, regional, and urban labor markets. While the last cannot be understood without the others, I want to make the argument for the urban labor market as a fundamental unit of analysis within the hierarchy for exactly the same reason as I see it as a fundamental arena of class struggle and labor-force evolution. The political processes that transmit demands from urban to state levels and back again are, however, rather complex. State regulation may be concentrated in a few sectors and so have differential rather than uniform impacts upon urban labor markets. Enforcement can also vary from one place to another depending upon class consciousness and mobilization and the pressure among capitalists to circumvent the law. And to the degree that the state apparatus is itself decentralized, as in the United States, much regulation of labor markets dissolves into a mosaic of regional and even local differentiations. Collective bargaining at the national level likewise always leaves room for local variation, while unionization also varies from place to place. The strong local implantation of labor unionism still makes the title of "union town" meaningful. In the United States, for example, antiunion manuals advise keeping plants small (fewer than one hundred employees) and at least two hundred miles apart.

But there is much more to class struggle and the evolution of labor power than legal regulation and collective bargaining. All manner of informal arrangements can be arrived at, a whole culture of work, struggle, co-operation and social interaction evolved, which gives a unique coloration to labor qualities within an urban region. Religion, education, tradition, individual motivations, and patterns of collective mobilization integrate with the laborer's instincts for survival to produce a mosaic of urban labor markets which, though they may overlap and interpenetrate and integrate upward into regional and national configurations, form important units of analysis, if only because they remain the basic frame within which the working day finds its geographical range of possibilities. I shall therefore hold the "focus of resolution" at this level for purposes of further analysis, though with the clear recognition that it is not the only relevant geographical scale for looking at labor market behaviors.

II. SPACE, TECHNOLOGY, AND CAPITALIST COMPETITION
IN URBAN LABOR MARKETS

The entrepreneurial search for excess profit is fundamental within the social relations of capitalism. Excess profits can be had by virtue of superior technology and organization or by occupying superior locations. In itself, of course, location means nothing: the capitalist needs privileged access (measured in time and cost) to raw materials, to intermediate products, services, and infrastructures (physical and social), final markets, and, of course, to labor supplies of the requisite quantity and quality.

The coercive laws of competition force capitalists to search out superior technologies and locations. This imparts strong technological and geographical dynamism to production, exchange, and consumption. Strong checks exist, however, to an unlimited dynamism. Change of technology entails costs, as does locational shift. A rational capitalist should not change either unless the excess profits outweigh the costs. But competition does not necessarily promote such rationality. In the same way that individual laborers may see the streets of every city paved with gold, so individual capitalists often see gold shimmering out of every technological gimmick and every new locational niche. Lured on, they may take action with disastrous consequences not only for themselves but also for the whole capitalist class. The search for excess profit means speculation, and speculation too easily breeds excess. In the face of that experience, a countervailing capitalist rationality can arise. Capitalists can seek to convert control over technology or location into monopoly privileges that put themselves outside of rather than merely ahead of their competition. Labor processes can be protected by industrial secrecy, patent laws, and the like. In some industries, such protections are weak (anyone can set up a sweatshop just by buying a few sewing machines and hiring labor), whereas in others (pharmaceuticals and electronics) the protections are usually stronger. The capacity to convert the "natural monopoly" of spatial location into business monopoly also varies from the strong protections inherent in the provision of utilities to the weak protections afforded builders and contractors.

Most capitalists would probably prefer to be outside of rather than merely ahead of their competition. The search for excess profit therefore divides into two streams: first, a competitive path searching out new technologies and locations for temporary gain; second, the search for monopoly power through exclusive command of technological or locational advantage. The drive to convert temporary into permanent monopoly advantage is more important than is generally realized. It is of particular relevance in explaining capitalist behavior in urban labor markets. Once favorably positioned, they may push to consolidate monopoly powers, move to prevent the infiltration of competition, try to seal in access to special qualities of labor supplies, lock up flows of inputs by exclusive subcontracting, and monopolize market outlets by equally exclusive franchises, dealerships, and the like. In so doing, they necessarily become deeply embroiled in the totality of political-economic processes operating within a particular labor market. They try, in effect, to manage their own positive externality effects and to capture the benefits of the urban synergism which they consciously help to promote.

This dual path to excess profit splits into another important duality to the degree that trade-offs exist between technological and locational advantages. A superior technology can compensate for an inferior location, and the opposite is also true. Under competition, some rough equilibrium should arise within the landscape of capitalist production in which trade-offs between technological and locational advantages would be nicely balanced for all producers. It would be a highly unstable landscape. The range of spatial competition is technologically defined (by economies of scale and the range of a good) at the same time as the appropriate technology depends upon the size and scale of the market area for both inputs and outputs (to say nothing of the fluid movement of labor supply). The search for excess profits through technological change is not, therefore, independent of the search for excess profits from location. Even in the absence of excessive speculation, competition simultaneously provokes shifts in spatial configurations and technological mixes, making "spatial equilibrium" (in the sense of classical location theory) an impossibility. The closer a space-economy approaches an equilibrium condition, the more the accumulation of capital and the search for excess profits will disrupt it.

But the pace of change of either sort is held back by the turnover time of the capitals engaged. Different kinds of goods require different working periods (varying from the daily baking of bread through the annual productions of agriculture, to the even longer times taken to produce, say, a hydroelectric dam or a power station). Furthermore, the different inputs can be turned over at different rates (machinery, buildings, etc.). The longer these working periods and turnover times (see Harvey 1982, chap. 8), the greater the geographical and technological inertia. New technologies and locations cannot be achieved until after the value embodied in the fixed capital employed has been fully recovered; unless, that is, a portion of the value is devalued, written off before its economic lifetime is out.

The longer these lifetimes, the more vulnerable such production systems become. Any withdrawal of the daily flow of labor (through strikes, out-migration, or transfer to other job opportunities within the urban labor market) spells danger for capitalists employing large quantities of fixed capital. Any introduction of new methods, new product lines, or new input configurations also puts existing systems of production and the fixed capital they employ in jeopardy. These problems are so serious that capitalists will not undertake long-term investments without the assurance of some stability in labor markets and without protection against excessive speculative innovation. Under such conditions, monopoly control of technology and location appears necessary, a vital means to guarantee conditions for long-term investment. But the trade-off between location and technology also enters in. Highly competitive firms in the realm of technology may carve up the world into monopolistically controlled spaces, while firms that are highly competitive in local markets (like building contractors) may be weakly competitive when it comes to technology. We thus end up with a four-way classification of monopolistic or competitive styles of seeking excess profits from technology or location. In practice, most firms probably end up closer to the center than to the peripheries of that frame.

The greater the monopoly power, the more the geographical landscape of capitalist production tends toward a relatively stationary state. The rhythms of technological and locational change are slowed down even beyond the point required to guarantee the proper amortization of fixed capital. The trouble, of course, is that such fixity is inconsistent with the further accumulation of capital. It may even undermine the capacity to wage class struggle against labor effectively. Herein lies a basis for stagnation and then crisis formation. A sudden break with past technological mixes and spatial configurations often entails massive devaluations of the preexisting capital and the breaking of powerful monopoly privileges, including those built up by labor organizations. The crisis "liberates" capital from the stagnation of its quasi-monopolistic chains; it permits new technologies to be deployed and new spatial configurations to be created. It also implies new patterns of labor bargaining and of social relations in production. The trade-offs between technology and location are radically disturbed, and new interurban, inter-regional, and international divisions of labor arise, only to embody new monopolistic elements. The geographical and technological landscape of capitalism is torn between a stable but stagnant calm incompatible with accumulation and disruptive processes of devaluation and "creative destruction."

When we look at these processes from the standpoint of the social, spatial, and technological divisions of labor, however, we note another set of restraints. The complementarity of many production flows and the "round-aboutness" of production techniques make it hard for firms to shift technique or location without parallel moves on the part of other firms. Considerable economies of scale attach to agglomeration in areas where a wide range of substitution (of inputs or of markets) is possible. The effect is to tend to confine innovation possibilities to restricted locations for competitive firms — hence the significance of large metropolitan areas (Chinitz 1958). Only in relatively monopolistic sectors can innovation disperse (to rural R & D establishments, for example). Shifts of location are likewise constrained by the difficulty of ensuring simultaneous moves by suppliers or market outlets. Only when firms have sufficient monopoly power can they drag their own suppliers and market outlets with them or economize on the use of transportation systems so that location no longer matters. The dynamism I have depicted in the case of individual competitive firms is therefore modified by conditions of complementarity within an overall spatial division of labor.

Capitalist behavior is thus ambiguous in relation to spatially defined urban labor markets. On the one hand, the thrust to gain monopoly privileges that put them above their competition, coupled with economies of agglomeration within a spatial division of labor, can lead firms to be both covetous and solicitous of tapping into and preserving the special privileges of exclusive access to labor supplies of a certain quantity and quality. They may even take active steps to help preserve labor qualities, compromise with labor demands in return for labor cooperation, and put some of their own resources behind the drive to enhance labor qualities (though always, of course, with an eye to those qualities they regard as advantageous to themselves). On the other hand, competition (either spatial or technological) can push them to ride roughshod from one type of labor market (social or spatial) to another with scant regard for the consequences of plundering the qualities and quantities of labor power. They are then forced to visit the costs of creative destruction on the labor force within the urban region with all manner of consequences, including the eruption of labor discontent and the triggering of awesome class struggle.

To summarize this section: The search for excess profits based on technological and locational advantage is limited by the monopolistic element of both. The trade-off between technology and location is an active factor within the formation of the geographical landscape of production and becomes more so to the degree that monopoly privileges attach to both within a spatial and technological division of labor. The process of accumulation requires, however, that monopoly privileges be broken. And that can be done only through processes of creative destruction, which means the devaluation of both capital and labor power. The capitalist landscape of production therefore lurches between the stabilizing stagnation of monopoly controls and the disruptive dynamism of competitive growth.

III. THE TENDENCY TOWARD "STRUCTURED COHERENCE" IN THE ECONOMY OF URBAN REGIONS

The class relation between capital and labor tends, under the conditions described, to produce a "structured coherence" of the economy of an urban region. At the heart of that coherence lies a particular technological mix – understood not simply as hardware but also as organizational forms – and a dominant set of social relations. Together these define models of consumption as well as of the labor process. The coherence embraces the standard of living, the qualities and style of life, work satisfactions (or lack thereof), social hierarchies (authority structures in the workplace, status systems of consumption), and a whole set of sociological and psychological attitudes toward working, living, enjoying, entertaining, and the like. We shall later see how the coherence also spawns a distinctive urban politics. How is this tendency toward structured coherence produced?

Laborers, we saw, are free – depending on their skills, the degree of competition between them, the forms of segmentation, and the levels of demand – to substitute job opportunities daily within a socially given commuting range. Wage rates and working conditions within sectors should therefore be more finely adjusted within than between urban labor markets. To reproduce labor power on a daily basis, workers must also spend much of what they earn on goods and services retailed within a similar socially given commuting range. Within that range, they are free to patronize this or that establishment, purchase this or that service, bid for this or that house, and press for this or that level of social provision. In so doing, they convert their wage into a certain style, standard, and pattern of consumption within a system of market areas for goods and geographically defined labor markets. Though the two market areas may not be coterminous for any one individual or family (those on the fringes in particular may work in one market area and shop in another), the effect is to tend to define an urban area as a unity of job and consumption opportunities. To be sure, the skills and status system and the various labor market segmentations prevent any equalization of wage rates, working conditions, living standards, or social provision within that urban region, while equally vigorous discrimination on the consumption side (racial, sexual, or religious discrimination in housing markets, in social provision, etc.) creates another layer of barriers to the equalization of living standards and life-styles. There is, nevertheless, a certain merit to considering an underlying unity of job and consumption opportunities as a norm around which such deviations pivot. This norm fixes, for example, a standard against which the sense of relative deprivation may be measured.

The conception to which this leads is of a daily exchange of labor power and a daily reproduction of labor power caught within the confines of some loosely defined field of commuting possibilities. From a purely technical standpoint this positions labor as an appendage of the circulation of capital within the urban region. Wage revenues circulate out of production only to enter back into production as a living laborer, fed, housed, rested, and ready for work. This "company store" image does not imply powerlessness on the part of the laborer, though it does limit the exercise of that power, short of revolution. Collective struggles within the confines of this appendage relation frequently affect the exact form of structured coherence achieved. This applies as much to the public provision of services (hence the significance of local politics) as it does to struggles over local wage rates, working conditions, and the nature, price, and quality of consumption goods and services. Within the frame I have defined, therefore, there is abundant oportunity for laborers to pursue the enhancement of skills, the construction of class organizations for mutual support (e.g., savings associations, mutual benefit societies), and the building of a basis for political power. Employers are likewise caught in the same dependency relation. They are as deeply beholden to the daily exchange of labor power for their profit as laborers are beholden to them for daily sustenance. Ownership and control over the means, mechanisms, and forms of production gives them key advantages in class struggle, but they can never escape the dependency relation, which, in the first instance, is necessarily articulated through daily labor markets.

Consider the broad contours of the struggle between capital and labor within the confines of the urban region. Technology offers capitalists a vital means of control which mediates the production of labor surpluses and wage rates and ranges as well as job structures and hierarchies. Struggles over the deployment of new technologies are fundamental to the kind of structured coherence achieved within the urban region. Struggles waged by either capitalists or laborers to sustain and enhance labor quantities and qualities are likewise important, since they define the range of technological possibilities. Cooperation, cooptation, and consent are also a part of class struggle. They have the advantage, for capitalist and laborer alike, of giving a certain measure of stability and security to both work and the standard of living, albeit under the overall domination of capital. Accommodation plays a vital role in giving a relatively stable structured coherence to production and consumption within the urban region.

Capitalists, however, can choose to buy and sell commodities on a daily basis within or without the urban region, depending, of course, on the nature of the good, transport costs, effective demand, relative prices, and the like. Commodity and service production within an urban region roughly divides (as economic base theory long ago argued) into locally produced and consumed goods and services and an "export" trade counterbalanced by "imports" of goods and services from other urban regions. The volume and qualities of the internal market are, however, important parameters for much of the capital operating there. Effective demand in that market depends upon wages paid out, new investments made, and revenues received (rents, interest, taxes, profits). Distribution relations therefore affect the kind of structured coherence achieved (the balance of luxury versus wage goods, between final consumption and new investment, for example). Struggles over distribution and over the forms of consumption unfold unevenly from one urban region to another and likewise contribute to the uniqueness of each (cf. Katznelson 1981).

Consider, now, the complexities that arise through spatial competition and complementarity between urban regions within a geographical division of labor. Low wage costs in a particular industry may make it easier to compete in other markets as well as internally. But low wages mean less local effective demand, which may reduce economies of scale for locally oriented production and thus undermine the capacity to compete within a geographical division of labor. I use tht example to illustrate the idea that high wage costs do not always undermine competitiveness but can sometimes improve it, depending on the sector. Processes of this type underline the unique position of each urban region in the kind of structured coherence achieved in relation to its position within the geographical division of labor. The principle I am working toward is this: that class struggles over wage rates, working conditions, consumption (public or private), distribution relations, and so forth within an urban region intersect with export-import relations within a geographical division of labor in highly specific ways. Determinations are reciprocal and, as we shall see, necessarily fluid and dynamic. The tendency toward structured coherence takes shape and is shaped by these reciprocal relations. The effect is to emphasize the uniqueness of geographical position as well as of the qualities of each urban region.

Within this broad idea there are two issues I want to take up for closer inspection. Consider, first, how the technological mix within an urban region tends to define production and consumption processes simultaneously. There are, to begin with, certain important sectors (transportation being one) where an industry serves both production and consumption simultaneously, automatically unifying the technology deployed in both. In other cases, the push to serve both producer and consumer markets arises out of the quest for economies of scale in the market (this is very much the case with electronics). Then there are less tangible but no less important unifying forces. Designers and workers familiar with a technology (its functions, maintenance, etc.) in the workplace can quickly adapt it to uses in the living space. But the inverse relation is also true. The kinds of skills children pick up from the technology of play form a basis for the skills they can bring to production: computer games are an important educational device. Indeed, pressure for innovation can just as easily begin in the home as in the workplace (the demand for labor-saving household gadgets, innovative games, etc.). The motivations and logic of development are, however, quite different. Competition, class struggle, and the need to coordinate production push capitalists toward innovation even in the face of the barrier of amortization of past investments.

In the consumption sphere, premature and planned obsolescence has to be produced by the mobilization of fashion, style, status-seeking, possessive individualism, or appeals to social progress. The effect, however, is to accentuate the parallel evolutions of the technologies of production and consumption within the urban region. Only in "export enclave" economies of some Third World cities do we find a strong separation in the technologies of the two spheres. The tendency in the urban economies of advanced capitalist economies is to forge powerful and significant links between the technologies of the two spheres. Indeed, a case can be made that the stronger the link, the more dynamic the urban economy will become.

Consider, second, the links between social relations in the workplace and in the living space. Here, too, the tendency toward structured coherence rests on parallel evolutions, though again under very different circumstances and with quite different motivations. Patriarchal relations within the family, for example, can be taken over wholesale in the organization of social relations in the workplace. Modifications in the workplace – themselves influenced by patterns of technological change and of labor demand (the need to mobilize women as part of an industrial reserve army, for example) – have implications for social relations in the household (cf. *Capital* 1:490). Ties of family and kinship and relations of gender and age adapt to new forms of industrial organization (cf. Hareven 1982) at the same time as employers are drawn willy-nilly to use those familial and familiar relations as means of control and cooptation. These qualities of labor power evolve jointly through the daily experience of living and working.

But I speak only of the *tendency* toward structured coherence because it exists in the midst of a maelstrom of forces that tend to undermine and disrupt it. Competition over technological change, product innovation, and social organization; class struggles over distribution; social relations of production and reproduction; shifting space relations; and the push to accelerate turnover times and accumulation all make for constant imbalances. Equilibrium could be achieved only by accident, and then only momentarily. To the degree that capitalism internalizes powerful contradictions – between growth and technological progress, between the growth of productive forces and the dominant social relations of production – so the economy of any urban region is always potentially crisis-prone. Overaccumulation and devaluation are perpetual threats that have to be contained.

The potential responses to that threat are very different and take the urban economy in quite different directions. First, increasing monopolization provides a way to control the disequilibrating processes. We have already seen how private monopolization (of space, technology, or both) is one effective solution to excessive and destructive competition, and we have also argued that the thrust toward monopolization within an urban economy is the first level at which the monopolization due to space may be procured. We now encounter a collective version of that solution. Vested interests in the status quo actively cooperate to contain the forces of disruption. And in so doing they reinforce, perhaps even try to institutionalize, the kind of structured coherence already achieved within the economy of the urban region. The pursuit of such a strategy has two disadvantages. It leads to both internal stagnation and loss of external competitiveness within the geography of accumulation.

The second direction seeks to resolve the contradictions through temporal and spatial displacement (cf. Harvey 1982, 1985). Surpluses of capital and labor are then absorbed through some mix of long-term growth strategies (usually the debt-financing of long-term investments, which puts off crisis formation into the future) and geographical expansionism (export of money capital, expanding exports of goods and services to other regions, and the like). The problem, of course, is that all other urban economies experience the same dilemmas. To the degree that each strives to rid itself of its own internal contradictions through geographical expansion, the result is economic and geopolitical conflict within the international division of labor (wars over jobs, investment, commodity prices and exchange, money, capital flows, labor migration, and the like). Even in the situation where a particular urban economy has evolved (perhaps through monopolization) toward a point of strongly structured coherence, external influences of this sort also threaten to disrupt it.

We shall return to the geopolitical aspects of this later. For the moment, I simply want to insist upon the power of the tendency toward structured coherence in an urban economy and to insist also that the same processes that push in that direction tend to undermine and disrupt what they produce. So do the internal contradictions of capitalism come home to roost within the economies of urban regions.

IV. PHYSICAL AND SOCIAL INFRASTRUCTURES

The reproduction of both capital and labor power requires a wide range of physical and social infrastructures. These consolidate and reinforce the trend toward structured coherence within an urban labor market.

Some of these infrastructures are embedded in the land as a built environment of roads, bridges, sewers, houses, schools, factories, shopping centers, medical facilities, and so on. They hang together as a spatially specific resource complex of humanly created assets to support both production (fixed capital) and consumption (the consumption fund). They absorb often large quantities of long-term and geographically immobile capital investment and require further capital during their lifetime to compensate for wear and tear and maintenance needs. The aging of this capital stock does not fit any unified schema. It usually has to be renewed piecemeal, under conditions where the relations within the spatial configuration of the resource complex as a whole constrain what can happen to the parts because of the need to preserve the harmony of the whole. The stock of fixed capital and of consumption fund assets does, however, provide a solid form of wealth that can be used to produce and consume more wealth. The urban region acquires another meaning – it can be defined as a particular spatial configuration of a built environment for production, consumption, and exchange.

I have elsewhere examined the general conditions for the production of these kinds of assets and the tensions that exist between them and the dynamics of accumulation (Harvey 1982). I need state here only those general points necessary to my argument. First, the assets themselves embody or support a dominant technological mix, giving added strength to the idea of structured coherence of production and consumption. Second, privileged access to any unique bundle of assets in the built environment is a potential source of excess profit. Capitalists therefore have a direct interest in the creation and location of such investments and will seek an advantageous location with respect to them (this can lead to strong competitive bidding for sites and locations). Third, the production of the built environment means withdrawing capital from current consumption and production, and that is usually done through debt-financing. Government and financial institutions are usually involved in their production and maintenance. This carries the added advantage that the configuration of the resource complex as a whole can be planned on "rational" lines with an eye to the working harmony of the whole. Fourth, the capital embodied in the built environment is vulnerable to devaluation if the pattern of uses envisaged does not materialize. Put the other way round, this means that employers and consumers are confined to certain kinds of uses and activity patterns for the lifetime of such investments if devaluation is to be avoided. Substitutions of uses are always possible, of course, so that some degree of flexibility exists within these patterns. Finally, the protection of the value of such assets is a vital objective for those who hold the debt on them (primarily financial institutions, governments, and private individuals). Protection in this case means pressure on users to confine themselves to the possibilities that the assets define. In all of these respects, powerful forces are at work to maintain and even institutionalize the structured coherence of the urban-regional economy.

Social infrastructures are harder to pin down. They are not immobile and fixed in space in the same way as built environments (though to the degree they use the latter they also are confined spatially), and they have a variety of orientations (from care of the aged and maintenance of the labor reserve in a state of readiness to enter production, through active policies to enhance labor qualities and ensure discipline and respect for authority, to essential governmental, legal, technical, and scientific services for capitalists). The market area for each kind of service is often vague, and in any case varies in scale from local day care centers to cultural institutions that serve a large region. But they absorb large quantities of capital, and their aggregate effect is to help consolidate the tendency toward structured coherence within the urban region. Furthermore, the social institutions that support life, work, and the circulation of capital are not created overnight and require a certain degree of stability if they are to be effective. The institutions are often national and regional rather than local in scope, but no matter how centralized the degree of financial or political power which lies behind them, some degree of local autonomy is always granted. Social infrastructural provision tends to be hierarchically organized (like labor and commodity markets), with the urban region forming one layer of the structure. Within the urban region, however, institutions and the people who run them tend to coalesce, sometimes tightly and sometimes loosely but rarely without conflict, into a matrix of interlocking and interdependent social resources offering a specific mix of social possibilities. This matrix affects the qualities of labor power in all their aspects (from skills to work attitudes), the condition of the industrial reserve army, and other crucial aspects of labor power supply. But it has equal significance for the reproduction of capital, affecting the production of scientific and technical knowledge and the evolution of managerial and financial know-how and entrepreneurial abilities. Some of the infrastructures are public; some, like education, may be mixed; and still others may be organized outside the framework of the state (religion being a prime example). The reproduction of social infrastructures is therefore open to a curious mix of private and class pressures, social conventions and traditions, and political processes contained within a hierarchically organized state apparatus.

Under such conditions, initial diversities of culture, religion, racial heritage, social attitudes, class consciousness, and so forth can be reproduced and even magnified to form the basis of labor market segmentations. Bourgeois interests may become similarly fragmented through, for example, religious or ethnic domination of economic activity in certain sectors. The effect is to produce further fragmentations in political ideology and allegiance. But taken together, these features give unique coloration to socioeconomic and political processes within each urban region. The social infrastructures are themselves produced by a long history of social interactions and evolution. They are not entirely imposed from above or given from outside. Local industrialists may support scientific and educational institutions in the hope of drawing upon the technologies and managerial skills produced there, while access to such centers (Stanford and MIT, for example) can give competitive advantages. Labor struggles within the urban region can likewise produce strong local commitment to traditions of public education to which the capitalists may also rally in their own class interest. The overall effect of such processes is to emphasize the trend toward structured coherence within the social structure and economy of the urban region.

There are, however, limits to the coherence that can be achieved. The social infrastructures absorb vast quantities of capital and labor power and are limited by the availability of surpluses of both. And to the degree that they become caught up in the circulation of capital so their capacity to enhance local surplus value productivity becomes an important issue. The problem in this case is rendered even more complicated because the benefits of local investments can spread quickly and widely. Interurban "brain drains" of skilled labor and of entrepreneurial and managerial know-how are easily accomplished. New technologies designed in one place can be instantaneously implemented in another. The financing can likewise entail all sorts of redistributions of resources from one urban region to another (through government budgets but also through private transfers, such as alumni donations to colleges). Under such conditions, local exposure to threats of overaccumulation and devaluation becomes hard to estimate. Writing off the value of assets embodied in this resource complex, to say nothing of the human capacities employed there, is, however, a tricky and dangerous affair. Like the built environment, it is hard to change one aspect without affecting the rest. Devaluation entails the modification or sometimes even the destruction of a whole system of community reproduction. Social infrastructures, themselves the product of struggle and history, are hard to transform except through the same kind of creative destruction applied to built environments.

An examination of physical and social infrastructures will help to broaden the conception of what an urban region is all about. It is more than a set of overlapping and interpenetrating commodity and labor markets; more than a set of intersecting labor processes and productive forces; more, even than a simple structured coherence of production and consumption. It is also a living community endowed with certain physical and social assets, themselves the product of a long process of historical development and class struggle. These assets define the wealth of a community, and it is through their proper maintenance, enhancement, deployment, and use that the productivity of labor power stands to be continuously preserved and enhanced at the same time as the reproduction and expansion of capital is assured. The problem, of course, is that this wealth is produced and sustained through the circulation of capital, which is itself crisis-prone. The viability of the physical and social infrastructures is perpetually threatened by the cold winds of overaccumulation, devaluation, and dissolution.

Nevertheless, we now see the urban as a community in which daily processes of living and working occur against a seemingly solid, secure, and relatively permanent background of social and physical infrastructures strongly implanted within the social and physical landscape of capitalism. This implies that a class-bound mode of production and consumption cannot function without some operative geographical conception of community. "Community" is not defined, however, as some autonomous entity but as a set of processes which produce a geographical product. The latter is real and tangible enough. For that reason it leads directly to the question, to what degree is the process set in motion through human agency then dominated by its own product? Put another way, do produced communities act as a barrier to class-bound accumulation? Important political implications then follow.

V. CLASS-ALLIANCE FORMATION IN URBAN REGIONS

The tendency toward structured coherence of the economy gives a material base to class-alliance formation within urban regions. The objective of the class alliance is to preserve or enhance achieved models of production and consumption, dominant technological mixes and patterns of social relations, profit and wage levels, the qualities of labor power and entrepreneurial-managerial skills, social and physical infrastructures, and the cultural qualities of living and working. The class alliance is always unstable (for reasons I shall shortly take up), and its spatial range is in any case fuzzy and usually internally fragmented to some degree (e.g., city versus suburb). Its posture may be defensive or aggressive with respect to other urban regions, but its strength is of particular importance at times of crisis when struggles erupt over the when and where of place-specific devaluation. It can also form alliances with political forces in other urban regions and so build toward regional or national configurations of political power. The class alliance that forms within an urban region is, nevertheless, a powerful shaping force in the landscape of capitalism. The product of capital accumulation and class struggle unfolding in geographical space, it in turn shapes their dynamics in fundamental ways.

Three questions have to be addressed about such class alliances. First, who participates in them and why? Second, how are the diverse interests shaped and articulated politically? And third, what renders such class alliances both unstable and vulnerable?

The short answer to the first question is, everyone but no one in particular. All economic agents occupy a space and have some interest in controlling activities in the spaces around them. If, as we have argued, there is an inevitable tendency toward the production of structured coherence of an urban economy, then it follows that everyone has some interest in finding political means to affect the form that structured coherence takes. But some have a greater interest than others. We know, for example, that capital invested in the built environment cannot be moved without being destroyed. The capital flowing into social infrastructures, though more flexible, is also hard to render mobile without destroying many of its essential qualities. We also know that if the value of this vast capital investment is to be preserved, then production and consumption have to continue at a certain level and of a certain type for a relatively long period. The owners of this capital (or of titles to the public and private debt incurred thereon) have an enormous stake in defending their assets and the models of production and consumption which underpin their value. The ownership of such assets and of the debt can spread widely across social classes, from the working-class homeowner to the large financial institutions that may hold much of the mortgage and municipal debt. All have a vested interest in the continued prosperity of the urban region and have very good reasons to participate in a class alliance to defend their interests. But some factions of capital and labor are more committed by immobile investment than others. Land and property owners (including that faction of the working class that has gained access to homeownership), developers and builders, the local state, and those who hold the mortgage and public debt have much more to gain from forging a local alliance to protect their interests and to ward off the threat of localized devaluation than do transient laborers, itinerant salesmen, and peripatetic multinationals.

But the quantities and qualities of physical and social infrastructures affect the competitive position of the urban region in the international division of labor, the profits of enterprise, the standard of living of labor, and a whole host of other possibilities for the qualities of living and working within the urban region. There are, therefore, broader class interests behind their production and proper utilization than the immediate interests of those who own them. Peripatetic multinationals have a fine appreciation of them. Itinerant tenants are not indifferent to their accommodations either. A broad consensus of interest therefore exists behind the principle (though not necessarily the detailed practices) of enhancing investment in social and physical infrastructures within the urban region (providing, of course, the investment is productive, profitable, and does not unduly favor or burden one class faction rather than another). To the degree that class alliances form within the urban region around the theme of protection and enhancement of immobile physical and social infrastructures, all classes and factions have an interest in participating in the political game.

But interest in class-alliance formation does not end there. Producers who

cannot easily move because of fixed capital commitments or who have
acquired some degree of monopoly power through privileged access to
markets or inputs (including special qualities of the labor supply) can join
with an immense array of merchants, professions, services, and state
personnel who draw their incomes from the local circulation of revenues to
support and preserve the development of the urban economy. Factions of
labor that have, through organization and struggle, managed to create islands
of relative privilege within a sea of exploitation will rally to such an alliance if
its themes are protection of jobs and of living standards already achieved and
will see active participation in such an alliance as a means to further enhance
their own position. We see the basis here for the rise of some kind of alliance
between all classes, in defense of social reproduction (of both accumulation
and the reproduction of labor power) within the urban region. The alliance
typically engages in community boosterism and strives to create community
solidarity behind ideals of social progress and defense of local interests. Such
activities, I want to stress, are not aberrations of class struggle but are a
necessary and particular manifestation of the way class relations and accumulation unfold in space.

Such alliances are, however, inherently unstable. Both internal divisions
and external pressures make it hard to hold them together in the face of a
social dynamic restlessly powered by the pursuit of profit, the accumulation
of capital, and the multifaceted lines of class cleavage and struggle embodied
therein. Divisions become immediately apparent when it comes to mapping
the future. Different interests pull in different directions, each usually
claiming that the public interest lies wherever it itself is headed. Factional
divisions within the bourgeoisie (between financial, commercial, producer,
real estate, and landed property interests, or between local neighborhood
producers and multinational organizations) match factional divisions within
the working class (between men and women, between skilled blue collar and
white collar and the unskilled, between the employed and the unemployed,
between the varied segmentations) to make it hard to talk of any coherent
class interest in class-alliance formation. Worse still, individuals occupy
multiple roles and can be torn in many different directions – workers may also
be homeowners, consumers, parents, and investors and may seek to participate in the class alliance in quite inconsistent roles. And there is no way a
class alliance can act that does not unduly favor or burden one faction or class
rather than another. Decisions on public investment, to take the clearest case,
have uneven class impacts and benefits at the same time as they alter the
spatial configuration of assets and their relative accessibility. Work-force
segmentations that have become manifest as spatial segregations stand to be
undermined or reinforced, depending upon the nature of such decisions.
Competition (between workers, between producers of goods and services,

retailers, etc.) and the struggle to procure monopoly powers do not disappear
with class-alliance formation. They are, rather, perpetually disruptive forces
that the class alliance has to contain. Much of the art of urban and regional
politics, as we shall shortly see, consists in finding ways to trade off costs and
benefits between groups and interests while containing competition and
monopoly powers so as to maintain majority support for a ruling alliance.

The external pressures on the alliance's stability are of two sorts. First, all
economic agents internalize a choice between staying in place and striving for
local improvement or moving elsewhere to where profits, wage rates, working
conditions, life-styles, environmental qualities, hopes for the future, and so
on appear better. That tension, common to all, is not evenly balanced for all.
Different factions and classes have different capacities for geographical
mobility depending upon the privileges they command, the assets they own,
and the intangible restraints that tend to keep them place-bound. A single
male with a sack of gold (or, what amounts to the same thing, letters of
credit) has more options as a rule than does the owner of a local steel mill or a
married woman with extensive family and kinship ties and cares. Some are
more solid partners in a class alliance than others simply because they have
fewer options to move elsewhere. But appearances can sometimes be
deceptive. Bankers and financiers control the most geographically mobile
asset of all – money – but are also often heavily committed to an urban region
through their holdings of local debt (this was the dilemma of many of New
York's international banks during that city's fiscal crisis of 1974–75).
Multinational firms appear able to relocate production rapidly, yet sometimes
depend upon such a particular mix of fixed capital, local labor qualities, and
infrastructures that movement comes hard. A worker with extensive kinship
obligations may use them to command geographical mobility rather than to
remain locked in place. These examples illustrate that decisions to support or
abandon, build or undermine a class alliance must come out of the resolution
of complex and conflicting tensions. The same group interest may even
actively undermine on the one hand what they actively strive to support on
the other. Financial institutions, for example, may undermine the quality of
their own debt and the power of their local class alliance by financing
suburbanization or the export of money capital to wherever the rate of return
is highest. Workers, by pushing for high wages, can stimulate the loss of
jobs. Such examples of unintended and often contradictory consequences are
legion in this context.

Second, disruptive forces can be brought to bear on the class alliance from
outside. The in-migration of labor power of lower cost and different qualities,
the takeover of local production and retailing by outside capital, the import
of commodities once locally produced, inflows of money capital, and
redistributions of revenues alter power balances between the participants in

an alliance. Indeed, the import may be organized by one faction with just such an aim: employers encourage in-migration of cheaper labor power; merchants, the import of cheaper commodities compared to those produced locally; and so on. The ability to mobilize external relations and possibilities becomes an important bargaining strength in negotiations within the class alliance. The class or faction that can most easily summon up external assistance (the labor unions that can bring in strike support funds, the capitalists who can mobilize outside support to quell unrest) have an advantage over groups who lack such power. Conversely, groups that can threaten to move elsewhere if they do not get local satisfaction of their demands are in a more powerful position relative to those that cannot.

The same forces that counteract the tendency toward a structured coherence of an urban economy also render class alliances unstable and insecure. But there is a further dimension to all of this, which we must now subject to rather close scrutiny. This concerns the political means available to define, articulate, and act upon class-alliance aims and the political art of forging a ruling-class alliance out of the conflictual and contradictory impulses that lie behind the tendency toward local class-alliance formation.

VI. URBAN POLITICS AND THE SEARCH FOR A RULING-CLASS ALLIANCE

The confusions and instabilities of class-alliance formation create a political space in which a relatively autonomous urban politics can arise. The confusions of roles, orientations, and interests of individuals, groups, factions, and classes, taken together with the disruptions of capital accumulation (growth, technological change, class conflict, and crises of overaccumulation), keep social relations in a perpetual state of flux and often plunge them into the ambiguous tensions of social transformation. The art of politics here comes into its own. The politician of genius and craft can forge a relatively permanent and powerful coalition of interests so as to unify and articulate a sense of place-bound community. Indeed, so open is the situation that a whole class of politicians can arise given over entirely to its exploitation. "Nowhere do 'politicians' form a more separate, powerful section of the nation than in North America," wrote Engels, pushing the "process of the state power making itself independent in relation to society" to extremes (Marx and Lenin 1968, 20). It is into this breach that a whole class of "urban managers" can also insert themselves as a seemingly independent source of social power (Saunders 1981, 118–36). Both politicians and urban managers (and there often seems little point in distinguishing between them from this standpoint) play the game of coalition politics in such a way as to build a ruling class that sees itself as the symbol of community and appropriates the necessary means (traditional and symbolic as well as legal, financial, and technical) to legitimize its authority and power. It usually speaks "in the public interest" and finds ways to command sufficient authority or mass support (by way of concessions, cooptation, horse-trading, and repression) so as to still the opposition that is bound to arise to its activities.

The local government is, of course, a central political means around which a ruling coalition tends to forge its identity and modes of action within an urban region. But I want to resist the idea that it is the only or even the most important means. The political processes at work in civil society are much broader and deeper than the local government's particular compass. Indeed, there are many facets that make it ill-suited to the task of coalition building. Its boundaries do not necessarily coincide with the fluid zones of urban labor and commodity markets or infrastructural formation; and their adjustment through annexation, local government reorganization, and metropolitan-wide cooperation is cumbersome, though often of great long-run significance. Local jurisdictions frequently divide rather than unify the urban region, thus emphasizing the segmentations (such as that between city and suburb) rather than the tendency toward structured coherence and class-alliance formation. Other means then have to be found within the higher tiers of government or within civil society (informal groupings of business and financial interests, for example) to forge a ruling-class alliance. On the one hand, Robert Moses reshaped New York without any popular mandate by using state and federal powers, backed by a network of powerful financial, business, construction (including unions), and real estate interests, to dominate an otherwise segmented local government apparatus. Mayor Schaefer uses Baltimore's City Hall, on the other hand, as a base to reach out into civil society and build a coalition of public and private interests capable of dominating the whole urban region. It is, we conclude, the interpenetration of class, group, and individual relations within and between the state and civil society which provides the matrix of possibilities for building a ruling coalition.

To the degree that all economic agents have some interest in joining a ruling coalition, the composition of the latter is open rather than predetermined. Its exact composition is a matter of negotiation out of which many different configurations can arise. Alliances can shift from issue to issue (capital and labor may agree upon the need for new jobs but disagree about the need to regulate working conditions), and different working coalitions define varied and sometimes quite contrary objectives. Some coalitions may be pro-growth and others anti-growth, and elements of capital and labor can be found on both sides of that divide. And the politics can point in many different directions. On the one hand, there are the urban-based revolutionary movements such as that of the Paris Commune, and the strong traditions of "municipal socialism" – Milwaukee in the 1900s; Vienna in the 1920s;

Bologna, the Greater London Council, and Santa Monica today — which sustain themselves through electoral command of the local government apparatus. On the other hand, there are the seemingly all-powerful pro-growth coalitions that emerged in many American cities after 1945, in some cases using and in other cases by-passing (like Robert Moses) local government (Molotch 1976; Mollenkopf 1983). In between lie all kinds of hybrids from the hotly contested politics described in Katznelson's (1982) *City Trenches* to the stable but authoritarian machine politics of New York's Boss Tweed, Chicago's Mayor Daley, and Baltimore's Mayor Schaefer. Each kind of politics depends upon the forging of a particular coalition of interests; and each is, in its own way, unique. Furthermore, each coalition has different means and resources open to it which limit what it can or cannot do (political control over the state apparatus, the local budget, and land-use regulation, for example, gives very different powers from control over the strings of investment finance). Herein lies the sort of tension that sparks conflict and that can bring a ruling coalition down. When Mayor Kucinich tried to take the local government apparatus of Cleveland against the banking community, he eventually lost, to be replaced by a new ruling-class alliance in which financier and City Hall cooperated.

The impact of the ruling coalition upon the pace of local growth, innovation, social transformation and reproduction can be far-reaching and profound in its implications. Not only can it exercise direct control over the formation of physical and social infrastructures (and through them influence the basic economic and social attributes of the urban region), but it can also go out of its way to attract or repulse jobs (of this or that sort), people (of this or that class or sort), and business, commercial, financial, real estate, cultural, and political activities. It can strive to create an appropriate "business climate," fashion new kinds of living environments, encourage new kinds of life-style, facilitate and attract new kinds of development. It can be innovative or defensive, passive or aggressive in its pursuit of social objectives and economic goals. Even new patterns of social relations can be affected — segmentations of one sort may be diminished (for example, between the races and sexes), while discrimination of another sort can be highlighted (for example, a privileged and politically conscious faction of labor may be detached from the rest of the working class by acquisition of special privileges within a ruling-class alliance). From all of these standpoints, the political-economic evolution of an urban region appears relatively autonomous and certainly unique and particular to every instance.

The multidimensional ferment and unique qualities of such political processes within the urban region, the forging of unique ruling coalitions out of all kinds of individual, group, and class fragments, the unique directions taken, and the powerful mobilization of the spirit of a place-bound geographical community appear at first sight as quite incompatible with the basic presuppositions of a capitalist mode of production and consumption. But there is a deep sense in which such features are not only compatible with but integral to capitalism's processes and contradictions as these necessarily operate in geographical space. It is important to see how and why.

Any ruling-class alliance has to accommodate to the basic logic of capital circulation and accumulation if it is to remain within the capitalist system and successfully reproduce the conditions of its own existence. A successful ruling-class alliance has to be, in spirit as well as in practice, a procapitalist class alliance. The trouble, of course, is that there are many ways to be procapitalist, while the inner contradictions of capitalism render any attempt to be consistent moot. Being procapitalist certainly does not mean selling out to a local capitalist class, since such groups do not necessarily act in their own class interest any more than individuals do (particularly when these groups exert some degree of monopoly control). And when we introduce the uncertainties of spatial competition under geographical conditions of changing space relations, it becomes evident that no single line of argument or action can define what it means exactly to be procapitalist. Even if capitalists mounted a powerful conspiracy (and from time to time they do), the odds are that it would not work.

This is the kind of situation which Marxists find so discouraging and their critics delight in. It underlies all the debates over the virtues of class analysis versus urban managerialism, over the "relative autonomy" of local political processes, over "place as historically contingent process," as Pred (1984) termed it, versus a general theory of uneven capitalist development in geographical space. How, then, can we cut the Gordian knots in these tangled debates?

VII. THE URBAN REGION AS A GEOPOLITICAL UNIT IN THE UNEVEN GEOGRAPHICAL DEVELOPMENT OF CAPITALISM

Daily life is reproduced under capitalism through the circulation of capital. That circulation process has a certain contradictory logic, entails class relations and struggle, promotes perpetual revolutions in productive forces and modes of consumption, and requires a mass of supporting organization and infrastructure to reproduce itself. We know a great deal about that contradictory logic (cf. Harvey 1982). The problem is to show how the phenomena of the urban process are contained within it. I say "contained within" rather than "reduced to" precisely because I regard any account of the circulation of capital as incomplete that does not include, among other things, its geographical specification. Though I will concede, therefore, that there are aspects of urban life and culture which seem to remain outside the immediate grasp of the contradictory logic of accumulation, there is nothing of significance that lies outside its context, not embroiled in its implications. The task of the urban theorist, therefore, is to show where the integrations lie and how the inner relations work.

Capital accumulation, when considered as a geographical process from the very start, tends to produce distinctive urban regions within which a certain structured coherence is achieved and around which certain class alliances tend to form. Conceding the instability of that process (including the instability of the geographical space and its definition) opens a space for seemingly autonomous political processes and for seemingly unique ruling coalitions to form, taking each urban region down a distinctive political-economic path of development. I now have to show how and why the autonomy and the uniqueness are not only compatible with but also vital to the logic of accumulation in geographical space. Once the question is posed that way, it proves not too hard to at least sketch in an answer. I shall do so through consideration of four basic points.

Consider, first, the idea of "the city as a growth machine." I use Molotch's (1976) telling image in part because it reflects the capitalistic imperative of "accumulation for accumulation's sake, production for production's sake." But deeper consideration of it takes us past the mere convenience of analogue and into more fruitful theoretical territory. Accumulation entails the conversion of surplus capital through combination with surplus means of production and surplus labor power into new commodity production. That activity is inherently speculative. But accumulation also requires the prior production of the necessary preconditions of production, the social and physical infrastructures being of the greatest significance in this regard. The production of these preconditions by capital entails a double and compound speculation. Prior speculative investments have to match the requirements of further speculative growth. And these prior investments are at least in part embedded in the land as immobile and fixed capital of long duration. For the individual capitalist, of course, the most convenient condition is that in which they can either freely appropriate prior conditions as they find them (for example, assets generated under some prior mode of production) or make minimal investments on their own account (a rail connection, some worker housing, a company store). But that is insufficient for sustained accumulation. The politics then have to precede the economy.

It is at just such a point that a ruling coalition and the autonomy of its politics come into their own. A ruling coalition in effect speculates on the production of the preconditions for accumulation; it collectivizes risks through finance capital and the state. This is precisely what the "growth machine" is all about. Yet it is, as Molotch insists, a *capitalistic* growth machine in which certain dominant interests – of banking and finance capital, of property capital and construction interests (including laborers and their unions), of developers and ambitious agents of the state apparatus – typically call the tune. They seek profit from the production of preconditions. The realization of that profit depends on the profitability of the accumulation that such preconditions help promote. The growth coalition uses its political and economic power to push the urban region into an upward spiral of perpetual and sustained accumulation. Such a process has its inner tensions and conflicts and cannot, given the contradictory logic of capital accumulation, be permanently sustained. We shall return to its instabilities shortly.

Consider, second, invention and innovation. Intercapitalist competition and class struggle force periodic revolutions in productive forces. Such conditions vary from one urban region to another. But the search for excess profit also spurs innovation for innovation's sake as well as attempts to counter that thrust through monopoly controls and locational shifts. Jane Jacobs (1969, 1984) has long argued, for example, that the fundamental role of cities is to produce "new work" and that some cities are better at it than others. Those with chaotic industrial and entrepreneurial structures allow of the unexpected collision of new ideas, techniques, and possibilities out of which new products and methods can spring. Those in which monopoly power is deeply entrenched are less open and more prone to stagnation. That thesis, partly plausible for the nineteenth century, is less so today. If innovation has become a business (as Marx long ago argued it must), then the creation of preconditions of that business becomes more and more important. These preconditions can be more easily sustained within the large multi-national corporation and the state than by the small firm. And while spatial agglomeration of such preconditions (the "high-tech" innovation centers around Boston, Palo Alto, North Carolina, Long Island, etc.) may be relevant, the spatial transfer of technology, albeit often under monopoly control, is now so rapid as to render its specifically urban qualities moot. Yet there is a broader version of Jacobs's thesis that makes more, though still only partial, sense.

Innovation, after all, entails more than invention. It calls for venture capital and specific labor skills in its development, access to distribution systems for marketing, and openness on the part of recipients which may entail the redesign of consumer markets and the transformation of taste and fashion. It affects the hegemonic technological mix within the structured coherence toward which every urban economy tends. Innovation, in short, is not and can never be confined to the sphere of production. It necessarily spills over into consumption, household reproduction, social services (e.g., education, health care), administration, cultural activities, and political processes. There is also a strong demand for it in the military and in other branches of government concerned with surveillance and control. Innovation in all these spheres is as important to the dynamics of capitalism as are direct changes in the labor process. This social and political innovation has to be "rational," however, in relation to accumulation. How is such a result achieved? From this standpoint we can view the urban region as a social and political innovation center within which the search for some appropriate mix of life-styles, social provision, cultural forms, and politics and administration parallels the perpetual thrust toward technological and organizational dyna-mism in production. The autonomy of the urban region's ruling-class alliance and of its politics is vital to this kind of social and political dynamism. Furthermore, the liberty of individuals and groups to intervene in that politics is as fundamental as is the liberty of entrepreneurs to pursue technological changes and product innovation. The social ferment and conflict of urban social movements born out of class struggle, possessive individualism, community rivalries, and segmentations and segregations based on labor qualities and life-style preferences can be mobilized into creative processes of sociopolitical innovation. The successful urban region is one that evolves the right mix of life-styles and cultural, social, and political forms to fit with the dynamics of capital accumulation.

But how do we know when the right mix is achieved? This brings me to a third point. We can view the urban region as a kind of competitive collective unit within the global dynamics of capitalism. Like individual entrepreneurs, each urban region has the autonomy to pursue whatever course it will, but in the end each is disciplined by the external coercive laws of competition. Its industry has to compete within an international division of labor, and its competitive strength depends upon the qualities of labor power; the efficiency and depth of social and physical infrastructures; the "rationality" of life-styles, cultures, and political processes; the state of class struggle and social tension; and geographical position and natural resource endowments. Urban regions that make wrong choices lose out to their competition in much the same way that erring entrepreneurs do. Urban regions wracked by class struggle or ruled by class alliances that take paths antagonistic to accumu-lation (toward no-growth economies or municipal socialism) at some point have to face the realities of competition for jobs, trade, money, investments, services, and so forth. Urban regions can be left behind, stagnate, decay, or drift into bankruptcy, while others surge ahead. But this is not to say that all kinds of successful specializations, particular mixes of urban economy and divisions of labor, ruling-class alliances and divergent political forms, cannot coexist. The uniqueness of each urban region is not eliminated by capitalism any more than the individual firm loses its unique qualities. Some urban regions specialize in the production of surplus value, while others seem to specialize in consuming it. Some appear at a certain historical moment as leading centers of cultural and political innovation, only to fade under the heavy hand of some dominant ruling class that so stifles dissent that innovation lags. Other class alliances use strong coercive powers to force a recalcitrant population into the forefront of accumulation through the disciplining of labor movements and the reduction of wage rates and worker resistance. All kinds of combinations are possible. But the uniqueness has to be seen as historically and geographically contingent. The combinations, arrived at through voluntaristic and autonomous struggles, are in the end contingent upon processes of capital accumulation and the circulation of associated revenues in space and time.

But now I shall modify that conception somewhat through consideration of a fourth point. The political power of a ruling-class alliance is not confined to an urban region: it is projected geopolitically onto other spaces. We now have to see the urban region as a geopolitical entity within the uneven geographical development of capitalism. How that geopolitical power is projected and used has important consequences, not only for the fate of the individual urban region but for the fate of capitalism. Let us see how that can be so.

The power that a ruling-class alliance projects depends in part upon the internal resources it can mobilize. Financial and economic leverage is crucial. That in part depends upon the urban region's competitive position. But competition is not always between equals: urban regions with enormous and complex economies cast a long and often dominant shadow over the spaces that surround them. Economic power is deployed within a hierarchical structure of urban regions. Those urban regions, like New York and London, which command power within the realms of credit and finance (the central nervous system of capitalism) can use that power across the whole capitalist world. The hierarchy of size is reemphasized by hierarchies of function. The power of innovation, in social and political affairs as well as in the production of goods and services, also confers a particular influence. But political leverage within a hierarchically organized state apparatus is also important in its own right. Power, in this case, depends largely upon the coherence and legitimacy of the local ruling coalition in relation to national politics.

These different sources of local power are not always consistent with each other. Divisions and fragmentations abound and frequently check the geopolitical influence of the urban region as a coherent entity. The conflict that attaches to social and political innovation, for example, may fragment and divide a local alliance, leaving it open to external influence and manipulation. Capitalists may appeal to capitalists in other regions or to state authority to put down labor unrest, while workers may likewise build coalitions across urban regions and seek command of central state power for their own advantage. Whoever is excluded from a local ruling coalition will likely seek outside help. Different coalitions also command different resources. A local socialist movement may have a great deal of local legitimacy and popular support but lack command over the levers of finance and trade. The exercise of geopolitical power may under such circumstances split into two or more factions: the "city" of London has a far different kind and range of influence than the Greater London Council. The fragmentations can just as easily be geographical as social. Political jurisdictions can be defined, for example, which emphasize the split between city and suburb.

We here encounter the fascinating issue of the scope and extent of local political authority in relation to economic interests within the urban region. The trend in the nineteenth century was to try to extend and enhance local political authority so as to make the major cities geopolitical entities that reflected the main lines of economic influence and power. But after universal suffrage and the growth of labor movements, the trend has been in the opposite direction, toward political fragmentation of urban regions and cleavage between economic and political scales of operation. The problem for practical urban political economy is, therefore, to establish the urban region as a coherent geopolitical presence in the face of the fragmentations. To this end, a ruling-class alliance will seek to mobilize sentiments of community boosterism and solidarity, to coopt and create loyalties to place, to invent and appropriate local tradition. It will use local newspapers, radio, and television to reinforce the sense of place (this process is particularly powerful in the United States) in a world of universal exchange. It will strive to build a political machine, not necessarily confined to conventional political channels, to wage geopolitical struggle in a world of uneven geographical development.

Geopolitical strategies become part of the arsenal of weapons employed by a ruling coalition. At the very minimum, the coalition will struggle politically within the nation state over the allocation of public investments, tax incidence and revenues, political representation, and the like. It will seek ways to enhance its geographical position through political concessions and public investments (particularly in transport and communications, in which regard the ruling coalition tends to act as a glorified collective land speculator). Building a powerful political machine able to deliver the vote and other kinds of political support often pays off in political and economic favors. But economic, cultural, and innovative powers can also be used as instruments of domination over other urban regions. Surpluses of capital and labor generated within the urban region can be put to use elsewhere under controlled conditions; branch plants can be set up in different urban regions, exclusive trading outlets cultivated, and powerfully dominant financial links forged. Tentacles of economic power can reach outward to dominate other urban regions, while invading tentacles from elsewhere are vigorously combated by political maneuvers and monopolistic controls. Competition between urban regions is thus transformed into a raw geopolitical power struggle between them.

The ruling coalition has, after all, much to defend in the way of sunken investments, standards of living, conditions of work, life-styles and culture, social organization, and modes of politics and governance. It also has much to gain from rapid and often conflictual innovation in all these areas. When times are good, it can look to improve its competitive position and bring the fruits of capitalist "progress" into the community. It can look to mobilize internal and external forces into an upward spiral of local development. In times of crisis it has just as much to gain by warding off the devaluation and destruction of productive capacity, labor power, local markets, and social and physical infrastructures. It can look to mobilize competitive and geopolitical power to export the threat of local overaccumulation and to bar the import of such problems onto its own terrain.

In all of these respects the ruling coalition has to act like a kind of collective entrepreneur. Its role is double-edged. Competition between different urban regions and the coalitions that represent them helps co-ordinate the political and social landscape with capitalism's exacting require-ments. It helps discipline geographical variations in accumulation and class struggle within the bounds of capitalism's dynamic at the same time as it opens fresh spaces and possibilities within which that dynamic can flourish. The different coalitions become key agents in the uneven geographical development of capitalism. Insofar as that uneven geographical development, as I have argued elsewhere (Harvey 1982, chaps. 12 and 13), is a stabilizing outlet for capitalism's contradictions, so the agency that helps promote it becomes indispensable. Capitalism's pursuit of a spatial fix for its own inner contradictions is actively mediated through the actions of a ruling coalition attentive to the fate of accumulation and class struggle within each urban region. But like all entrepreneurs, the coalition is caught between the fires of open and escalating competition with others and the stagnant swamp of monopoly controls fashioned out of the geopolitics of domination. The latter entails the crystallization of the geographical landscape of capitalism into stable but in the long run stagnant configurations of hierarchical domination within a system of urban regions. The problem, of course, is that capitalism cannot so easily be contained; stagnation is not its forte but merely compounds and exacerbates internal contradictions. The coherence of a ruling coalition is put at risk under such conditions, at the very moment when external opposition to its domination necessarily hardens. The collective entrepreneur, we must recall, is fashioned out of an uneasy and unstable coalition of individuals, factions, and classes, each of which internalizes a tension between seeking advantage by breaking from or even undermining the coalition and remaining solidary and so seeking to secure gains already made. The fragments are, in any case, always caught between postures of conflict and accommodation. To the degree that a ruling coalition does not deliver on its promises – as must in the long run be the case under monopoly control – so the forces making for its overthrow, always latent, move explicitly into open and sometimes even violent revolt. The weakening of internal coherence gives abundant opportunity to reshape external links and alliances as well as to shape new internal combinations of forces. New urban regions arise as power centers within the international division of labor; innovation and competitive growth resume at the same time as the forces of competitive restructuring through creative destruction are put to work. The geopolitical landscape of capitalism, like that of production, "lurches between the stabilizing stagnations of monopoly control and the disruptive and often destructive dynamism of competitive growth."

That process is stressful in the extreme. And it provokes its own particular forms of resistance, sometimes spilling over into revolts against the very logic of capitalism itself. Urban regions are constructed as communities replete with traditions of labor market behavior, capitalist forms of action, class alliances, and distinctive styles of politics. These constructions, built out of the class relations of capital accumulation, are not so easily overthrown. The ruling-class alliances, the urban political processes, and the geopolitical rivalries that capitalism produces therefore appear, at a certain point, as major barriers to further capitalist development. The revolutionary power of capitalism has to destroy and reshape the sociopolitical forms it has created in geographic space. The seeming autonomy and perpetual ferment of urban political processes lies at the very heart of that contradiction. But then, so too does the potentiality of urban politics to shape the cutting edge of revolution. The urban region either submits to the forces that created it or becomes the hearth of a revolutionary movement.

VIII. CONCLUSION

I have long argued that capitalism builds a physical and social landscape in its own image, appropriate to its own condition at a particular moment in time, only to have to revolutionize that landscape, usually in the course of crises of creative destruction at a subsequent point in time (cf. Chaps. 1 and 2). We now encounter a particular version of that thesis, worked out on a particular geographical scale, that of urban regions, and with a much stronger political content. I do not, however, want for one moment to give the impression that this is the only scale on which such a geopolitical representation can be constructed. I have elsewhere sought to represent it from the standpoint of larger-scale regions and nation states (Harvey 1982, 1985). But observers of the urban process, of no matter what political or methodological persuasion, at least agree on this: that social, economic, and political processes have a particular meaning at the urban level of analysis and that such a scale of generalization has real implications for the way in which individuals and other economic agents relate daily actions to global processes. The urban realm is, as it were, a "concrete abstraction" that reflects how individuals act and struggle to construct and control their lives at the same time as it assembles within its frame real powers of domination over them. Urban politics is a realm of action which individuals can easily understand and to which individuals can immediately relate. The sorts of processes we have studied in this chapter provide a real context of conditions to which individuals, groups, and classes must accommodate and respond. The processes appear as abstract forces, to be sure, but they are not the kind of forces that we can ever afford to abstract from. To argue, for example, that class struggle can unfold independently of geopolitical representations and confrontations is a totally unwarranted abstraction. It is, unfortunately, an abstraction to which Marxists have all too frequently been prone. From this standpoint, the critics and defectors from the Marxist tradition of urban analysis are correct in the complaints they voice. Where they in turn err is in seeking to deny that the urban community and its distinctive politics are produced under capitalist relations of production and consumption as these operate in and on geographical space.

The fundamental Marxist conception, as I see it, is of individuals and social groups, including classes, perpetually struggling to control and enhance the historical and geographical conditions of their own existence. How they struggle – individually or collectively, through coalitions or confrontations – has important implications. But we also know that the historical and geographical conditions under which they struggle are given, not chosen. And this is true no matter whether the conditions are given by nature or socially created. The relevant conditions can be specified many ways, however, and some ways appear more relevant than others. Where we put the emphasis matters. In a capitalist society, we know that social life is reproduced through the circulation of capital, which implies class relations and struggle, accumulation and innovation, and periodic crises. But we also have to say something more concrete about the historical and geographical conditions of that process. Marxists have paid close attention to the history – the creation of wage labor, the rise of money forms and commodity production, the formation of necessary social and institutional supports, the emergence of certain kinds of political theory and authority, the constructions of scientific and technical understandings, and the like. But they have paid little attention to the geography. Putting the geography back in immediately triggers concern for the urbanization of capital as one of the key conditions under which struggles occur. It also focuses our attention on how capitalism creates spatial organization as one of the preconditions of its own perpetuation. Far from disrupting the Marxian vision, the injection of real geographical concerns enriches it beyond all measure. By that path we might hope to liberate ourselves from the chains of a spaceless Marxist orthodoxy as well as from the futility of bourgeois retreat into partial representations and naïve empiricism. The stakes of historical and geographical struggle are far too great to allow the luxury of such retreats. The historical geography of capitalism has to be the central object of theoretical enquiry in the same way that it is the nexus of political action.

6

Money, Time, Space, and the City

I am looking to understand the forces that frame the urban process and the urban experience under capitalism. I focus on the themes of money, space, and time because thinking about them helps clear away some of the clutter of detail and lay bare the frames of reference within which urbanization proceeds. That way we can get a better handle on the meaning of the urban experience, find ways to interpret it, and think through viable alternatives. The themes I explore are, on the surface, very abstract. But the abstractions are not of my making. They are embedded in a social process that creates abstract forces that have concrete and personal effects in daily life. The "rationality" of money and the power of the rate of interest, the partitioning of time by the clock and of space according to the cadastral register, are all abstractly conceived features of social life. Yet each in its own way seems to have more power over us than we have over them.

I argue that the very existence of money as a mediator of commodity exchange radically transforms and fixes the meanings of space and time in social life and defines limits and imposes necessities upon the shape and form of urbanization. The particular use of money as capital hardens these connections at the same time as the dynamics of accumulation (accelerating growth, technological revolutions, crises, etc.) render them less and less coherent. This lack of coherence renders the urban process under capitalism a peculiarly open affair, in the sense that confusion, conflict, and struggle are a normal condition and that fixed outcomes cannot be determined in advance. What this seeming openness conceals, however, is an underlying process that precludes liberation from the more repressive aspects of class-domination and all of the urban pathology and restless incoherence that goes with it.

Interior to this general argument I want to construct another, which will, I hope, help us understand the politics of urban protest, the forms of urban power, and the various modes of urban experience. Confusions arise, I shall show, because command over money, command over space, and command over time form independent but interlocking sources of social power, the repressive qualities of which spark innumerable movements of revulsion and revolt. The demands to liberate space from its various forms of domination, to liberate time for free use, and to exist independently of the crass vulgarity of pure money valuations can each be built into social protest movements of enormous breadth and scope. Yet creative use of money, space, and time also lies at the heart of constructive urban experience. It is exactly this dialectic that many of the great urban novelists — some of whose insights I use as raw material — pick up on and weave into their plots and sentiments. The confusion is compounded, however, by the restless and contradictory dynamic of capital circulation and accumulation. Though class struggle then surges to the fore as the principal axis of revulsion and revolt, the other axes do not disappear but take on curiously warped and contorted forms, which in turn undermine the clarity of class struggle and its objectives. Precisely for this reason, urban social movements take on mixed political coloration and can quickly change their spots according to shifting circumstances. The vision of possible alternatives is put up for grabs, and political-economic analysis appears either unduly rigid or just plain dumb in the face of an urban history that is as confused as the multiple forces that shape it. Part of this confusion, I hold, can be rendered tractable by looking carefully at money, capital, space, and time as frameworks binding the political economy of the urban process into particular configurations.

I. MONEY

"It is very difficult to write a novel about money," said Zola (1967, 1236) — "it is cold, glacial, devoid of interest." Money, Simmel (1978) likewise complained, though central to every aspect of our life and culture, is itself devoid of any content "save that of possession" (325); it is "the representation of abstract group forces" (301) which "in every domain of life and in every sense strive to dissolve substance into free-floating processes" (168). "To the extent that money, with its colorlessness and its indifferent quality can become a denominator of all values," Simmel (1971, 330) wrote, "it becomes the frightful leveler — it hollows out the core of things, their specific values and their uniqueness and incomparability in a way which is beyond repair. They all float with the same specific gravity in the constantly moving stream of money."

This was hardly promising raw material for grand literature or even, as Simmel discovered to his cost, good philosophizing. Marx's lengthy enquiries on the subject (including the third chapter of *Capital*) make for dull reading compared with his inspired prose when he confronts exploitation in the labor process. Zola's *L'argent* (as he himself foretold) was uninspired; and Dreiser, who explored themes of distance, desire, and commodification with such dramatic intensity in *Sister Carrie,* came quite unstuck when he tried to construct an epic trilogy on the heartless, undifferentiated world of money and financial manipulation. So even though the truly epic novelists of the nineteenth-century urban scene, like Dickens and Balzac, typically used the circulation of money to tie together their "totalizing vision" (Williams 1960, 28) of city life, they evidently judged it safer to treat money itself as a fact of nature (or at least of human nature) that was as immutable as it was all-encompassing. "Papa! what's money?" asks little Paul of a startled Mr. Dombey, whose stumbling evasions on the subject leave the very junior partner-to-be "still cogitating and looking for an explanation in the fire." Having no answer either, Dickens lets the question dissipate up the chimney (as it were), perhaps to reappear as that "dark and invisible cloud" that he sees hovering over the teeming social life of the city. For money lies not only at the center of Mr. Dombey's concerns. It forms, in the novel as in the social world, the thread of connection that binds men and women, each pursuing their individual courses, "into an effective common life within which all individual lives are eventually held and shaped" (Williams 1960, 28).

The profundity of little Paul's question is matched only by the depth of our inability to provide satisfactory answers. Money is simultaneously everything and nothing, everywhere but nowhere in particular, a means that poses as an end, the profoundest and most complete of all centralizing forces in a society where it facilitates the greatest dispersion, a representation that appears quite divorced from whatever it is supposed to represent. It is a *real* or *concrete abstraction* that exists external to us and exercises real power over us.

The meaning of the phrase "concrete abstraction" deserves elaboration. Money, Marx shows us, arises out of concrete social practices of commodity exchange and the division of labor. The grand diversity of actual labor processes given over to the production of all manner of goods of specific qualities (concrete labor applied to produce use values) gets averaged out and represented in the single abstract magnitude of money (exchange value). Bonds of personal dependency are thereby broken and replaced by "objective dependency relations" between individuals who relate to each other through market prices and money and commodity transactions. "Individuals are now ruled by abstractions," says Marx (1973, 146–68), "whereas earlier they depended on one another." With the growth of the division of labor, money appears more and more as a "power external to and independent of the producers," so what "originally appears as a means to promote production becomes a relation alien (to them)." The "form-giving fire" of the labor process is represented and fetishized as a passive thing – money. Furthermore, "the power which each individual exercises over the activity of others or over social wealth exists in him as the owner of exchange values, of money."

Money becomes the mediator and regulator of all economic relations between individuals; it becomes the abstract and universal measure of social wealth and the concrete means of expression of social power.

Money, Marx (1973, 224–25) goes on to observe, dissolves the community and in so doing "becomes the *real community.*" But what kind of community does money define? What does money represent for it? And how can we locate the meaning of that particular kind of community called "urban" within its frame?

Consider, first, what money represents. "Since labor is motion, time is its natural measure," writes Marx (1973, 205), and from this we see that money is "objectification of general labor time" on the world market (abstract labor). The community of money cannot, therefore, be understood independently of the social meaning of either space or time. I lay aside these crucial interrelations for the moment; they will be taken up later.

The community of money is strongly marked by individualism and certain conceptions of liberty, freedom, and equality backed by laws of private property, rights to appropriation, and freedom of contract. Such personal freedoms and liberties exist, of course, in the midst of an "objective bondage" defined through mutual dependency within the social division of labor and a money economy. But the freedoms are of great social significance: "Since freedom means independence from the will of others, it commences with independence from the will of specific individuals. . . . The inhabitants of a modern metropolis are independent in the positive sense of the word, and even though they require innumerable suppliers, workers and cooperators and would be lost without them, their relationship to them is completely objective and is only embodied in money" (Simmel 1978, 300). The owners of money are free (within constraints) to choose how, when, where, and with whom to use that money to satisfy their needs, wants, and fancies (a fact that the free-market ideologues perpetually dwell upon to the exclusion of all else). The tremendous concern with personal freedoms and the pursuit of liberty (and the anger felt at its frustration) must in Simmel's view, be traced back to the qualities of money economies. Marx likewise attaches bourgeois notions of constitutionality to the inherent qualities of the money form.

There is also something very democratic about money. It is a "great leveler and cynic," says Marx, because it eliminates all other marks of distinction save those contained in its possession. "The existence of the infinite, quantitative grading of money ownership," says Simmel (1978, 391), "permits (social) levels to merge into one another and removes the distinctive formation of aristocratic classes which cannot exist without secure boundaries." The erosion of traditional class distinctions and their replacement by the crass democracy of money was the sort of social transformation that Henry James, for one, viewed with wistful regret. The tendency to eliminate clear class distinctions is reinforced, in Simmel's view, by the rise of a variety of occupations (from the street vendor to the banker) which have no other content than making money. The typical turbulence of the circulation and making of money also incites "the awareness of difference" that underlies the demand for egalitarian reforms, some of which are bound to see the light of day (Simmel 1978, 270, 433).

The style of urban life necessarily reflects such conditions. The breakdown of clear class distinctions is accompanied by rising barriers between individuals. While Simmel will ultimately translate this into a tragic vision of the loneliness of creative individualism (a condition which, unlike Marx, he can see no way to transcend), he nevertheless sees it as "indispensable for the modern form" of urban life: "The pecuniary character of relationships, either openly or concealed in a thousand forms, places an invisible functional distance between people that is an inner protection and neutralization against the overcrowded proximity and friction of our cultural life" (477).

The sense of social structure which Simmel presents is very different from that traditionally associated with Marx. Yet there is nothing here that is actually inconsistent with Marx's theory of money. What is missing, of course, is any consideration of the circulation of capital (as opposed to money) and the class relations implied therein. The processes we have so far described are real enough, but the contrast with the rules of capital circulation is of more than passing interest. It indicates a deep tension between the individualism and equality that the possession of money implies and the class relations experienced in the making of that money.

The objective, measurable, and universal qualities of money call forth other forms of social transformation within the community that money defines. "The idea that life is essentially based on intellect, and that intellect is accepted in practical life as the most valuable of our mental energies," says Simmel (1978, 152), "goes hand in hand with the growth of a money economy." Two aspects of this intellectual activity call for comment. First, the more we deal with abstract symbols of money (like bank notes) rather than with a tangible commodity of intrinsic value (like gold), the more we are forced to resort to abstract and symbolic modes of thought that match the "concrete abstraction" of the money form. "Consider," says Simmel, "the complicated psychological pre-conditions required to cover bank notes by cash reserves" and what this means for the symbolic content of our own thinking. Marx, too, emphasizes how the faith needed to operate on paper money or credit has to have a quasi-religious quality if it is to sustain the complex transactions of a modern money economy. Second, the content of this intellectual activity is deeply affected by the nature of money operations. "The measuring, weighing and calculating exactness of modern times" stands in "a close causal relationship to the money economy," which demands "continuous mathematical operations in our daily transactions." A money economy demands a certain kind of rationalism, based on exact, precise, and rigorous measurement of calculable magnitudes (Godelier 1972). This is the kind of positivist intellectual equipment we necessarily use every time we confront something as simple as a market price.

A money economy, Simmel (1978, 411) concludes, presupposes "a remarkable expansion" and intensification of mental processes to produce "a fundamental re-orientation of culture towards intellectuality." From this derives the growth of independent intellectual activities and professions oriented to exploring the rational calculus of economic life. A material basis is here defined for the rise of powerful vested interests in principles of objective measurement, rational computation, and economic calculation. Such modes of thought can extend over all spheres of social concern. It was, for example, no accident that Sir Isaac Newton was also, for a time, Master of the King's Mint. The kind of materialist and positivist science produced is, however, as great a leveler and cynic as the money form it mimics. All phenomena are brought under a single homogeneous and supposedly universal form of thought. Everything is reduced to a common plane of intellectuality, which functions as the secular religion of the money economy. And such modes of thought have, in turn, to be powerfully protected. For, as Simmel (1978, 172) notes, "Only in a stable and closely organized society that assures mutual protection and provides safeguards against a variety of elemental dangers, both external and psychological, is it possible for such a delicate and easily destroyed material as paper to become [money]."

This sketch, constructed with the aid of Marx and Simmel, of the kind of "community" that money defines is by no means complete. But it does provide a sufficient base out of which to evolve an understanding of other facets of the social process (including, as we shall see, revulsion and revolt against the money calculus) which invest urban life under capitalism with its specific qualities. The first step down that path, however, entails the integration of conceptions of space and time into the argument.

II. TIME

"Economy of time," says Marx (1973, 173), "to this all economy ultimately reduces itself." But what are the qualities of this time to which all economy is to be reduced? We here encounter a paradox. For though money may represent social labor time, the rise of the money form transforms and shapes the meaning of time in important and specific ways. Simmel (1978, 505–6) thus argues that "the modern concept of time – as a value determined by its usefulness and scarcity" became widely accepted only to the degree that market capitalism flourished. Le Goff (1980, 35–36) agrees. The enlarge-

ment of the monetary sphere of circulation and the organization of commercial networks over space, he argues, forced the merchant, at least as long ago
as the fourteenth century, to construct "a more adequate and predictable
measurement of time for the orderly conduct of business." This need was
reinforced to the degree that merchants became the organizers of urban-based
production. Thus, the "cultivation of urban labor in the fourteenth century"
spawned a "fundamental change in the measurement of time which was
indeed a change in time itself." Symbolized by clocks and bells that called
workers to labor and merchants to market, separated from natural rhythms
and divorced from religious significance, "a sort of chronological net in which
urban life was caught" was created by merchants and masters. The new
definition of time did not pass undisputed by religious authority any more
than by the urban laborers called to accept the new temporal discipline.
"These evolving mental structures and their material expressions," Le Goff
concludes, "were deeply implicated in the mechanisms of class struggle."

But the reach and fineness of mesh of this new chronological net was no
greater than the class power that lay behind it. For though bureaucratic and
state interests might rally behind it as a convenient framework for social
control, the compelling necessity to respect the new definitions of time lay
primarily with the merchants and masters who long maintained only a local,
and then often by no means dominant, power within the broader society in
which they were inserted (Thrift 1981). The issue of time and its proper
notation consequently remained, E. P. Thompson assures us, a lively focus of
class struggle throughout the birth-throes and even unto the consolidation of
urban industrial capitalism. The long historical passage to the domination of
this new sense of time was partly a matter of technology, due to the
introduction of cheap timepieces (Landes 1983) and of gas and electric
lighting to overcome the constraints of the "natural" working day.[1] But more
fundamentally it was a question of class relations which forced the use of those
technological possibilities along lines dictated by capital circulation. Society
became enmeshed in a single and universal chronological net only to the
degree that class forces mobilized in both production and exchange came
together. And that happened most spectacularly toward the end of the
nineteenth century.

The struggle over time in production goes back, both Le Goff and
Thompson agree, to at least the medieval period. For his part, Marx notes
that the struggle over the length of the working day goes back to the
Elizabethan period when the state legislated an increase in the length of the
customary working day for laborers freshly released from the land by violent

---

[1] Engels (1971, 336–52) has a most interesting account of the labor struggles waged by
carpenters in Manchester after 1844 when gas lighting was introduced as part of a strategy to .
increase the length of the working day.

primitive accumulation and consequently prone to be unstable, undisciplined, and itinerant. The incarceration of the unemployed with the mad (which Marx highlights and Foucault erects into a whole book) was but one of many means to bring the labor force to heel. Over several generations, "new labor habits were formed, and a new time-discipline imposed," E. P. Thompson (1967, 90) confirms, forged under the pressure to synchronize both the social and the detail division of labor and to maximize the extraction of the laborer's surplus labor time (the basis of profit). Thus came into being "the familiar landscape of industrial capitalism, with the time-sheet, the timekeeper, the informers and the fines." The battle over minutes and seconds, over the pace and intensity of work schedules, over the working life (and rights of retirement), over the working week and day (with rights to "free time"), over the working year (and rights to paid vacations) has been, and continues to be, royally fought. For the worker learned to fight back within the confines of the newly internalized sense of time: "The first generation of factory workers were taught by their masters the importance of time; the second generation formed their short-time work committees in the ten-hour movement; the third generation struck for overtime or time-and-a-half. They had accepted the categories of their employers and learned to fight back within them. They had learned their lesson, that time is money, only too well" (Thompson 1967, 90).

But even though the new time discipline and its associated work ethic may have been successfully implanted fairly early on in the Manchesters, Mulhouses, and Lowells of the early industrial revolution, it did not so easily take root in the grand metropolis or in rural areas. Time literally sprawls in Dickens's world in a way that mainly reflects the time frame of the merchant capitalist. The High Street clock made it appear "as if Time carried on business there and hung out his sign." The mass of his characters are scarcely tied down to the tight Gradgrind schedule of industrial Coketown. It took revolutions in the realm of circulation rather than in production (as Thompson tends to imply) to impose the universal sense of abstract and objective time we now so commonly accept as basic to our material existence. And in this it was the extraordinary and rapid conquest of space through the advent of the railroad, the telegraph, the telephone, and the radio that finally forced matters (Pred 1973).

It was, after all, only in 1883, Kern (1983, 12) reminds us, that the more than two hundred local times that a traveler encountered on a rail journey from Washington to San Francisco were brought to order and the unprofitable confusion ended that had, for example, the Pennsylvania Railroad system operate on a Philadelphia time that was five minutes different from that of New York. It was only in 1884, also, that the first moves were made toward international agreement on the meridian, time zones, and the beginning of the global day. And it was many years before even the advanced capitalist countries coordinated their clocks.

The tightening of the chronological net around daily life had everything to do with achieving the necessary coordinations for profitable production and exchange over space. Simmel (1971, 328) spelled out the rationale with devastating accuracy. "If all the watches in Berlin suddenly went wrong in different ways even only as much as an hour," he wrote, "its entire economic and commercial life would be derailed for some time." Spatial separation (itself made more and more possible with increasing sophistication of the money economy) "results in making all waiting and breaking of appointments an ill-afforded waste of time." The "technique of metropolitan life," he continued, "is not conceivable without all of its activities and reciprocal relationships being organized and coordinated in the most punctual way into a firm, fixed framework of time which transcends all subjective elements." The tight scheduling of the newly emerging mass transit systems at the end of the nineteenth century, for example, profoundly changed the rhythm and form of urban life (though the idea of fixed time schedules over invariable routes at a fixed price had been around since the first omnibus routes in the 1820s). The coming of the railroad likewise "flaunted agricultural time keeping," for even "the comparatively slow haste of the back-country freight train rumbling from town to town," says Stilgoe (1983, 23), "suffused every structure and space" in the railroad corridors with a new sense of time. The early morning milk train in Thomas Hardy's *Tess* captures that new sense of time and of rural-urban connection across space magnificently.

But there were all kinds of equally significant indirect ways in which the conquest of space after 1840 shifted the whole sense and valuation of time for all social classes. The rise of the journey to work as a phenomenon of urban living was itself connected to the increasing partition of time into "working" and "living" in separate spaces. And there were all manner of secondary effects of such a journey to work upon customary meal times, household labor (and its sexual division), family interactions, leisure activities, and the like. The rise of mass-circulation newspapers, the advent of telegraph and telephone, of radio and television, all contributed to a new sense of simultaneity over space and total uniformity in coordinated and universally uniform time.

Under such conditions the qualities of money could further affect matters. The fact that money can function as a store of value, and hence of social power, that can be held over time allows individuals to choose between present and future satisfactions, and even allows consumption to be moved forward in time through borrowing (Sharp 1981, 163). Individuals are thereby forced to define their own time horizons, their individual "discount rate" or "time preference" as they contemplate whether to expend their social power now or conserve it for later. The social representation of time preference is given by financial institutions, which state time horizons and discount rates for borrowing. Mortgage and interest rates and terms then appear as "concrete abstractions" to which individuals, firms, and even governments have to respond.

The function of money as a store of value also permits the accumulation of social power in individual hands over time. Compared to other forms of social wealth, money power can, as Marx points out, be accumulated without limit – logistical curves of geometrical expansion over time become entirely feasible. Money here counters its democratizing function, since it also counts among its qualities the capacity for a most unequal distribution of a universal form of social power. The question of intergenerational transfer of wealth (or debts) then arises, hence the social significance that Marx and Engels attach to inheritance and the bourgeois form of the family. Even those with limited money resources can find ways, as Hareven (1982) brilliantly demonstrates, to integrate their sense and use of "family time" into the newly emerging demands and schedules of "industrial time."

The shaping of time as a measurable, calculable, and objective magnitude, though deeply resented and resisted by many, had powerful consequences for intellectual modes of thought. The nineteenth and twentieth centuries saw the birth of innumerable professions that had a deep and vested interest in a rigorous definition and measurement of time, since their whole *raison d'être* was to advise on the efficient allocation of what had become a scarce and quantifiable resource. Engineers, chemists, economists, industrial psychologists, to say nothing of the experts in time and motion study, computerization, automation, electronics, and information transfer, all have in common an abstract conception of time that can be used in concrete ways, usually directed toward making money. Small wonder that differential calculus, with its fine analytics of rate of change over measurable time, became the basis for much of modern technical education. Thus economists, while demanding calculus as a prerequisite to the understandings they have to offer, are also quick to point out that "time is a scarce resource that must be spent" and that "a basic problem of human existence" (with respect to which they stand to offer us the friendliest of advice) "is to spend it well, to use it to bring about the greatest return of happiness that can be achieved" (Sharp 1981, 2). The intellectual baggage that goes with the equation "time is money" is evidently of enormous extension and sophistication.

III. SPACE

"Tess . . . started on her way up the dark and crooked lane or street not made for hasty progress; a street laid out before inches of land had value, and when one-handed clocks sufficiently divided the day" (Thomas Hardy). So begins E. P. Thompson's (1967) classic piece on time and work-discipline under industrial capitalism. Yet Thompson makes nothing of the fact that the street that so impeded Tess's progress was formed "before inches of land had value." I make the remark because social historians and theorists all too rarely take Le Goff's (1980, 36) advice to put the simultaneous conquest of time and space at the center of their concerns. The medieval merchant, Le Goff argues, discovered the fundamental concept of "the price of time" only in the course of exploring space. And we have already seen how it was only through the conquest of space after 1840 that an abstract, objective, and universal sense of time came to dominate social life and practice.

The priority given to time over space is not in itself misplaced. Indeed, it mirrors the evolution of social practices in important ways. What is missing, however, is an appreciation of the practices that underlie the priority. Only in such a light can we understand those situations in which location, place, and spatiality reassert themselves as seemingly powerful and autonomous forces in human affairs. And such situations are legion. They vary from the urban speculator turning inches of land into value (and personal profit), through the forces shaping the new regional and international division of labor, to the geopolitical squabbles that pit city against suburb, region against region, and one half of the world in sometimes violent conflict with the other. Given the seriousness of such events, we ignore the question of space at our peril.

Space cannot be considered independently of money because it is the latter, as Marx (1973, 148) insists, that permits the separation of buying and selling in both space and time. The breaking of the bonds of personal dependency through money exchange is here paralleled by the breakdown of local barriers so that "my product becomes dependent on the state of general commerce and is torn out of its local, natural and individual boundaries." The world market ultimately defines the "community" of exchange interactions, and the money in our pocket represents our objective bond to that community as well as our social power with respect to it. Here, too, money is the great leveler and cynic, the great integrator and unifier across the grand diversity of traditional communities and group interests. Commodity exchange and monetization challenge, subdue, and ultimately eliminate the absolute qualities of *place* and substitute relative and contingent definitions of places within the circulation of goods and money across the surface of the globe. Zola (1980, 452–58) caught the rural impact of all this with great dramatic intensity in *La terre*. Frank Norris (1981, 44) saw the same integrations. Watching the prices coming over the wires that connected them to the world market, the California wheat ranchers lost their sense of individuality. "The ranch became merely the part of an enormous whole, a unit in the vast agglomeration of wheat land the whole world round, feeling the effects of causes thousands of miles distant." Under the impact of the transport and communications revolution, the world market and the space it embraced came to be felt as a very real, concrete abstraction in relation to everyone's social practice.

The social effects are legion. To begin with, money "permits agreements over otherwise inaccessible distances, an inclusion of the most diverse persons in the same project, an interaction and therefore a unification of people who, because of their spatial, social, personal and other discrepancies in interests, could not possibly be integrated into any other group formation" (Simmel 1978, 347). By the same token, money creates an enormous capacity to concentrate social power in space, for unlike other use values it can be accumulated at a particular place without restraint. And these immense concentrations of social power can be put to work to realize massive but localized transformations of nature, the construction of built environments, and the like. Yet such concentrations always exist in the midst of the greatest dispersion because the social power that money represents is tied to an immense diversity of activities across the world market.

We here encounter paradoxes with deep implications. The price system, for example, is the most decentralized (socially and spatially) of all socially coordinated decision-making mechanisms, yet it is also a powerful centralizing force that permits the concentration of immense money power in a few hands. Even the notion of distance takes on quite new meanings. Desire, Simmel (69–76) suggests, arises "only at a distance from objects," yet presupposes "a closeness between objects and ourselves in order that the distance should be experienced at all." Money and exchange across the world market turn the metropolis into a veritable bordello of consumer temptation in which money (or the lack of it) becomes itself the measure of distance. This was the theme that Dreiser got at so sensationally in *Sister Carrie*. And it has vital meanings. A whole world of commerce and money exchanges collapses into a confrontation on New York's Fifth Avenue or in Baltimore's Harborplace – between individual desire and a vast array of commodities drawn from all corners of the earth. The nature of political participation is no less dramatically affected. Money, Simmel (1978, 344) notes, permits political participation without personal commitment (people give money more easily than time) as well as participation in far-off causes, often to the neglect of those near at hand. Dickens parodies such a habit through the character of Mrs. Pardiggle in *Bleak House*; she is so obsessed with raising money for the Tookaloopo Indians that she quite neglects her own children.

But what is the nature of this "space" across which and within which such processes operate? The conquest of space first required that it be conceived of as something usable, malleable, and therefore capable of domination through human action. A new chronological net for human exploration and action was created through navigation and map making. Cadastral survey permitted the unambiguous definition of property rights in land. Space thus came to be represented, like time and value, as abstract, objective, homogeneous, and universal in its qualities. What the map makers and surveyors did through mental representations, the merchants and landowners used for their own class purposes, while the absolutist state (with its concern for taxation of land and the definition of its own domain of domination) likewise relished the clear definition of absolute spaces within a fixed spatial net. Builders, engineers, and architects for their part showed how abstract representations of objective space could be combined with exploration of the concrete, malleable properties of materials in space. But these were all just islands of practice, light chorological nets thrown over a totality of social practices in which all manner of other conceptions of place and space – sacred and profane, symbolic, personal, animistic – could continue to function undisturbed. It took something more to consolidate space as universal, homogeneous, objective, and abstract in most social practices. That "something" was the buying and selling of space as a commodity. The effect was then to bring all space under the single measuring rod of money value.

The subsumption of places and spaces under the uniform judgment of Plutus sparked resistance, often violent opposition, from all kinds of quarters. The struggle over the commodification of land and space goes back at least as far and was certainly as long drawn out and fiercely fought as that over the meaning and control of time. Here, too, it was the transport and communications revolution of the nineteenth century that finally consolidated the triumph of space as a concrete abstraction with real power in relation to social practices. The independent power of the landlord class was broken, and in the process land became nothing more than a particular kind of financial asset, a form of "fictitious capital" (Harvey 1982, chap. 11). Or, put the other way round, land titles became nothing other than "coined land" (Simmel 1978, 508).

But there is a contradiction in this. The homogeneity of space is achieved through its total "pulverization" into freely alienable parcels of private property, to be bought and traded at will upon the market (Lefebvre 1974, 385). The result is a permanent tension between the *appropriation* and use of space for individual and social purposes and the *domination* of space through private property, the state, and other forms of class and social power (Lefebvre 1974, 471). This tension underlies the further fragmentation of otherwise homogeneous space. For the ease with which both physical and social space could now be shaped – with all that this implies for the annihilation of the absolute qualities of place and of the privileged territoriality of traditional communities sealed off in aristocratic, religious, or royal quarters (among others) – poses a serious challenge to the social order. In whose image and to whose benefit is space to be shaped? Where the land market is dominated by money power, the democracy of money takes charge. Even the largest palace can be bought and converted into office or slum building. The land market sorts spaces to functions on the basis of land price and does so only on the basis of ability to pay, which, though clearly differentiated, is by no means differentiated enough to etch clear class and social distinctions into the social spaces of the city. The response is for each and every stratum in society to use whatever powers of domination it can command (money, political influence, even violence) to try to seal itself off (or seal off others judged undesirable) in fragments of space within which processes of reproduction of social distinctions can be jealously protected.

There was, then, a dramatic transformation in the sense of urban space as the democracy of money increasingly came to dominate the land market in the nineteenth century. As John Goode (1978, 91–107) perceptively notes, "The organization of space in Dickens is based on a tension between obscurity and proximity"; it is a space of accidental encounters in which the exploratory zeal of the merchant class can still hold sway. Characters can freely move across spaces precisely because to do so is not to challenge the prevailing class distinctions. But George Gissing's novels of the late nineteenth century portray a very different London. "The city is no longer the meeting-place of the classes; on the contrary, it is the structured space of separation" that can be "charted, literally mapped out," with "distances which have no contingency" and "zones functioning as class and economic differentials." The "social space of the city, insofar as it is created space," Goode concludes, "is partly organized to keep class relationships to an abstraction – suburbs, ghettoes, thoroughfares are all ways of keeping the possibilities of direct confrontation at bay." The irony, of course, is that at the very historical moment when the potentiality of the city as "a place of encounters" (to use a favorite expression of Lefebvre's) was at its apogee, it became a fragmented terrain held down and together under all manner of forces of class, racial, and sexual domination.

How can this fragmentation be reconciled with the homogeneity of universal and objective space? That question has provoked a variety of theoretical and practical responses. Durkheim (1965), for one, recognized the importance of the fragmentations and represented them as social spaces within the organic solidarity of society as a whole. The urban reformers (like Charles Booth, Octavia Hill, and Jane Addams) and sociologists (particularly of the Chicago School) set out to explore the fragments and to try to identify or impose some sense of "moral order" across them. And there arose a whole host of professionals – engineers, architects, urban planners, and designers – whose entire mission was to rationalize the fragments and impose coherence on the spatial system as a whole (Giedion 1941). These professionals, whose role became more and more marked as progressive urban reformers acquired political power, acquired as deep a vested interest in the concept of homogeneous, abstract, and objective space as their professional confrères did with respect to the concrete abstractions of time and money. Even art, Kern (1983, 144–52) suggests, succumbed in its turn to cubism in a culture that affirmed "the unreality of place" at the same time as it sought to confine forms to a flat surface in homogeneous and abstract space. The consequent tensions between "the world of three dimensions that was their inspiration and the two-dimensionality of painting that was their art" generated canvases that were as fragmented and shattered in their appearance as the urban social landscapes that they often sought to depict.

The growing consensus that space must be, in spite of its evident fragmentations, objective, measurable, and homogeneous (how else could it be ordered for the rational conduct of business?) was accompanied by another emerging consensus toward the end of the nineteenth century. Writers as diverse as Alfred Marshall and Proust concluded that space was a less relevant dimension to human affairs than time. In this, once more, the transport and communications revolution was fundamental. As early as the 1840s, Leo Marx (1964, 194) tells us, Americans were taken with the "extravagant" sentiment that the sublime paths of technological progress were leading inexorably to the "annihilation of space and time" (a phrase apparently borrowed from a couplet of Alexander Pope's: "Ye Gods! annihilate but space and time / And make two lovers happy"). The other Marx (Karl, 1973, 524–44) more soberly reduced this extravagant idea to the annihilation of space *by* time. For though the medieval merchant discovered the price of time through the exploration of space, it was, Marx insisted, labor *time* that defined money, while the *price of time* or *profit* was the fundamental dimension to the capitalist's logic of decision. From this Marx could derive what he saw as a necessary impulsion under capitalism to annihilate the constraints and frictions of space, together with the particularities of place. Revolutions in transport and communications are, therefore, a necessary rather than a contingent aspect of capitalist history.

The consequent victory of time over space and place had its price. It meant acceptance of a way of life in which speed and rush to overcome space was of the essence. Thomas Musil thought he caricatured when, in *The Man without Qualities,* he depicted "a kind of super-American city where everyone rushes about, or stands still, with a stop-watch in his hand. . . . Overhead trains, overground-trains, underground trains, pneumatic express mails carrying consignments of human beings, chains of motor vehicles all racing along horizontally, express lifts vertically pumping crowds from one traffic level to another. . . ." (quoted in Kern 1983, 127) but he was merely describing the kind of organization of flows over space that paralleled Simmel's description of time requirements for the modern metropolis. "Steady uninterrupted flow was becoming the universal American requirement" says Jackson (1972,

238), and engineers and planners raised the science of such flows (of goods, of people, of information, of production processes) to the very pinnacle of their professional expertise (Stilgoe 1983, 26). In this respect the United States quickly established itself as "the most modern form of existence of bourgeois society" (Marx 1973, 104). Gertrude Stein (1974, 93–5) more or less agreed. "The Twentieth Century has become the American Century," she wrote, and "it is something strictly American to conceive a space that is filled always filled with moving." Kerouac's (1955, 25, 111) characters rushing frantically *On The Road* from coast to coast are living embodiments of that spirit: "We were leaving confusion and nonsense behind and performing our one and only noble function of the time, *move.*" Such a rush of movement implied, of course, the dissolution of any traditional sense of community. "There was nowhere to go but everywhere," wrote Kerouac, and the sociologists and urban planners belatedly rushed to catch up with concepts like Webber's (1963, 1964) "community without propinquity" situated in "the nonplace urban realm."

The kind of community money defines is, evidently, one in which the organization of space and time, including the precedence of the latter over the former, takes on particular qualities. Money is, in turn, not independent of these qualities, since money represents nothing more than abstract social labor, socially necessary labor time, developed, as Marx (1972, 253) puts it, "in the measure that concrete labor becomes a totality of different modes of labor embracing the world market." The interrelations between money, time, and space form, thus, intersecting nets of very specific qualities that frame the whole of social life as we now know it. But the constraints of that frame do not pass unnoticed or unchallenged. To these challenges we must now turn.

IV. REVULSION AND REVOLT

While the community that money defines through time and space permits all manner of freedoms and liberties, the constraints imposed by the intersecting spatial, chronological, and monetary nets are repressive enough to spark all manner of revulsions and revolts. And from time to time the incoherent pieces of resistance coalesce and well up as some deep-seated demand to construct an alternative society, subject to different rules, outside of and beyond the rational discourse and the disciplines and constraints determined within the community of money. The utopian elements within all such proposals and actions are, it is interesting to note, almost always seeking a different notion of value and different modes of operation in time and space from those that have increasingly come to dominate all aspects of social life.

The cynical leveling of all human activities and experiences to the heartless and colorless qualities of money has always proved hard to accept. "We experience in the nature of money itself something of the essence of prostitution," says Simmel (1978, 377); and Marx (1973, 163) expresses a parallel sentiment. Baudelaire returned again and again to this theme (see chap. 3). From this there arises "a deep yearning to give things a new importance, a deeper meaning, a value of their own" other than the "selling and uprooting of personal values" (Simmel 1978, 404). "Commerce," says Baudelaire (1983b, 65, 88), "is in its very essence satanic." It is "the vilest form of egoism" in which "even honesty is a financial speculation." There are, he goes on to proclaim, "only three beings worthy of respect: the priest, the warrior and the poet. To know, to kill and to create." Simmel (1978, 97) gives that wounded cry a deeper psychological meaning. "Some people consider violent robbery more noble than honest payment, for in exchanging and paying one is subordinated to an objective norm, and the strong and autonomous personality has to efface itself, which is disagreeable." The gangster, the crook, the messianic revolutionary, and even the financial swindler excite as much secret approbation as public condemnation (particularly when their exploits are spectacularly carried off).[2] The ability to live a way of life "that does not have to consider the money value of things" likewise has "an extraordinary aesthetic charm," comments Simmel (1978, 220), and Baudelaire, for one, lived out that aesthetic sense in being simultaneously impoverished poet and exquisite dandy. Sentiments of revulsion and gestures of defiance against the dull rationality of the monetary calculus abound in contemporary life.

Revulsion against the tightening chronological net around all aspects of social life has been no less marked. It took decades before the skilled workers, for example, would surrender their right to "blue Monday," and in certain occupations, such as mining and construction, absenteeism and intermittent employment are so normal as hardly to call for special comment. And the fight over minutes and moments within the labor process is as eternal as it has been fierce, forcing employers even in recent years to all manner of concessions (flexitime, quality circles, etc.) in order to contain the spirit of revolt in bounds.

[2] The peculiar and deeply paranoid bourgeois fear of the criminal classes in the nineteenth century, a reading of Chevalier (1973) suggests, had much to do with the idea that there was an alternative and subversive underworld that constituted a totally different form of society from that projected by bourgeois culture. "The thieves form a republic with its own manners and customs," wrote Balzac; "they present in the social scene a reflection of those illustrious highwaymen whose courage, character, exploits and eminent qualities will always be admired. Thieves have a language, leaders and police of their own; and in London, where their association is better organized, they have their own syndics, their own parliament and their own deputies" (quoted in Chevalier 1973, 70–71).

There were also many voices within the bourgeoisie, like that of Simmel, who worried about or openly revolted against the rigid discipline of the watch. "We are weighed down, every moment," complained Baudelaire (1983b, 97), "by the conception and sensation of Time." Its seeming scarcity arose, he felt, out of a pace and style of modern life in which "one can only forget Time by making use of it." "It was briefly fashionable," records Benjamin (1973, 54), for Parisians during the 1840s to express their contempt for the discipline of time by taking "turtles for a walk in the arcades." At the end of the nineteenth century in particular, the bourgeois literati sought refuge from the domination of universal and abstract public time through subjective explorations of their own private sense of time (Proust and Joyce spring most easily to mind). Conrad expressed the sense of revolt more directly: he had the anarchist in *The Secret Agent* take on the task of blowing up the Greenwich meridian. But although our thinking about time has never been the same since, this spirit of revolt, which Kern (1983) for one makes much of, was nourished out of a context in which time was becoming more and more rationally and universally defined. What the literati really discovered, of course, was something that had been evident to the working classes for generations: that it takes money to command free time, real as opposed to imaginary release from the rigid discipline of organized public time. In this respect poor Baudelaire lived under a double sufferance: despising money, he lacked the means to put himself outside of the discipline of time. Small wonder that he never ceased to rail against the crassness of bourgeois materialism and elevated the dandy and the flâneur to the status of heroes.

The capacity to appropriate space freely has likewise been held, in both thought and social practice, an important and vital freedom. Freedom to roam the city streets without fear of compromise is not necesarily given by money. Indeed, situations frequently arise where the least privileged in the social order have the greatest liberty in this regard (Cobb 1975, 126). Restriction of the freedom to appropriate space through private property rights and other social forms of domination and control (including that exercised by the state) often provokes all manner of social protest movements (from the reappropriation of central Paris during the Commune by the popular classes expelled therefrom by Haussmann's works, to civil rights sit-ins and "take-back-the-night" marches). The demand to liberate space from this or that form of domination and reconstitute it in a new image, or to protect privileged spaces from external threat or internal dissolution, lies at the center of many urban protest movements and community struggles (Lefebvre 1974; Castells 1983). And to the degree that the fragmentation of space which accompanies its homogenization allowed the formation of protected islands outside of direct social control, so opportunities arose for all manner of subversive visions of community and place, and their spatial integument, to take root. Innumerable dissident groups – anarchists like Kropotkin (1968), women of the sort that Hayden (1981) describes, communitarians like the religious and secular groups (the Cabetists, for example) that played such an important role in the settling of America, the alternative life-style movements that created the "communes" of the 1960s, and so forth – all sought to liberate and appropriate their own space for their own purposes. And in so doing they mounted a practical challenge to the supposed homogeneity of abstract, universalized space.

But such social movements must be understood in terms of what they are revolting against. The search for "authentic community" and a "sense of place" became all the more fierce as the community of money and the annihilation of absolute place under the domination of money became more powerfully felt. And the search bore partial fruit. Kinship ties were resurrected by urban dwellers (Hareven 1982), new networks of social contacts forged (Fischer 1982), and whole new communities created that often managed to seal themselves off in protected spaces behind all manner of symbols and signs (from gatehouses and walls to street names and postal codes) to emphasize the special qualities of neighbourhood and place. Urban style and fashion, Simmel (1978) points out, are convenient ways to reintroduce the social distinctions that the democracy of money tends to undermine. And so arose the modern sense of "community" so dear to sociologists, though they took a while to lose that prejudice that sees rurality as the true incarnation of authentic community and the city as merely the site of social breakdown, of pure individualism and social anomie. Gans (1962) thus brought to life in *The Urban Villagers* what had been evident to close observers of the urban scene for many years; that the struggle to create protected places and communities was as fiercely fought in urban areas (Gissing's London, for example) as its evident loss was felt in rural areas (like Hardy's Wessex). Under such conditions, too, the family can take on new meaning and significations, as a "haven in a heartless world" (Lasch 1977), a social center in which considerations of money, time, and space can be treated in a radically different way from those prevailing in public life (Hareven 1982).

The revolt within intellectual circles against the kind of rationality implied within the community of money – a rationality that extended, as we have seen, across conceptions of time and space as well as of value – is as broad as it is historically long. For if Auguste Comte, the father of positivism, anointed the bankers as managers of his utopia (a far from utopian condition, as we seem close to realizing in practice these days), there were many others, from Carlyle and Ruskin, to William Morris and Neitzsche, through Heidegger and Sartre, who saw things quite differently. And if liberals, those "historical representatives of intellectualism and of money transactions," as Simmel (1978, 432) calls them, have been inclined "to condone everything because they understand everything" and to represent it in a kind of passionless and objective scientific discourse, there have been many others, from conservatives to Marxists, prepared to dispute them with a passion liberals have found both disconcerting and distasteful.

More problematic are those social movements that reject rationality and seek solace in mysticism, religion, or some other transcendental or subjective ideology. Religious alternatives or proposals for alternatives to the community of money abound and frequently spark social practices outside of the overwhelming rationalities of modern life. Fascism likewise defines an alternative sense of community to that defined by money, exalts absolute place (the soil, the fatherland), appeals to an entirely different sense of historical time (in which the playing out of myth has great importance), and worships values of a higher order than those embodied in money. Far from being a direct expression of capitalism, fascism as an ideology expresses violent opposition to the rationality implicit in the community of money, and the historical symbols of that community — Jews and intellectuals — are consequently singled out for persecution. Marxists also seek a society in which the value of human life is appraised in ways other than through the market. And while they usually cling to the idea of rational planning as a positive virtue, they have often embraced in practice nationalist definitions of community that are as opposed to their own ideology of internationalism as they are to the universality of money. Indeed, there has been hardly a single dissident cultural, political, or social movement these last two hundred years in the advanced capitalist world that has not had somewhere at its base some kind of striving to transcend the money form and its associated rational conceptions of the proper use of space and time. Most of the vivacity and color of modern life, in fact, arises precisely out of the spirit of revulsion and revolt against the dull, colorless, but seemingly transcendental powers of money in abstract and universal space and time.

Yet all such social movements, no matter how well articulated their aims, run up against a seemingly immovable paradox. For not only does the community of money define them in an oppositional sense, but the movements have to confront the social power of money directly if they are to succeed. Colorless and heartless it may be, but money remains the overwhelming source of social power, and what Marx calls its "dissolving effects" are perpetually at work within the family or within alternative "authentic communities" that social groups struggle to define. Such a tendency is writ large in the history of innumerable organizations, from communes that either founder on money questions or convert into efficient enterprises, religious organizations that become so obsessed with the accumulation of money that they pervert the message they propose, to socialist governments that come to power with noble visions only to find they lack the money to carry out their plans. All manner of oppositional movements have come to grief as they stumble upon the rock of money as the central and universal source of social power.

It takes money, we can conclude, to construct any alternative to the society predicated on the community of money. This is the essential truth that all social movements have to confront; otherwise, it confronts and destroys them. Money may be, as the moralists have it, the root of all evil, yet it appears also as the unique means of doing good. Zola (1967, 224–25) understood that truth very well:

Mme Caroline was struck with the sudden revelation that money was the dung-heap that nurtured the growth of tomorrow's humanity. . . . Without speculation there could be no vibrant and fruitful undertakings any more than there could be children without lust. It took this excess of passion, all this contemptibly wasted and lost life, to ensure the continuation of life. . . . Money, the poisoner and destroyer, was becoming the seed-bed for all forms of social growth. It was the manure needed to sustain the great public works whose execution was bringing the peoples of the globe together and pacifying the earth. She had cursed money, but now she prostrated herself before it in a frightening adulation: it alone could raze a mountain, fill in an arm of the sea, at last render the earth inhabitable to mankind. . . . Everything that was good came out of that which was evil.

Love and money may make the world go around, Zola seems to say, but love of money provides the raw energy at the center of the whirlwind.

V. MONEY, SPACE, AND TIME AS SOURCES OF SOCIAL POWER

That the possession of money confers enormous social powers upon its owners requires no substantial demonstration. Marx (1964b, 167) parodies (though not by much) the seeming magic of its powers thus:

The extent of the power of money is the extent of my power. . . . I am ugly, but I can buy for myself the most beautiful of women. Therefore I am not ugly. . . . I am stupid, but money is the real mind of all things and how then should its possessor be stupid? Besides, he can buy talented people for himself, and is he who has power over the talented not more talented than the talented? Do not I, who thanks to money am capable of all that the human heart longs for, possess all human capacities? Does not my money, therefore, transform all my incapacities into their contrary?

The social power of money has, therefore, ever been the object of desire, lust, and greed. Thus does the concrete abstraction of money acquire its powers relative to and over us.

But what of space and time? Once constituted as concrete abstractions within the community of money, do they not also become sources of social power? Do not those who dominate them also possess strong powers of social control? Such a thesis calls for at least some minimal demonstration. The demonstration will lack point, however, unless we also bear in mind that it is the interconnections between command of money, space, and time as intersecting sources of social power that in the end matter.[3] Money can thus be used to command time (including that of others) and space, while command over time and space can easily be parlayed back into command over money. The property speculator who has the money to wait and who can influence the development of adjacent spaces is in a better situation than someone who lacks powers in any one of these dimensions.

Command over space, as every general and geopolitician knows, is of the utmost strategic significance in any power struggle. The same principle also applies within the world of commodity exchange. Every supermarket manager also knows that command over a strategic space within the overall construction of social space is worth its weight in gold. This value of space lies at the root of land rent. But spatial competition is always monopolistic competition, simply because two functions cannot occupy exactly the same location. Capture of strategic spaces within the overall space can confer much more than its aliquot share of control. The struggle between diverse railroad interests in the nineteenth century provides abundant examples of this principle at work, while Tarbell (1904, 146) pictures Rockefeller "bent over a map and with military precision [planning] the capture of the strategic locations on the map of East Coast oil refineries." Control over strategic land parcels within the urban matrix confers immense power over the whole pattern of development. And although the liberation of space and the annihilation of space by time erode any permanent power that may attach to control of strategic spaces, the monopolistic element is always recreated afresh. Indeed, control over the production of spatial organization then becomes fundamental to the creation of new spatial monopolies. The importance of such monopoly power is precisely that it gives rise to monopoly rent and can thereby be converted into money.

But the created space of society is also, as Lefebvre (1974) insists, the space of social reproduction. Thus, control over the creation of that space also confers a certain power over the processes of social reproduction. We can see

---

[3] These intersections are, I suspect, at the root of Benjamin's (1973) fascination with the figures of the *flâneur*. the dandy, and the gambler in nineteenth-century culture. He comments, for example, "To the phantasmagoria of space, to which the flâneur was addicted, corresponded the phantasmagoria of time, to which the gambler dedicated himself. Gambling transformed time into a narcotic" (174).

this principle at work within the most diverse of social circumstances. The organization of space within the household says much about power and gender relations within the family, for example, while hierarchical structures of authority or privilege can be communicated directly through forms of spatial organization and symbolism. Control over spatial organization and authority over the use of space become crucial means for the reproduction of social power relations. The state, or some other social grouping such as financiers, developers, or landlords, can thus often hide their power to shape social reproduction behind the seeming neutrality of their power to organize space (Lefebvre 1974, 369). Only at certain moments — gross gerrymandering of political boundaries, the dismantling of spaces of opposition by a higher power (the suppression of the Paris Commune or recent attempts to do away with the Greater London Council), corruption within a system of planning permissions — does the nonneutrality of the creation of space become evident. The power to shape space then appears as one of the crucial powers of control over social reproduction. And it is exactly on this basis that those who have the professional and intellectual skills to shape space materially and effectively — engineers, architects, planners, and so on — can themselves acquire a certain power and convert their specialized knowledge into financial benefit.

The relation between command over money and command over time as sources of social power is no less compelling. Those who can afford to wait always have an advantage over those who cannot. The case is at its most obvious during strikes and lockouts when workers (in the absence of any extensive money reserves) can quickly be reduced to starvation while the owners, however much their profits may be singed, continue to dine at full tables. Capitalists can continue to command the surplus labor time of workers in part because they can wait them out during phases of active class struggle. The same principle applies within the bourgeoisie. The merchant who can wait on payment has a power advantage over a producer who cannot, and at moments of crisis well-heeled financiers can dispose of rivals who have to roll over their debts — thus did James Rothschild dispose of the Pereires's Crédit Mobilier in 1867. Differential capacity to command time consolidates the hierarchy of money power within the bourgeoisie.

Similar pressures exist within the work force and in the hidden interiors of family life. If, for example, there is any sense at all to that strange concept of "human capital formation," it is simply that those who can afford to defer present gratification have the opportunity to acquire skills that may form the basis for improved life chances. In effect, workers use time (their own or that of their children) in the hope, sometimes vain, that education will yield a long-run increase in money power. The organization of money and time within the family for this and other purposes is a complex affair; for as Hareven (1982) shows, different trade-offs exist between members of a family (the capacity to mobilize time is not always a matter of money), and different ways for capturing any monetary benefits can also be devised. For while male wage earners may assume that bringing home money gives them the right to command the time of spouse and children, the worktime of women in the home can also be viewed as one of the crucial assets within the family for freeing the time of others to capture monetary benefits in the marketplace (Pahl 1984). Small wonder that the relations between the command of money and time within family life form a crucial zone of gender conflict.

Also, while many within the bourgeoisie fritter away the "free time" given by money wealth in immediate and luxurious self-indulgence (a practice viewed as doubly outrageous when indulged in by workers), there are also those who use the free time so liberated to engage in scientific, artistic, and cultural endeavors that can in turn be parlayed into enormous power in the realms of scientific knowledge, technological understanding, and ideology. Power over research or cultural production time (including the time of others) is a vital power over social reproduction which resides with the wealthy or the state. Many an artist and researcher has tried to revolt against the hegemony of money power over their time. The most successful, of course, have been those who have converted a technical expertise over the efficient disposal of other people's time into the kind of monopoly power that allows them to extract a monopoly price. Herein, to a large degree, lies the significance of the buying and selling of scientific and technical know-how over the proper use of time, space, and money in contemporary society.

Money, time, and space all exist as concrete abstractions framing daily life. Universal, objective, and minutely quantifiable, they each acquire these particular qualities through certain dominant social practices of which commodity exchange and the social division of labor are in the first instance of the greatest importance. Prices, the movements of the clock, rights to clearly marked spaces, form the frameworks within which we operate and to whose signals and significations we perforce respond as powers external to our individual consciousness and will. And no matter how fiercely the spirit of revulsion and revolt may occasionally flare, the tight norms defined by such concrete abstractions are by now so deeply entrenched that they appear almost as facts of nature. To challenge these norms and the concrete abstractions in which they are grounded (to challenge, for example, the tyranny of the public clock or the necessity of the price system) is to challenge the central pinions of our social life.

But the concrete abstractions of money, time, and space are not defined independently of each other. Money, for example, arises out of exchange and the spatial division of labor and represents social labor time. But by the same token the formation of the world market depends crucially upon the rise of an appropriate money form and the spread of the psychological preconditions necessary to its proper use. I insist upon the significance of such interrelations in part because other commentators (ranging from neoclassical economists to time-space geographers) so frequently ignore them. But I also insist that the power relations between individuals, groups, and even whole social classes, and the consequent capacity to find feasible paths of social transformation, are broadly defined through the meshing of monetary, spatial, and chronological nets that define the parameters of social action. For it is hard to go outside of these parameters. Even Conrad's secret agent, who wanted to blow up the Greenwich meridian, might be aghast at the social chaos that would surely now result.

VI. THE CIRCULATION AND ACCUMULATION OF CAPITAL

What happens when we inject the circulation and accumulation of capital into this framework of thought? Capitalists most certainly make use of the social power of money and carefully cultivate command over time and space as sources of social power.[4] But capitalist practices give money, time, and space even more specific (and in some cases restrictive) meanings than they have within the simple community of money. At the same time, these practices create incoherency and contradiction within the intersecting nets of social power.

All money is not capital. But capital is the social power of money used to make more money, most typically through a form of circulation in which money is used to buy commodities (labor power and means of production) which, when combined within a particular labor process, produce a fresh commodity to be sold at a profit. The importance of this form of circulation can be judged by the fact that most of the commodities sustaining daily life under advanced capitalism are produced this way.

Marx lays bare the essential characteristics of such a mode of production and circulation. The perpetual search for profit means "accumulation for accumulation's sake," the perpetual expansion of the value and the physical quantity of output over time. Logistical growth, necessary to maintain stability, is commonly regarded as inevitable and good. But expansion occurs through the exploitation of living labor in production. This presupposes the buying and selling of labor power as a commodity, a class relation between capital and labor, and struggle between them within the labor process as well as in the labor market. This class struggle, when coupled with intercapitalist competition, forces the system to be technologically dynamic. Technological

---

[4] This is one of the profounder and often unrecognized themes worked out in Marx's *Economic and Philosophic Manuscripts*.

change is also seen as inevitable and good. Marx's genius, of course, was to show how and why such a system was necessarily unstable. Technological change tends to remove living labor, the agent of expansion, from production and so undermines the capacity to expand. Periodic crises are, therefore, as inevitable as the twin compulsions toward logistical growth and technological revolution (cf. Harvey 1982, 1985).

Capitalism consequently creates a more and more universal sense of what Hareven (1982) calls "historical time." Cyclical rhythms of prosperity and depression integrate into periodic revolutions in the labor process. From 1848 to 1933, and from then until now, the world has experienced an ever-increasing synchronization of its economic activities. Our experiences, our life chances, and even our conceptual understandings increasingly depend upon where we are situated on the logistical growth curves and their periodic interruptions and descents into confusion and crisis. The temporal net of possibilities appears less and less open and more attached to the lawlike behavior of capitalist development over time.

This history occurs within a geography that is likewise subject to radical transformations. Capitalism, Marx (1973, 407–10) insists, necessarily accelerates spatial integration within the world market, the conquest and "liberation" of space, and the annihilation of space by time. In so doing it accentuates rather than undermines the significance of space. Capitalism has survived, says Lefebvre (1976, 21), "only by occupying space, by producing space." The ability to find a "spatial fix" to its inner contradictions has proven one of its saving graces (cf. Harvey 1982, 1985). While the community of money implies the formation of the world market, therefore, the community of capital requires the geographical deepening and widening of processes of capital accumulation at an accelerating rate.

Although the temporal and spatial rhythms of expansion and contraction are broadly given within the laws of accumulation, there are all manner of cross-cutting tensions that render the historical geography of capitalism an unpredictable and often incoherent affair. If, for example, the fundamental condition of crisis is one of overaccumulation – the existence of excess capital and labor side by side – then such surpluses can be absorbed by temporal displacement (debt-financed long-term investments), spatial expansion (the production of new spaces), or some combination of the two. Which dominates and where cannot be specified in advance. But we can say that the mechanics of urban growth (and indebtedness) and geographical construction (peripherally or within a system of cities) are embedded within such an overall process.

Other tensions exist. Consider, first, the time it takes for capital to complete its circulation from money back to money plus profit. Each labor process has its own turnover time, and increasing fragmentation in the division of labor poses serious problems of coordination under conditions where profit is the sole objective. The problems are overcome through new uses of money. The credit system steps center stage to coordinate devergent turnover times. Furthermore, the acceleration of turnover time yields competitive advantage and so becomes an objective of technological change. This acceleration largely depends, however, on the deployment of fixed capital, which turns over slowly. Again, the technical problems of arranging such forms of investment can be resolved only through appeal to the credit system. The special relation between time and money is put to special use. But a tension arises because the circulation of a part of the capital has to be slowed down in order to accelerate the circulation of the remainder. There is no necessary net gain here. Pressure then arises to accelerate the turnover time of the fixed capital, to write off the value of fixed capital at an accelerating rate (no matter what its physical lifetime), and even to replace it before its economic lifetime is out. Machinery, buildings, and even whole urban infrastructures and life-styles are made prematurely obsolescent; "creative destruction" becomes necessary to the survival of the system. But the capacity to set such processes in motion depends upon conditions within the credit system — the supply and demand for money capital, the rate of money growth, and so on. Cyclical rhythms of investment and disinvestment in machinery and in built environments connect to interest rate movements, inflation, and growth of the money supply, and hence to phases of unemployment and expansion. Time horizons are more and more tightly defined via the credit system. But we also note that the meaning of value and the stability of money as its measure (its devaluation through inflation) also become more elastic in response to changing time horizons. The concrete abstractions of money and time become even more closely intertwined.

Consider, second, how pressures within the circulation of capital lead to the systematic pursuit of the annihilation of space by time. Again, we encounter a contradiction. Space can be overcome only through the production of space, of systems of communication and physical infrastructures embedded in the land. Natural landscapes are replaced by built landscapes shaped through competition to the requirements of acclerating accumulation. The "pulverization" and fragmentation necessary to homogenize space have to take definite forms. Landownership has to be rendered subservient to money power as a higher-order form of property, and land becomes a form of "fictitious capital"; thus, control over the production of space is passed to the interior of the credit system. The uneven development of space then becomes a primary expression of its homogeneity. Immense concentrations of productive force and labor power are assembled in urban areas in the midst of the greatest possible spatial dispersal of commodity flows within a spatially articulated urban hierarchy organized so as to minimize turnover time. This fixed landscape of uneven development then becomes the barrier to be overcome. And overcome it is, but only through the same processes of "creative destruction" which wash away the dead weight of past investments from current concerns. The annihilation of space by time proceeds apace. But it is now the created spaces of capitalism, the spaces of its own social reproduction, that have to be annihilated.

Consider now the social implications of these dual contradictions. Space can be overcome only through the production of a fixed space, and turnover time can be accelerated only by fixing a portion of the total capital in time. The fixed spaces and times can be overcome only through creative self-destruction. We look at the material solidity of a building, a canal, a highway, and behind it we see always the insecurity that lurks within a circulation process of capital, which always asks: how much more time in this relative space? The rush of human beings across space is now matched by an accelerating pace of change in the produced landscapes across which they rush. Processes as diverse as suburbanization, deindustrialization and restructuring, gentrification and urban renewal, through to the total reorganization of the spatial structure of the urban hierarchy, are part and parcel of a general process of continuous reshaping of geographical landscapes to match the quest to accelerate turnover time. The destruction of familiar places and secure spaces of social reproduction provokes many an anguished cry, not only from the poor and impoverished who are left "grieving for a lost home," deprived of even the minor "sources of residential satisfaction in an urban slum" (to appropriate two of Fried's [1963; Fried and Gleicher 1961] more trenchant titles). Zola (1954b, 293–95) records the distress of a businessman of humble origins who discovers his childhood lodgings exposed in the midst of Haussmann's demolitions. Henry James (1946) was not to be outdone. Returning to New York after many years of absence, he saw an urban landscape possessed by "the reiterated sacrifice to pecuniary profit" (191) and "in perpetual repudiation of the past" (53). "We are only installments, symbols, stop-gaps," the proud villas seem to say; "we have nothing to do with continuity, responsibility, transmission" (11). There was, James admitted, much about the past that deserved repudiation, "yet there had been an old conscious commemorated life too, and it was this that had become the victim of supersession" (53). The whole American landscape, he complained, sat there "only in the lurid light of business, and you know . . . what guarantees, what majestic continuity and heredity, that represents" (161). Familiar places and secure spaces were being annihilated within the "whirligig of time" – but it was the circulation of capital that was calling the tune.

Out of sentiments such as these many a movement of revulsion and revolt can build against the monstrous figure of the developer, the speculator, the urban renewer, and the highway builder who, like Robert Moses, takes a "meat-axe" to living communities. The evil inherent in such figures has become legendary. They are the centerpieces of what Berman (1982) defines as "the tragedy of development" whose epitome is Goethe's Faust, raging on the hilltop as he contemplates the one small piece of space, occupied by a venerable old couple, that has yet to be integrated into the rationalized and produced space appropriate for modern capitalist forms of development. Zola (1954b, 76–78) recaptures that very same image. Saccard, the archetypal speculator of Second Empire Paris, stands on the butte Montmartre with the "recumbent giant" of Paris at his feet, smiles into space, and "with his hand spread out, open and sharp-edged as a cutlass," cuts through space to symbolize Haussmann's wounding slashes through the veins of a living city, wounds that spurt gold and give sustenance "to a hundred thousand navvies and bricklayers." The perpetual reshaping of the geographical landscape of capitalism is a process of violence and pain.

Bourgeois objections to such consequences of capitalism are based on more than Baudelaire's (1983a, 90) lament that "no human heart changes half so fast as a city's face." They record more than nostalgia for the loss of a past, the destruction of the affectivity of "knowable communities" and familiar places (Williams 1973). They go deeper, too, than that anguished culture of modernity which Berman (1982, 15) evokes as a universally shared "mode of vital experience – experience of space and time, of the self and others, of life's possibilities and perils," experience that "promises us adventure, power, joy, growth, transformation of ourselves and the world – and at the same time, that threatens to destroy everything we have, everything we know, every-thing we are." What is being expressed, rather, is a pervasive fear that the dominant mode of production and social reproduction upon which the perpetuation of bourgeois power rests is itself nothing more than what Marx calls "a self-dissolving contradiction."

It is rather as if the strings within the monetary, temporal, and spatial nets that frame social life are pulled taut in the face of an accumulation process that demands their rapid adaptation and reorganization. Simultaneously tightened and stretched, the nets distort and snap, only to be hastily repaired into a patchwork quilt of new possibilities.

The sensation of disruption and incoherence in the framing of social life, in the true sources of social power, is universally felt but in different ways. For example, the social spaces of reproduction, which appeared so coherent to Gissing and which the Chicago sociologists could conveniently fit into some organic theory of urban form, lose their functional coherence and are transformed under contradictory pressures stemming from changing labor market demand on the one hand and the need to stimulate consumption through the mobilization of fashion and style as artificial marks of social distinction on the other. The obsolescence of "created community" becomes just as important as its firm implantation. The speed-up of labor processes and of the circulation of money, goods, information, and so forth provokes resistance and protest from workers who are nevertheless integrated into the mass expectation of instantaneous satisfaction of their own wants and needs. Control over space likewise loses its coherence. The annihilation of space by time proceeds differentially according to whether it is money, commodities, productive capacity, labor power, information, or technical know-how that is being moved – control within one of these networks of motion can be all too easily by-passed by movement in another (with money and information appearing as superior powers simply by virtue of the speed with which they can be moved). The buying and selling of futures (itself an extraordinary conception requiring psychological and intellectual preconditions that far exceed anything Simmel ever dreamed of) can even invert the realities of economic time so as to make the time incoherencies of a Robbe-Grillet novel appear as a realistic representation. The value of money, once a secure representation of value, gyrates as wildly as the time-space horizons of social action. Not only does inflation render the social power of money suspect, but money itself disintegrates into a cacophony of competing definitions (paper, private debts, coin, gold, state debt, special drawing rights, quantified by mysterious numbers like M1, M2, M3). The circulation of capital explodes the contradictions inherent in the money form and proves far more effective, ironically, than any secret agent at undermining the coherence of money, space, and time as secure frameworks of social power.

These incoherencies create all manner of opportunities for social transformation into which almost any interest group can step with hope of gain. Opportunities for successful class struggle arise for a working class threatened by transformations in labor markets, labor processes, and the spaces of their social reproduction. But the incoherence and the threat to existing power relations coupled with sentimental attachment to the past spark just as many oppositional movements within an increasingly fragmented bourgeoisie. Movements of revulsion and revolt against capitalism, its social basis or particular effects, become as diverse and incoherent as the system they arise in opposition to. That can in turn provoke a demand to impose coherence, to define secure sources and forms of social power. And if capitalism itself appears threatened by its own internal contradictions, then civil society, if it is to remain capitalist, must somehow bring order to the chaos, rout out the incoherencies, and contain the ferments of revulsion and revolt. The openings created for social transformation must be closed off or clearly defined. A higher power, that of the state, must be invoked as a matter of social survival.

State power and authority must be used not only to contain diverse oppositional movements directly but to anchor the frameworks of money, space, and time as sources of social power. State management of the quantity and qualities of money supply is one of its oldest and most venerable of functions. Central bank money now dominates other forms of money within an economy and is as secure as the state power on which it rests. The art of central banking becomes a litmus test of good government, because the state does not possess absolute powers of money creation but has to act as a powerful and secure mediator between the chaotic processes of money creation within its confines and the universal forms of money on the world market. The state manages and secures many of the basic time frames of decision making and coordination. It synchronizes clocks; it regulates the length of the working day, the length of a working life (through compulsory ages of school leaving and retirement), legal holidays and paid vacations, and hours of opening and closing (of commercial establishments and places of entertainment); and it enforces all the other bits and pieces of legislation that define the time frame of much of social life. The state affects the turnover time of capital either indirectly, through taxation procedures defined for amortization and depreciation and the setting of some social rate of time discount, or directly, by taking charge of many long-term investments and so thinking time horizons that the circulation of capital and financial markets cannot afford to contemplate. The state also facilitates planned obsolescence or spreading the costs of creative destruction (compensation for urban renewal or industrial restructuring, or amelioration of the social impacts of changing labor processes, for example). In all of these respects, the state intervenes to set a time frame within which private investment and individual decisions can be made. The state likewise protects rights to the appropriation of space (both private and public). The planning of the location of industry and population, of housing and public facilities, of transport and communications, of land uses, and so on, creates an overall spatial frame to contain and facilitate the innumerable and fragmented decisions that otherwise shape urban development. In all of these respects, the totalitarianism of the liberal capitalist state restrains the disintegrating tendencies of money, time, and space in the face of the contradictions of capital circulation.

To secure these frames of social action, the state needs more than the power, authority, and legitimacy to impose its will. It also must be able to call upon the requisite scientific and technical understandings. This gives added value to the rationality and intellectuality implied in the community of money. The professions that create and guard such knowledge acquire fresh importance, and their leading figures – Keynes, Le Corbusier, Wiener, and Koopmans, for example – enjoy great prestige. Such intellectuals acquire a well-grounded social power to the degree that their knowledge becomes a vital material force, not only with respect to techniques of production, but also with respect to the global framing of social action through control and management of money, space, and time. Those who can monopolize that kind of knowledge are in a powerful social position. It was no accident, therefore, that the tightening of the monetary, spatial, and chronological nets in the latter half of the nineteenth century was accompanied by the rise of distinctive professions, each with its own corner on the knowledge required to give coherence to those nets. The whole thrust of the Progressive movement in America, a movement that had enormous implications for urban and regional management and planning, was to convert power over knowledge into a class power of intellectuals, professionals, and academics over and above the class war between capital and labor. Though it never rose above that war in the manner they imagined, the power of engineers and managers, economists and architects, systems analysts and experts in industrial organization, could not be taken lightly. It became powerfully embedded in key state and corporate functions as planning became the order of the day. Intellectual conflicts over the meanings of money, space, and time had and continue to have very real material effects. The conflict over modernity and design in architecture, for example, is more than a conflict over taste and aesthetics. It deals directly with the question of the proper framing of the urban process in space and time (Giedion 1941).

The ideals of socialism and centralized planning can appear attractive to such a professional class, as the cases of Oskar Lange, Le Corbusier, Hans Blumenthal, and many others abundantly illustrate. Socialism seemed to hold out the possibility of doing everything that the bourgeois state wanted to do but could not. In intellectual circles the debate over socialism was in practice often reduced to debate over the superior organization of productive forces and the superior rationality of state-planned allocations of space and time as opposed to those achieved by market processes in which money power played a dominant role. It took many years of bitter experience and reluctant self-criticism to recognize that the total rationalization of the uses of space and time by some external authority was perhaps even more repressive than chaotic market allocations (cf. Lefebvre 1974; Duclos 1981). Certainly, to the degree that space and time are forms of social power, their control could all too easily degenerate into a replication of forms of class domination that the elimination of money power was supposed to abolish.

VII. THE URBAN PROCESS AND ITS POLITICAL CONFUSIONS

The urban process under capitalism is fraught with the most extraordinary political confusions, the roots of which can partially be exposed by consideration of how urbanization is framed by the intersecting concrete abstractions of money, space, and time and shaped directly by the circulation of money capital in time and space. The tension between the individualism that attaches to the spending of money and the class experience of earning that money splits the social and psychological foundations for political action. The struggle to command time (one's own or that of others) or to put oneself outside of the crass equation of time with money likewise leads to conflicting political perspectives. Those who are forced to give up surplus labor time to others in order to live will themselves engage in all kinds of struggles not only to limit the time taken from them but also to command the time of others (the time of other family members in housework or of those who offer services). And those who have sufficient money power may seek to define and use their own time in idiosyncratic ways. Money becomes the fundamental means to acquire free time. Only the *clochard*, or hobo, avoids that equation. Nevertheless, there is more than passing recognition on the part of even the most idiosyncratic user of free time that proper and efficient social coordination in universal time (in production as well as in exchange and communications) can be a means to liberate free time from the daily chores of production and reproduction. Even the most anarchistic of us like the traffic lights to be linked and the hours of opening and closing to be clearly marked. On the one hand, we recognize that rational social coordinations in universal time are necessary to sustain life in an urbanized world, while on the other we seek individual freedom from all such temporal discipline. The individualism that money imparts to the use of time conflicts with the social rationality required to be able to use that time creatively and well. State planning and regulation (of hours of labor, of opening and closing times, and so forth) appear unmitigated evils from one perspective and saving virtues from the other.

The struggle to command space is likewise plagued by all manner of ambiguities. The freedom to appropriate and move over space at will is highly valued. Money is an important but by no means exclusive means (as any tramp will tell you) of acquiring such freedom. But money is also often used to secure particular spaces against intrusion. The purchase of private property rights secures exclusive rights to dominate a parcel of space. I suspect the reason why car and homeownership make such an attractive combination is because it ensures an individualized ability to command and protect space simultaneously. Those without money power have to define their territorial privileges by other means. The urban gang protects its turf through violence, and low income and minority populations seek to define collective spaces within which they can exercise the strictest social control. Neighborhoods and communities may consequently be organized in ways antagonistic to pure market valuations, though it is surprising how much community action (particularly in more affluent areas) is oriented to purely market ends (from the defense of housing investments to controlled access to life chances within structured labor markets).

But the pulverization of space by private property and its segmentation into controlled social spaces are antagonistic to the ability to appropriate space freely. The inability to stroll a city out of fear of arrest for trespass or of violence because of some transgression of social space is frustrating. Fragmented powers of domination may also inhibit the structuring of urban space for the efficient use of time. Violently defended private and social spaces often render the structure of urban space relatively static and processes of spatial transformation highly conflictual. Even the vast power of money capital (with its penchant for reducing space to a form of fictitious capital) can be frustrated by such monopolies. Rational spatial planning and state control appear to be adequate respfonses to such problems, though such power can be used for radically different class purposes. The use of state power to free up space for capital (through forced expropriation, urban renewal, and the like) is very different from the use of state power to check the extraction of vast money revenues from those who have to appropriate spaces owned by others in order to live. On the other hand, nationalization of the land and abolition of private property rights does not necessarily liberate space for popular appropriation. It can even lead to the erosion of those limited rights to appropriate space given by private property and other mechanisms of securing social space. The prevention of one mode of dominating space merely creates another.

Such tensions obscure political consciousness and render all political programs problematic. Should the struggle to curb money power lead to curbing money uses? Should the struggle to curb the thirst for surplus labor be accompanied by an abandonment of concern for efficient means of producing a surplus product? Can the struggle to liberate space for free appropriation be waged without incurring new and even more damaging forms of domination? Should the struggle to free space and time from some dominant and repressive universal rationality entail abandonment of the search for super-efficient organizations of space and allocations of time to reproduce daily needs with the minimum of effort?

The analysis of money, space, and time in the context of capital accumulation with its dominant class relations reveals much about the dynamics of the urban process, its inner tensions, and the significance of urbanization to capitalism's evolution. It also helps us understand the dilemmas and confusions that the urban experience produces for political and intellectual consciousness. Given the intricate complexity and sheer scale of urbanization under capitalism and the peculiar mix of alienations and opportunities that arises out of the urban experience, the objectives of radical and revolutionary movements are bound to become confused. Political consciousness becomes multidimensional, often contradictory, and certainly fragmented. The history of urban social movements has to be read in exactly such a light. The history of class-based political movements also illustrates how easily these can be torn asunder by exactly such fragmentations. Small wonder that left political movements all too often studiously ignore urban social movements as peripheral froth but in so doing undermine their credibility and their power to undertake a total transformation of capitalism into some alternative mode of production.

Capitalism these last two hundred years has produced, through its dominant form of urbanization, not only a "second nature" of built environments even harder to transform than the virgin nature of frontier regions years ago, but also an urbanized human nature, endowed with a very specific sense of time, space, and money as sources of social power and with sophisticated abilities and strategies to win back from one corner of urban life what may be lost in another. And while it may be true that some are losers everywhere, the vast majority find at least minor compensations somewhere while the rest find solace and hope in the intricacy of the game. Every political movement against the domination of capital must, at some point, confront such confusions. This is also the kind of fragmented and often contradictory political consciousness that permeates our intellectual representations and proposals as to what a genuinely humanizing urban experience might be all about. It is, therefore, imperative that we step back and reflect upon the rationality and social meaning of our conceptions of money, time, and space as frames within which capitalist urbanization and the urban experience unfold. That way, we can more freely seek conceptions that liberate rather than imprison our thinking as to what a noncapitalist but urbanized human future could be all about.

7

Monument and Myth: The Building of the Basilica of the Sacred Heart

Strategically placed atop a hill known as the butte Montmartre, the Basilica of Sacré-Coeur occupies a commanding position over Paris. Its five white marble domes and the campanile that rises beside them can be seen from every quarter of the city. Occasional glimpses of it can be caught from within the dense and cavernous network of streets which makes up old Paris. It stands out, spectacular and grand, to the young mothers parading their children in the Jardins de Luxembourg, to the tourists who painfully plod to the top of Notre Dame or who painlessly float up the escalators of the Centre Beaubourg, to the commuters crossing the Seine by metro at Grenelle or pouring into the Gare du Nord, to the Algerian immigrants who on Sunday afternoons wander to the top of the rock in the parc des Buttes Chaumont. It can be seen clearly by the old men playing "boule" in the place du Colonel Fabien, on the edge of the traditional working class quarters of Belleville and La Villette – places that have an important role to play in our story.

On cold winter days when the wind whips the fallen leaves among the aging tombstones of the Père Lachaise cemetery, the basilica can be seen from the steps of the tomb of Adolphe Thiers, first president of the Third Republic of France. Though now almost hidden by the modern office complex of La Défense, it can be seen from more than twenty kilometers away in the Pavillion Henry IV in St. Germain-en-Laye, where Adolphe Thiers died. But by a quirk of topography, it cannot be seen from the famous Mur des Fédérés in that same Père Lachaise cemetery where, on May 27, 1871, some of the last few remaining soldiers of the Commune were rounded up after a fierce fight among the tombstones and summarily shot. You cannot see Sacré-Coeur from that ivy-covered wall now shaded by an aging chestnut. That place of pilgrimage for socialists, workers, and their leaders is hidden from a place of pilgrimage for the Catholic faithful by the brow of the hill on which stands the grim tomb of Adolphe Thiers.

Few would argue that the Basilica of Sacré-Coeur is beautiful or elegant (fig. 11). But most would concede that it is striking and distinctive, that its

Fig. 11. The Basilica of Sacré-Coeur

direct Byzantine style achieves a kind of haughty grandeur which demands respect from the city spread out at its feet. On sunny days it glistens from afar, and even on the gloomiest of days its domes seem to capture the smallest particles of light and radiate them outward in a white marble glow. Floodlit by night it appears suspended in space, sepulchral and ethereal. Thus does Sacré-Coeur project an image of saintly grandeur, of perpetual remembrance. But remembrance of what?

The visitor drawn to the basilica in search of an answer to that question must first ascend the steep hillside of Montmartre. Those who pause to catch their breath will see spread out before them a marvelous vista of rooftops, chimneys, domes, towers, monuments – a vista of old Paris that has not changed much since that dull and foggy October morning in 1872, when the archbishop of Paris climbed those steep slopes only to have the sun miraculously chase both fog and cloud away to reveal the splendid panorama of Paris spread out before him. The archbishop marveled for a moment before crying out loud: "It is here, it is here where the martyrs are, it is here that the Sacred Heart must reign so that it can beckon all to it!" (Jonquet n.d.). So who are the martyrs commemorated here in the grandeur of this basilica?

The visitor who enters into that hallowed place will most probably first be struck by the immense painting of Jesus which covers the dome of the apse. Portrayed with arms stretched wide, the figure of Christ wears an image of the Sacred Heart upon his breast. Beneath, two words stand out directly from the Latin motto – GALLIA POENITENS. And beneath that stands a large gold casket containing the image of the Sacred Heart of Jesus, burning with passion, suffused with blood and surrounded with thorns. Illuminated day and night, it is here that pilgrims come to pray.

Opposite a life-size statue of Saint Marguerite-Marie Alacoque, words from a letter written by that saintly person – date, 1689; place, Paray-le-Monial – tell us more about the cult of the Sacred Heart:

THE ETERNAL FATHER WISHING REPARATION FOR THE BITTERNESS AND ANGUISH THAT THE ADORABLE HEART OF HIS DIVINE SON HAD EXPERIENCED AMONGST THE HUMILIATIONS AND OUTRAGES OF HIS PASSION DESIRES AN EDIFICE WHERE THE IMAGE OF THIS DIVINE HEART CAN RECEIVE VENERATION AND HOMAGE.

Prayer to the Sacred Heart of Jesus, which, according to the scriptures, had been exposed when a centurion thrust a lance through Jesus' side during his suffering upon the cross, was not unknown before the seventeenth century. But Marguerite-Marie, beset by visions, transformed the worship of the Sacred Heart into a distinctive cult within the Catholic church. Although her life was full of trials and suffering, her manner severe and rigorous, the predominant image of Christ which the cult projected was warm and loving, full of repentance and suffused with a gentle kind of mysticism (Jonquet n.d.; Dansette 1965).

Marguerite-Marie and her disciples set about propagating the cult with great zeal. She wrote to Louis XIV, for example, claiming to bring a message from Christ in which the king was asked to repent, to save France by dedicating himself to the Sacred Heart, to place its image upon his standard and to build a chapel to its glorification. It is from that letter of 1689 that the words now etched in stone within the basilica are taken.

The cult diffused slowly. It was not exactly in tune with eighteenth-century French rationalism, which strongly influenced modes of belief among Catholics and stood in direct opposition to the hard, rigorous, and self-disciplined image of Jesus projected by the Jansenists. But by the end of the eighteenth century it had some important and potentially influential adherents. Louis XVI privately took devotion to the Sacred Heart for himself and his family. Imprisoned during the French Revolution, he vowed that within three months of his deliverance he would publicly dedicate himself to the Sacred Heart and thereby save France (from what, exactly, he did not say, nor did he need to). And he vowed to build a chapel to the worship of the Sacred Heart. The manner of Louis XVI's deliverance did not permit him to fulfill that vow. Marie-Antoinette did no better. The queen delivered up her last prayers to the Sacred Heart before keeping her appointment with the guillotine.

These incidents are of interest because they presage an association, important for our story, between the cult of the Sacred Heart and the reactionary monarchism of the *ancien régime*. This put adherents to the cult in firm opposition to the principles of the French Revolution. Believers in the principles of liberty, equality, and fraternity, who were in any case prone to awesome anticlerical sentiments and practices, were, in return, scarcely enamored of such a cult. Revolutionary France was no safe place to attempt to propagate it. Even the bones and other relics of Marguerite-Marie, now displayed in Paray-le-Monial, had to be carefully hidden during those years.

The restoration of the monarchy in 1815 changed all that. The Bourbon monarchs sought, under the watchful eye of the European powers, to restore whatever they could of the old social order. The theme of repentance for the excesses of the revolutionary era ran strong. Louis XVIII did not fulfill his dead brother's vow to the Sacred Heart, but he did built, with his own moneys, a Chapel of Expiation on the spot where his brother and his family had been so unceremoniously interred – GALLIA POENITENS. A society for the propagation of the cult of the Sacred Heart was founded, however, and proceedings for the glorification of Marguerite-Marie were transmitted to Rome in 1819. The link between conservative monarchism and the cult of the Sacred Heart was further consolidated.

The cult spread among conservative Catholics but was viewed with some suspicion by the liberal progressive wing of French Catholicism. But now another enemy was ravaging the land, disturbing the social order. France was undergoing the stress and tensions of capitalist industrialization. In fits and starts under the July Monarchy (installed in 1830 and just as summarily dispensed with in the revolution of 1848) and then in a great surge in the early years of the Second Empire of Napoleon III, France saw a radical transformation in certain sectors of its economy, in its institutional structures, and in its social order (Price 1975; Braudel and Labrousse 1976). This transformation threatened much that was sacred in French life, since it brought within its train a crass and heartless materialism, an ostentatious and morally decadent bourgeois culture, and a sharpening of class tensions. The cult of the Sacred Heart now assembled under its banner not only those devotees drawn by temperament or circumstance to the image of a gentle and forgiving Christ, not only those who dreamed of a restoration of the political order of yesteryear, but also all those who felt threatened by the materialist values of the new social order.

To these general conditions, French Catholics could also add some more specific complaints in the 1860s. Napoleon III had finally come down on the side of Italian unification and committed himself politically and militarily to the liberation of the central Italian states from the temporal power of the pope. The latter did not take kindly to such politics and under military pressure retired to the Vatican, refusing to come out until such time as his temporal power was restored. From that vantage point, the pope delivered searing condemnations of French policy and the moral decadence which, he felt, was sweeping over France. In this manner he hoped to rally French Catholics in the active pursuit of his cause. The moment was propitious. Marguerite-Marie was beatified by Pius IX in 1864. The era of grand pilgrimages to Paray-le-Monial began. The pilgrims came to express repentance for both public and private transgressions. They repented for the materialism and decadent opulence of France. They repented for the restrictions placed upon the temporal power of the pope. They repented for the passing of the traditional values embodied in an old and venerable social order. GALLIA POENITENS.

Just inside the main door of the Basilica of Sacré-Coeur in Paris, the visitor can read the following inscription:

THE YEAR OF OUR LORD 1875 THE 16TH JUNE IN THE REIGN OF HIS HOLINESS POPE PIUS IX IN ACCOMPLISHMENT OF A VOW FORMULATED DURING THE WAR OF 1870–71 BY ALEXANDER LEGENTIL AND HUBERT ROHAULT DE FLEURY RATIFIED BY HIS GRACE MSGR. GUIBERT ARCHBISHOP OF PARIS; IN EXECUTION OF THE VOTE OF THE NATIONAL ASSEMBLY OF THE 23D JULY 1873 ACCORDING TO THE DESIGN OF

THE ARCHITECT ABADIE; THE FIRST STONE OF THIS BASILICA ERECTED TO THE
SACRED HEART OF JESUS WAS SOLEMNLY PUT IN PLACE BY HIS EMINENCE CARDINAL
GUIBERT. . . .

Let us flesh out that capsule history and find out what lies behind it. As
Bismarck's battalions rolled to victory after victory over the French in the
summer of 1870, an impending sense of doom swept over France. Many
interpreted the defeats as righteous vengeance inflicted by divine will upon an
errant and morally decadent France. It was in this spirit that the empress
Eugene was urged to walk with her family and court, all dressed in
mourning, from the Palace of the Tuileries to Notre Dame, to publicly
dedicate themselves to the Sacred Heart. Though the empress received the
suggestion favorably, it was, once more, too late. On September 2, Napoleon
III was defeated and captured at Sedan; on September 4, the Republic was
proclaimed on the steps of the Hotel-de-Ville and a Government of National
Defense was formed. On that day also the empress Eugene took flight from
Paris having prudently, and at the emperor's urging, already packed her bags
and sent her more valuable possessions on to England.

The defeat at Sedan ended the Empire but not the war. The Prussian armies
rolled on, and by September 20 they had encircled Paris and put that city
under a siege that was to last until January 28 of the following year. Like
many other respectable bourgeois citizens, Alexander Legentil fled Paris at
the approach of the Prussian armies and took refuge in the provinces.
Languishing in Poitiers and agonizing over the fate of Paris, he vowed in early
December that "if God saved Paris and France and delivered the sovereign
pontiff, he would contribute according to his means to the construction in
Paris of a sanctuary dedicated to the Sacred Heart." He sought other
adherents to this vow and soon had the ardent support of Hubert Rohault de
Fleury (1903, 1905, 1907).

The terms of Legentil's vow did not, however, guarantee it a very warm
reception, for as he soon discovered, the provinces "were then possessed of
hateful sentiments towards Paris." Such a state of affairs was not unusual, and
we can usefully divert for a moment to consider its basis.

Under the *ancien régime*, the French state apparatus had acquired a strongly
centralized character which was consolidated under the French Revolution
and Empire. This centralization thereafter became the basis of French
political organization and gave Paris a peculiarly important role in relation to
the rest of France. The administrative, economic, and cultural predominance
of Paris was assured. But the events of 1789 also showed that Parisians had
the power to make and break governments. They proved adept at using that
power and were not loath, as a result, to regard themselves as privileged
beings with a right and duty to foist all that they deemed "progressive" upon

a supposedly backward, conservative, and predominantly rural France. The Parisian bourgeois despised the narrowness of provincial life and found the peasant disgusting and incomprehensible (Zeldin 1973, 1977).

From the other end of the telescope, Paris was generally seen as a center of power, domination, and opportunity. It was both envied and hated. To the antagonism generated by the excessive centralization of power and authority in Paris were added all of the vaguer small town and rural antagonisms toward any large city as a center of privilege, material success, moral decadence, vice, and social unrest. What was special in France was the way in which the tensions emanating from the "urban-rural contradiction" were so intensely focused upon the relation between Paris and the rest of France.

Under the Second Empire these tensions sharpened considerably. Paris experienced a vast economic boom as the railways made it the hub of a process of national spatial integration. At the same time, falling transport costs and the free trade policies signaled by the Anglo-French Treaties of Commerce in 1860 brought the city into a new relationship with an emerging global economy. Its share of an expanding French export trade increased dramatically, and its population grew rapidly, largely through a massive immigration of rural laborers (Gaillard 1977). Concentration of wealth and power proceeded apace as Paris became the center of financial, speculative, and commercial operations. The contrasts between affluence and poverty became ever more startling and were increasingly expressed in terms of a geographical segregation between the bourgeois quarters of the west and the working class quarters of the north, east, and south. Belleville became a foreign territory into which the bourgeois citizens of the west rarely dared to venture. The population of that place, which more than doubled between 1853 and 1870, was pictured in the bourgeois press as "the dregs of the people" caught in "the deepest depths of poverty and hatred" where "ferments of envy, sloth and anger bubble without cease" (Lepidis and Jacomin 1975). The signs of social breakdown were everywhere. As economic growth slowed in the 1860s and as the authority of Empire began to fail, Paris became a cauldron of social unrest, vulnerable to agitators of any stripe.

And to top it all, Haussmann, at the emperor's urging, had set out to "embellish Paris" with spacious boulevards, parks, and gardens, monumental architecture of all sorts. The intent was to make Paris a truly imperial city, worthy not only of France but of Western civilization. Haussmann had done this at immense cost and by the slipperiest of financial means, a feat which scarcely recommended itself to the frugal provincial mind. The image of public opulence which Haussmann projected was only matched by the conspicuous consumption of a bourgeoisie, many of whom had grown rich speculating on the benefits of his improvements (Pinkney 1958).

Small wonder, then, that provincial and rural Catholics were in no frame of mind to dig into their pockets to embellish Paris with yet another monument, no matter how pious its purpose.

But there were even more specific objections which emerged in response to Legentil's proposal. The Parisians had with their customary presumptuousness proclaimed a republic when provincial and rural sentiment was heavily infused with monarchism. Furthermore, those who had remained behind to face the rigors of the siege were showing themselves remarkably intransigent and bellicose, declaring they would favor a fight to the bitter end, when provincial sentiment showed a strong disposition to end the conflict with Prussia.

And then the rumors and hints of a new materialist politics among the working class in Paris, spiced with a variety of manifestations of revolutionary fervor, gave the impression that the city had, in the absence of its more respectable bourgeois citizenry, fallen prey to radical and even socialist philosophy. Since the only means of communication between a besieged Paris and the nonoccupied territories was pigeon or balloon, abundant opportunities arose for misunderstanding, which the rural foes of republicanism and the urban foes of monarchism were not beyond exploiting.

Legentil therefore found it politic to drop any specific mention of Paris in his vow. But toward the end of February the pope endorsed it, and from then on the movement gathered some strength. And so on March 19, a pamphlet appeared which set out the arguments for the vow at some length (Rohault de Fleury 1903, 10–13). The spirit of the work had to be national, the authors urged, because the French people had to make national amends for what were national crimes. They confirmed their intention to build the monument in Paris. To the objection that the city should not be further embellished they replied, "Were Paris reduced to cinders, we would still want to avow our national faults and to proclaim the justice of God on its ruins."

The timing and phrasing of the pamphlet proved fortuitously prophetic. On March 18, Parisians had taken their first irrevocable steps toward establishing self-government under the Commune. The real or imagined sins of the communards were subsequently to shock and outrage bourgeois opinion. And as much of Paris was indeed reduced to cinders in the course of a civil war of incredible ferocity, the notion of building a basilica of expiation upon these ashes became more and more appealing. As Rohault de Fleury noted, with evident satisfaction, "In the months to come, the image of Paris reduced to cinders struck home many times" (1903, 10–13). Let us rehearse a little of that history.

The origins of the Paris Commune lie in a whole series of events which ran into each other in complex ways. Precisely because of its political importance within the country, Paris had long been denied any representative form of municipal government and had been directly administered by the national government. For much of the nineteenth century, a predominantly republican Paris was chafing under the rule of monarchists (either Bourbon "legitimists" or "Orleanists") or authoritarian Bonapartists. The demand for a democratic form of municipal government was long-standing and commanded widespread support within the city.

The Government of National Defense set up on September 4, 1870, was neither radical nor revolutionary (Guillemin 1956), but it was republican. It also turned out to be timid and inept. It labored under certain difficulties, of course, but these were hardly sufficient to excuse its weak performance. It did not, for example, command the respect of the monarchists and lived in perpetual fear of the reactionaries of the right. When the Army of the East, under General Bazaine, capitulated to the Prussians at Metz on October 27, the general left the impression that he did so because, being monarchist, he could not bring himself to fight for a republican government. Some of his officers who resisted the capitulation saw Bazaine putting his political preferences above the honor of France. This was a matter which was to dog French politics for several years. Rossel, who was later to command the armed forces of the Commune for a while, was one of the officers shocked to the core by Bazaine's evident lack of patriotism (Thomas 1967).

But the tensions between the different factions of the ruling class were nothing compared to the real or imagined antagonisms between a traditional and remarkably obdurate bourgeoisie and a working class that was beginning to find its feet and assert itself. Rightly or wrongly, the bourgeoisie was greatly alarmed during the 1860s by the emergence of working-class organization and political clubs, by the activities of the Paris branch of the International Working Men's Association, by the effervescence of thought within the working class and the spread of anarchist and socialist philosophies. And the working class – although by no means as well organized or as unified as their opponents feared – was certainly displaying abundant signs of an emergent class consciousness.

The Government of National Defense could not stem the tide of Prussian victories or break the siege of Paris without widespread working-class support. And the leaders of the left were only too willing to give it in spite of their initial opposition to the emperor's war. Blanqui promised the government "energetic and absolute support," and even the International's leaders, having dutifully appealed to the German workers not to participate in a fratricidal struggle, plunged into organizing for the defense of Paris. Belleville, the center of working-class agitation, rallied spectacularly to the national cause, all in the name of the Republic (Lissagaray 1976).

The bourgeoisie sensed a trap. They saw themselves, wrote a contemporary commentator drawn from their ranks, caught between the Prussians and those whom they called "the reds." "I do not know," he went on, "which of these two evils terrified them most; they hated the foreigner but they feared the Bellevillois much more" (Bruhat, Dautry, and Tersen 1971, 75). No matter how much they wanted to defeat the foreigner, they could not bring themselves to do so with the battalions of the working class in the vanguard. For what was not to be the last time in French history, the bourgeoisie chose to capitulate to the Germans, leaving the left as the dominant force within a patriotic front. In 1871, fear of the "enemy within" was to prevail over national pride.

The failure of the French to break the siege of Paris was first interpreted as the product of Prussian superiority and French military ineptitude. But as sortie after sortie promised victory only to be turned into disaster, honest patriots began to wonder if the powers that be were not playing tricks which bordered on betrayal and treason. The government was increasingly viewed as a "Government of National Defection."[1]

The government was equally reluctant to respond to the Parisian demand for municipal democracy. Since many of the respectable bourgeois had fled, it looked as if elections would deliver municipal power into the hands of the left. Given the suspicions of the monarchists of the right, the Government of National Defense felt it could not afford to concede what had long been demanded. And so it procrastinated endlessly.

As early as October 31, these various threads came together to generate an insurrectionary movement in Paris. Shortly after Bazaine's ignominious surrender, word got out that the government was negotiating the terms of an armistice with the Prussians. The population of Paris took to the streets and, as the feared Bellevillois descended en masse, took several members of the government prisoner, agreeing to release them only on the verbal assurance that there would be municipal elections and no capitulation. This incident was guaranteed to raise the hackles of the right. It was the immediate cause of the "hateful sentiments towards Paris" which Legentil encountered in December. The government lived to fight another day. But, as events turned out, they were to fight much more effectively against the Bellevillois than they ever fought against the Prussians.

So the siege of Paris dragged on. Worsening conditions in the city now added their uncertain effects to a socially unstable situation. The government proved inept and insensitive to the needs of the population and thereby added fuel to the smoldering fires of discontent (Lazare 1872; Becker 1969). The people lived off cats or dogs, while the more privileged partook of pieces of Pollux, the young elephant from the zoo (forty francs a pound for the trunk). The price of rats – the "taste is a cross between pork and partridge" – rose

---

[1] Marx (1968) uses this phrase to telling effect in his passionate defense of the Commune. The idea was widespread throughout Paris at that time; see Marcel Cerf (1971).

from sixty centimes to four francs apiece. The government failed to take the elementary precaution of rationing bread until January when it was much too late. Supplies dwindled, and the adulteration of bread with bone meal became a chronic problem which was made even less palatable by the fact that it was human bones from the catacombs which were being dredged up for the occasion. While the common people were thus consuming their ancestors without knowing it, the luxuries of café life were kept going, supplied by hoarding merchants at exorbitant prices. The rich that stayed behind continued to indulge their pleasures according to their custom, although they paid dearly for it. The government did nothing to curb profiteering or the continuation of conspicuous consumption by the rich in callous disregard for the feelings of the less privileged.

By the end of December, radical opposition to the Government of National Defense was growing. It led to the publication of the celebrated *Affiche Rouge* of January 7. Signed by the central committee of the twenty Parisian arrondissements, it accused the government of leading the country to the edge of an abyss by its indecision, inertia, and foot-dragging; suggested that the government knew not how to administer or to fight; and insisted that the perpetuation of such a regime could end only in capitulation to the Prussians. It proclaimed a program for a general requisition of resources, rationing, and mass attack. It closed with the celebrated appeal "Make way for the people! Make way for the Commune!" (Bruhat, Dautry, and Tersen 1971; Edwards 1971).

Placarded all over Paris, the appeal had its effect. The military responded decisively and organized one last mass sortie, which was spectacular for its military ineptitude and the carnage left behind. "Everyone understood," wrote Lissagaray, "that they had been sent out to be sacrificed" (1976, 75). The evidence of treason and betrayal was by now overwhelming for those close to the action. It pushed many an honest patriot from the bourgeoisie, who put love of country above class interest, into an alliance with the dissident radicals and the working class.

Parisians accepted the inevitable armistice at the end of January with sullen passivity. It provided for national elections to a constituent assembly which would negotiate and ratify a peace agreement. It specified that the French army lay down its arms but permitted the National Guard of Paris, which could not easily be disarmed, to remain a fighting force. Supplies came into a starving city under the watchful eye of the Prussian troops.

In the February elections, the city returned its quota of radical republicans. But rural and provincial France voted solidly for peace. Since the left was antagonistic to capitulation, the republicans from the Government of National Defense seriously compromised by their management of the war, and the Bonapartists discredited, the peace vote went to the monarchists.

republican Paris was appalled to find itself faced with a monarchist majority in the National Assembly. Thiers, by then seventy-three years old, was elected president in part because of his long experience in politics and in part because the monarchists did not want to be responsible for signing what was bound to be an ignoble peace agreement.

Thiers ceded Alsace and Lorraine to Germany and agreed to a huge war indemnity. He was enough of a patriot to resist Bismarck's suggestion that Prussian bankers float the loan required. Thiers reserved that privilege for the French and turned this year of troubles into one of the most profitable ones ever for the gentlemen of French high finance (Guillemin 1971; Bruhat, Dautry, and Tersen 1971, 104–5; Dreyfus 1928, 266). The latter informed Thiers that if he was to raise the money, he must first deal with "those rascals in Paris." This he was uniquely equipped to do. As minister of the interior under Louis Philippe, he had, in 1834, been responsible for the savage repression of one of the first genuine working-class movements in French history. Ever contemptuous of "the vile multitude," he had long had a plan for dealing with them – a plan which he had proposed to Louis Philippe in 1848 and which he was now finally in a position to put into effect (Allison 1932; Guillemin 1971). The plan was simple. He would use the conservatism of the country to smash the radicalism of the city.

On the morning of March 18, the population of Paris awoke to find that the remains of the French army had been sent to Paris to relieve that city of its cannons in which was obviously a first step toward the disarmament of a populace which had, since September 4, joined the National Guard in massive numbers (fig. 12). The populace of working-class Paris set out spontaneously to reclaim the cannons as their own. On the hill on Montmartre, weary French soldiers stood guard over the powerful battery of cannons assembled there, facing an increasingly restive and angry crowd. General Lecomte ordered his troops to fire. He ordered once twice, thrice. The soldiers had not the heart to do it, raised their rifle butts in the air, and fraternized joyfully with the crowd. An infuriated mob took General Lecomte prisoner. They stumbled across General Thomas, remembered and hated for his role in the savage killings of the June Days of 1848. The two generals were taken to the garden of No. 6, rue des Rosiers and, amid considerable confusion and angry argument, put up against a wall and shot.

This incident is of crucial importance to our story. The conservatives now had their martyrs. Thiers could brand the insubordinate population of Paris as murderers and assassins. But the hilltop of Montmartre had been a place of martyrdom for Christian saints long before. To these could now be added the names of Lecomte and Clément Thomas. In the months and years to come, as the struggle to build the Basilica of Sacré-Coeur unfolded, frequent appeal was to be made to the need to commemorate these "martyrs of yesterday who

Fig. 12.   The hillside of Montmartre on the eve of March 18, 1871

died in order to defend and save Christian society."[2] On that sixteenth day of
June in 1875 when the foundation stone was laid, Rohault de Fleury rejoiced
that the basilica was to be built on a site which, "after having been such a
saintly place had become, it would seem, the place chosen by Satan and where
was accomplished the first act of that horrible saturnalia which caused so
much ruination and which gave the church two such glorious martyrs."
"Yes," he continued, "it is here where Sacré-Coeur will be raised up that the
Commune began, here where generals Clément Thomas and Lecomte were
assassinated." He rejoiced in the "multitude of good Christians who now
stood adoring a God who knows only too well how to confound the evil-
minded, cast down their designs and to place a cradle where they thought to
dig a grave." He contrasted this multitude of the faithful with a "hillside,
lined with intoxicated demons, inhabited by a population apparently hostile
to all religious ideas and animated, above all, by a hatred of the Church"
(Rohault de Fleury 1903, 264). GALLIA POENITENS.

   Thiers's response to the events of March 18 was to order a complete
withdrawal of military and government personnel from Paris. From the safe
distance of Versailles, he prepared methodically for the invasion and
reduction of Paris. Bismarck proved not at all reluctant to allow the

   [2] This phrase was actually used by the Committee of the National Assembly appointed to
report on the proposed law that would make the Basilica a work of public utility. See Rohault
de Fleury (1903, 88).

Fig. 13. Executions at the Mur des Fédérés in Père Lachaise cemetery, May 1871; gouache by Alfred Darjon. (Musée Carnavelet.)

reconstitution of a French army sufficient to the task of putting down the radicals in Paris and released prisoners and material for that purpose.

Left to their own devices, and somewhat surprised by the turn of events, the Parisians, under the leadership of the Central Committee of the National Guard, arranged for elections on March 26. The Commune was declared a political fact on March 28. It was a day of joyous celebration for the common people of Paris and a day of consternation for the bourgeoisie.

The politics of the Commune were hardly coherent. While a substantial number of workers took their place as elected representatives of the people for the first time in French history, the Commune was still dominated by radical elements from the bourgeoisie. Composed as it was of diverse political currents shading from middle-of-the-road republican through the Jacobins, the Proudhonists, the socialists of the International, and the Blanquist revolutionaries, there was a good deal of factionalism and plenty of contentious argumentation as to what radical or socialist path to take. Much of this proved moot, however, since Thiers attacked in early April and the second siege of Paris began. Rural France was being put to work to destroy working-class Paris.

What followed was disastrous for the Commune. When the Versailles forces finally broke through the outer defense of Paris — which Thiers had had

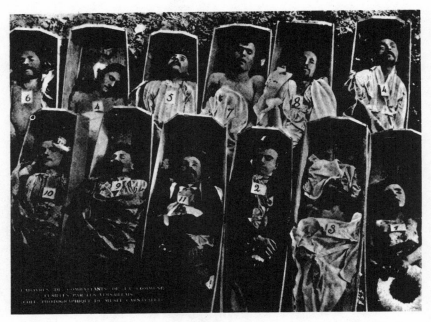

Fig. 14. Bodies of communards shot by Versaillese troops, May 1871. (Musée Carnavelet.)

constructed in the 1840s – they swept quickly through the bourgeois sections of western Paris and cut slowly and ruthlessly down the grand boulevards that Haussmann had constructed into the working-class quarters of the city. So began one of the most vicious bloodlettings in an often bloody French history. The Versailles forces gave no quarter. To the deaths in the street fighting, which were not, by most accounts, too extensive, were added an incredible number of arbitrary executions without judgment. The Luxemburg Gardens, the barracks at Lobau, the celebrated and still venerated wall in the cemetery of Père Lachaise, echoed ceaselessly to the sound of gunfire as the executioners went to work. Between twenty and thirty thousand communards died thus. GALLIA POENITENS – with vengeance (figs. 13 and 14).

Out of this sad history there is one incident which commands our attention. On the morning of May 28, an exhausted Eugène Varlin – bookbinder, union and food cooperative organizer under the Second Empire, member of the national guard, intelligent, respected, and scrupulously honest, committed socialist, and brave soldier – was recognized and arrested. He was taken to that same house on rue des Rosiers where Lecomte and Clément Thomas died. Varlin's fate was worse. Paraded around the hillside of

Fig. 15.   The toppling of the Vendôme Column during the Commune.
(Illustrated London News.)

Montmartre, some say for ten minutes and others for hours, abused, beaten, and humiliated by a fickle mob, he was finally propped up against a wall and shot. He was just thirty-two years old. They had to shoot twice to kill him. In between fusillades he cried, evidently unrepentant, "Vive la Commune!" His biographer called it "the Calvary of Eugène Varlin." The left can have its martyrs too. And it is on that spot that Sacré-Coeur is built (Foulon 1934).

The "bloody week," as it was called, also involved an enormous destruction of property. Paris burned. To the buildings set afire in the course of the bombardment were added those deliberately fired for strategic reasons by the retreating communards. From this arose the myth of the "incendiaries" of the Commune who recklessly took revenge, it was said, by burning everything they could. The communards, to be sure, were not enamored of the privileges of private property and were not averse to destroying hated symbols. The Vendôme Column – which Napoleon III had doted upon – was, after all, toppled in a grand ceremony to symbolize the end of authoritarian rule (fig. 15). The painter Courbet was later held responsible for this act and condemned to pay for the construction of the monument out of his own pocket. The communards also decreed, but never carried out, the destruction of the Chapel of Expiation by which Louis XVIII had sought to impress upon Parisians their guilt in executing his brother. And when Thiers had shown his true colors, the communards took a certain delight in dismantling his Parisian residence, stone by stone, in a symbolic gesture which de Goncourt felt had an "excellent bad effect" (Becker 1969, 288). But the wholesale burning of Paris was another matter entirely (fig. 16).

Fig. 16.   View of Paris burning from Père Lachaise cemetery. (Musée Carnavelet.)

No matter what the truth of the matter the myth of the incendiaries was strong. Within a year, the pope himself was describing the communards as "devils risen up from hell bringing the fires of the inferno to the streets of Paris."

The ashes of the city became a symbol of the Commune's crimes against the Church and were to fertilize the soil from which the energy to build Sacré-Coeur was to spring. No wonder that Rohault de Fleury congratulated himself upon that felicitous choice of words — "were Paris to be reduced to cinders." That phrase could strike home with redoubled force, he noted, "as the incendiaries of the Commune came to terrorize the world" (1903, 13).

The aftermath of the Commune was anything but pleasant. The bloodletting began to turn the stomachs of the bourgeoisie until all but the most sadistic of them had to cry "stop!" The celebrated diarist Edmond de Goncourt tried to convince himself of the justice of it all when he wrote:

It is good that there was neither conciliation nor bargain. The solution was brutal. It was by pure force. The solution has held people back from cowardly compromises . . . the bloodletting was a bleeding white; such a purge, by killing off the combative part of the population defers the next revolution by a whole generation. The old society has twenty years of quiet ahead of it, if the powers that be dare all that they may dare at this time. (Becker 1969, 312)

These sentiments were exactly those of Thiers. But when de Goncourt passed through Belleville and saw the "faces of ugly silence," he could not help but feel that here was a "vanquished but unsubjugated district." Was there no other way to purge the threat of revolution?

The experiences of 1870–71, when taken together with the confrontation between Napoleon III and the pope and the decadent "festive materialism" of the Second Empire, plunged Catholics into a phase of widespread soul-searching. The majority of them accepted the notion that France had sinned, and this gave rise to manifestations of expiation and a movement of piety that was both mystical and spectacular (Dansette 1965, 340–45). The intransigent and ultramontane Catholics unquestionably favored a return to law and order and a political solution founded on respect for authority. And it was the monarchists, generally themselves intransigent Catholics, who held out the promise for that law and order. Liberal Catholics found all of this disturbing and distasteful, but they were in no position to mobilize their forces – even the pope described them as the "veritable scourge" of France. There was little to stop the consolidation of the bond between monarchism and intransigent Catholicism. And it was such a powerful alliance that was to guarantee the building of Sacré-Coeur.

The immediate problem for the progenitors of the vow was, however, to operationalize a pious wish. This required official action. Legentil and Rohault de Fleury sought the support of the newly appointed archbishop of Paris.

Monseigneur Guibert, a compatriot of Thiers from Tours, had required some persuading to take the position in Paris. The three previous archbishops had suffered violent deaths: the first during the insurrection of 1848, the second by the hand of an assassin in 1863, and the third during the Commune. The communards had early decided to take hostages in response to the butchery promised by Versailles. The archbishop was held as a prime hostage for whom the communards sought the exchange of Blanqui. Thiers refused that negotiation, apparently having decided that a dead and martyred archbishop (who was a liberal Catholic in any case) was more valuable to him than a live one exchanged against a dynamic and aggressive Blanqui. During the "bloody week," the communards took whatever vengeance they could. On May 24, the archbishop was shot. In that final week, seventy-four hostages were shot, of whom twenty-four were priests. That awesome anticlericalism was as alive under the Commune as it had been in 1789. But with the massive purge which left more than twenty thousand communards dead, nearly forty thousand imprisoned, and countless others in flight, Thiers could write reassuringly on June 14 to Monseigneur Guibert: "The 'reds,' totally vanquished, will not recommence their activities tomorrow; one does not engage twice in fifty years in such an immense fight as they have just lost" (Guillemin 1971, 295–96; Rohault de Fleury 1905, 365). Reassured, Monseigneur Guibert came to Paris.

The new archbishop was much impressed with the movement to build a monument to the Sacred Heart. On January 18, 1872, he formally accepted responsibility for the undertaking. He wrote to Legentil and Rohault de Fleury thus:

You have considered from their true perspective the ills of our country. . . . The conspiracy against God and Christ has prevailed in a multitude of hearts and in punishment for an almost universal apostasy, society has been subjected to all the horrors of war with a victorious foreigner and an even more horrible war amongst the children of the same country. Having become, by our prevarication, rebels against heaven, we have fallen during our troubles into the abyss of anarchy. The land of France presents the terrifying image of a place where no order prevails, while the future offers still more terrors to come. . . . This temple, erected as a public act of contrition and reparation . . . will stand amongst us as a protest against other monuments and works of art erected for the glorification of vice and impiety. (Rohault de Fleury 1903, 27)

By July 1872, an ultraconservative Pope Pius IX, still awaiting his deliverance from captivity in the Vatican, formally endorsed the vow. An immense propaganda campaign unfolded, and the movement gathered momentum. By the end of the year, more than a million francs were promised, and all that remained was to translate the vow into its material, physical representation.

The first step was to choose a site. Legentil wanted to use the foundations of the still-to-be-completed Opera House, which he considered "a scandalous monument of extravagance, indecency and bad taste" (Jonquet n.d., 85–87). Rohault de Fleury's initial design of that building had, in 1860, been dropped at the insistence of Count Walewski ("who had the dubious distinction of being the illegitimate son of Napoleon I and the husband of Napoleon III's current favorite") (Pinkney 1958, 85–87). The design that replaced it (which exists today) most definitely qualified in the eyes of Legentil as a "monument to vice and impiety," and nothing could be more appropriate than to efface the memory of Empire by constructing the basilica on that spot. It probably escaped Legentil's attention that the communards had, in the same spirit, toppled the Vendôme Column.

By late October 1872, however, the archbishop had taken matters into his own hands and selected the heights of Montmartre because it was only from there that the symbolic domination of Paris could be assured. Since the land on that site was in part public property, the consent or active support of the government was necessary if it was to be acquired. The government was considering the construction of a military fortress on that spot. The archbishop pointed out, however, that a military fortress could well be very unpopular, while a fortification of the sort he was proposing might be less offensive and more sure. Thiers and his ministers, apparently persuaded that ideological protection might be preferable to military, encouraged the archbishop to pursue the matter formally. This the latter did in a letter of March 5, 1873 (Rohault de Fleury 1903, 75). He requested that the government pass a special law declaring the construction of the basilica a work of public utility. This would permit the laws of expropriation to be used to procure the site.

Such a law ran counter to a long-standing sentiment in favor of the separation of church and state. Yet conservative Catholic sentiment for the project was very strong. Thiers procrastinated, but his indecision was shortly rendered moot. The monarchists had decided that their time had come. On May 24, they drove Thiers from power and replaced him with the archconservative royalist Marshal MacMahon who, just two years before, had led the armed forces of Versailles in the bloody repression of the Commune. France was plunged, once more, into political ferment; a monarchist restoration seemed imminent.

The MacMahon government quickly reported out the law which then became part of its program to establish the rule of moral order in which those of wealth and privilege – who therefore had an active stake in the preservation of society – would, under the leadership of the king and in alliance with the authority of the church, have both the right and the duty to protect France from the social perils to which it had recently been exposed and thereby prevent the country falling into the abyss of anarchy. Large-scale demonstrations were mobilized by the church as part of a campaign to reestablish some sense of moral order. The largest of these demonstrations took place on June 29, 1873, at Paray-le-Monial. Thirty thousand pilgrims, including fifty members of the National Assembly, journeyed there to dedicate themselves publicly to the Sacred Heart (Dansette 1965, 340–45).

It was in this atmosphere that the committee formed to report on the law presented its findings on July 11 to the National Assembly, a quarter of whose members were adherents to the vow. The committee found that the proposal to build a basilica of expiation was unquestionably a work of public utility. It was right and proper to build such a monument on the heights of Montmartre for all to see, because it was there that the blood of martyrs – including those of yesterday – had flowed. It was necessary "to efface by this work of expiation, the crimes which have crowned our sorrows," and France, "which has suffered so much," must "call upon the protection and grace of Him who gives according to His will, defeat or victory" (Rohault de Fleury 1903, 88).

The debate which followed on July 22 and 23 in part revolved around technical-legal questions and the implications of the legislation for state-church relations. The intransigent Catholics recklessly proposed to go much further. They wanted the assembly to commit itself formally to a national undertaking which "was not solely a protestation against taking up of arms by the Commune, but a sign of appeasement and concord." That amendment was rejected. But the law passed with a handsome majority of 244 votes.

A lone dissenting voice in the debate came from a radical republican deputy from Paris:

When you think to establish on the commanding heights of Paris – the fount of free thought and revolution – a Catholic monument, what is in your thoughts? To make of it the triumph of the Church over revolution. Yes, that is what you want to extinguish – what you call the pestilence of revolution. What you want to revive is the Catholic faith, for you are at war with the spirit of modern times. . . . Well, I who know the sentiments of the population of Paris, I who am tainted by the revolutionary pestilence like them, I tell you that the population will be more scandalized than edified by the ostentation of your faith. . . . Far from edifying us, you push us towards free thought, towards revolution. When people see these manifestations of the partisans of monarchy, of the enemies of the Revolution, they will say to themselves that Catholicism and monarchy are unified, and in rejecting one they will reject the other. (Rohault de Fleury 1903, 88)

Armed with a law which yielded powers of expropriation, the committee formed to push the project through to fruition acquired the site atop the butte Montmartre. They collected the moneys promised and set about soliciting more so that the building could be as grand as the thought that lay behind it. A competition for the design of the basilica was set and judged. The building had to be imposing, consistent with Christian tradition, yet quite distinct from the "monuments to vice and impiety" built in the course of the Second Empire. Out of the seventy-eight designs submitted and exhibited to the public, that of the architect Abadie was selected. The grandeur of its domes, the purity of the white marble, and the unadorned simplicity of its detail impressed the committee – what, after all, could be more different from the flamboyance of that awful Opera House?

By the spring of 1875, all was ready for putting the first stone in place. But radical and republican Paris was not, apparently, repentant enough even yet. The archbishop complained that the building of Sacré-Coeur was being treated as a provocative act, as an attempt to inter the principles of 1789. And while, he said, he would not pray to revive those principles if they happened to become dead and buried, this view of things was giving rise to a deplorable polemic in which the archbishop found himself forced to participate. He issued a circular in which he expressed his astonishment at the hostility expressed toward the project on the part of "the enemies of religion." He found it intolerable that people dared to put a political interpretation upon thoughts derived only out of faith and piety. Politics, he assured his readers, "had been far, far from our inspirations; the work had been inspired, on the contrary, by a profound conviction that politics was powerless to deal with the ills of the country. The causes of these ills are moral and religious and the remedies must be of the same order." Besides, he went on, the work could not be construed as political because the aim of politics is to divide, "while our work has for its goal the union of all. . . . Social pacification is the end point of the work we are seeking to realize" (Rohault de Fleury 1903, 244).

The government, now clearly on the defensive, grew extremely nervous at the prospect of a grand opening ceremony which could be the occasion for an ugly confrontation. It counseled caution. The committee had to find a way to lay the first stone without being too provocative. The pope came to their aid and declared a day of dedication to the Sacred Heart for all Catholics everywhere. Behind that shelter, a much scaled-down ceremony to lay the first stone passed without incident. The construction was now under way. GALLIA POENITENS was taking shape in material symbolic form.

The forty years between the laying of the foundation stone and the final consecration of the basilica in 1919 were often troubled ones. Technical difficulties arose in the course of putting such a large structure on a hilltop rendered unstable by years of mining for gypsum. The cost of the structure increased dramatically, and, as enthusiasm for the cult of the Sacred Heart diminished somewhat, financial difficulties ensued. And the political controversy continued.

The committee in charge of the project had early decided upon a variety of stratagems to encourage the flow of contributions. Individuals and families could purchase a stone, and the visitor to Sacré-Coeur will see the names of many such inscribed upon the stones there. Different regions and organizations were encouraged to subscribe toward the construction of particular chapels. Members of the National Assembly, the army, the clergy, and the like all pooled their efforts in this way. Each particular chapel has its own significance.

Among the chapels in the crypt, for example, the visitor will find that of Jésus-Enseignant, which recalls, as Rohault de Fleury put it, "that one of the chief sins of France was the foolish invention of schooling without God" (Rohault de Fleury 1903, 269). Those who were on the losing side of the fierce battle to preserve the power of the church over education after 1871 put their money here. And next to that chapel, at the far end of the crypt, close to the line where the rue des Rosiers used to run, stands the Chapel to Jésus-Ouvrier.

That Catholic workers sought to contribute to the building of their own chapel was a matter for great rejoicing. It showed, wrote Legentil, the desire of workers "to protest against the fearsome impiety into which a large part of the working class is falling" as well as their determination to resist "the impious and truly infernal association which, in nearly all of Europe, makes of it its slave and victim" (Rohault de Fleury 1903, 165). The reference to the International Working Men's Association is unmistakable and understandable, since it was customary in bourgeois circles at that time to attribute the Commune, quite erroneously, to the nefarious influence of that "infernal" association. Yet, by a strange quirk of fate, which so often gives an ironic twist to history, the chapel to Jésus-Ouvrier stands almost exactly at the spot where ran the course of the "Calvary of Eugène Varlin." Thus it is that the basilica, erected on high in part to commemorate the blood of two recent martyrs of the right, commemorates unwittingly in its subterranean depths a martyr of the left.

Legentil's interpretation of all this was in fact somewhat awry. In the closing stages of the Commune, a young Catholic named Albert de Munn watched in dismay as the communards were led away to slaughter. Shocked, he fell to wondering what "legally constituted society had done for these people" and concluded that their ills had in large measure been visited upon them through the indifference of the affluent classes. In the spring of 1872, he went into the heart of hated Belleville and set up the first of his *Cercles-Ouvriers* (Dansette 1965, 356–58; Lepidis and Jacomin 1975, 271–72). This signaled the beginnings of a new kind of Catholicism in France – one which sought through social action to attend to the material as well as the spiritual needs of the workers. It was through organizations such as this, a far cry from the intransigent ultramontane Catholicism that ruled at the center of the movement for the Sacred Heart, that a small trickle of worker contributions began to flow toward the construction of a basilica on the hilltop of Montmartre.

The political difficulties mounted, however. France, finally armed with a republican constitution (largely because of the intransigence of the monarchists) was now in the grip of a modernization process fostered by easier communications, mass education, and industrial development. The country moved to accept the moderate form of republicanism and became bitterly disillusioned with the backward-looking monarchism that had dominated the National Assembly elected in 1871. In Paris the "unsubjugated" Bellevillois, and their neighbors in Montmartre and La Villette, began to reassert themselves rather more rapidly than Thiers had anticipated. As the demand

Fig. 17.   Sacré-Coeur as the enemy. (Reproduced, with permission, from the "Collection d'Affiches Politiques" of Alain Gesgon.)

for amnesty for the exiled communards became stronger in these quarters, so did the hatred of the basilica rising to their midst (fig. 17). The agitation against the project mounted.

On August 3, 1880, the matter came before the city council in the form of

Fig. 18. The Statue of Liberty in its Paris workshop

a proposal – a "colossal statue of *Liberty* will be placed on the summit of Montmartre, in front of the church of Sacré-Coeur, on land belonging to the city of Paris." The French republicans at that time had adopted the United States as a model society which functioned perfectly well without monarchism and other feudal trappings. As part of a campaign to drive home the point of this example, as well as to symbolize their own deep attachment to the principles of liberty, republicanism, and democracy, they were then raising funds to donate the Statue of Liberty that now stands in New York harbor (fig. 18). Why not, said the authors of this proposition, efface the sight of the hated Sacré-Coeur by a monument of similar order? (Ville de Paris, Conseil Municipal, *Procès Verbaux*, August 3, October 7 and December 2, 1880).

No matter what the claims to the contrary, they said, the basilica symbolized the intolerance and fanaticism of the right — it was an insult to civilization, antagonistic to the principles of modern times, an evocation of the past, and a stigma upon France as a whole. Parisians, seemingly bent on demonstrating their unrepentant attachment to the principles of 1789, were determined to efface what they felt was an expression of "Catholic fanaticism" by building exactly that kind of monument which the archbishop had previously characterized as a "glorification of vice and impiety."

By October 7 the city council had changed its tactics. Calling the basilica "an incessant provocation to civil war," the members decided by a majority of sixty-one to three to request the government to "rescind the law of public utility of 1873" and to use the land, which would revert to public ownership, for the construction of a work of truly national significance. Neatly sidestepping the problem of how those who had contributed to the construction of the basilica — which had hardly yet risen above its foundations — were to be indemnified, it passed along its proposal to the government. By the summer of 1882, the request was taken up in the Chamber of Deputies.

Archbishop Guibert had, once more, to take to the public defense of the work. He challenged what by now were familiar arguments against the basilica with familiar responses. He insisted that the work was not inspired by politics but by Christian and patriotic sentiments. To those who objected to the expiatory character of the work he simply replied that no one can ever afford to regard their country as infallible. As to the appropriateness of the cult of the Sacred Heart, he felt only those within the church had the right to judge. To those who portrayed the basilica as a provocation to civil war he replied: "Are civil wars and riots ever the product of our Christian temples? Are those who frequent our churches ever prone to excitations and revolts against the law? Do we find such people in the midst of disorders and violence which, from time to time, trouble the streets of our cities?" He went on to point out that while Napoleon I had sought to build a temple of peace at Montmartre, "it is we who are building, at last, the true temple of peace" (Rohault de Fleury 1905, 71–73).

He then considered the negative effects of stopping the construction. Such an action would profoundly wound Christian sentiment and prove divisive. It would surely be a bad precedent, he said (blithely ignoring the precedent set by the law of 1873 itself), if religious undertakings of this sort were to be subject to the political whims of the government of the day. And then there was the complex problem of compensation not only for the contributors but for the work already done. Finally, he appealed to the fact that the work was giving employment to six hundred families – to deprive "that part of Paris of such a major source of employment would be inhuman indeed."

The Parisian representatives in the Chamber of Deputies, which, by 1882, was dominated by reformist republicans such as Gambetta (from Belleville) and Clemenceau (from Montmartre), were not impressed by these arguments. The debate was heated and passionate. The government for its part declared itself unalterably opposed to the law of 1873 but was equally opposed to rescinding the law, since this would entail paying out more than twelve million francs in indemnities to the church. In an effort to defuse the evident anger from the left, the minister went on to remark that by rescinding the law, the archbishop would be relieved of the obligation to complete what was proving to be a most arduous undertaking at the same time as it would provide the church with millions of francs to pursue works of propaganda which might be "infinitely more efficacious than that to which the sponsors of the present motion are objecting."

The radical republicans were not about to regard Sacré-Coeur in the shape of a white elephant, however. Nor were they inclined to pay compensation. They were determined to do away with what they felt was an odious manifestation of pious clericalism and to put in its place a monument to liberty of thought. They put the blame for the civil war squarely on the shoulders of the monarchists and their intransigent Catholic allies.

Clemenceau rose to state the radical case. He declared the law of 1873 an insult, an act of a National Assembly which had sought to impose the cult of the Sacred Heart on France because "we fought and still continue to fight for human rights, for having made the French Revolution." The law was the product of clerical reaction, an attempt to stigmatize revolutionary France, "to condemn us to ask pardon of the Church for our ceaseless struggle to prevail over it in order to establish the principles of liberty, equality and fraternity." We must, he declared, respond to a political act by a political act. Not to do so would be to leave France under the intolerable invocation of the Sacred Heart (Rohault de Fleury 1905, 71 et seq.).

With impassioned oratory such as this, Clemenceau fanned the flames of anticlerical sentiment. The chamber voted to rescind the law of 1873 by a majority of 261 votes to 199. It appeared that the basilica, the walls of which were as yet hardly risen above their foundations, was to come tumbling down.

The basilica was saved by a technicality. The law was passed too late in the session to meet all the formal requirements for promulgation. The government, genuinely fearful of the costs and liabilities involved, quietly worked to prevent the reintroduction of the motion into a chamber which, in the next session, moved on to consider matters of much greater weight and moment. The Parisian republicans had gained a symbolic but Pyrrhic parliamentary victory. A relieved archbishop pressed on with the work.

Yet somehow the matter would not die. In February 1897, the motion was reintroduced (Lesourd 1973, 224–25). Anticlerical republicanism had by then made great progress, as had the working-class movement in the form of a vigorous and growing socialist party. But the construction atop the hill had likewise progressed. The interior of the basilica had been inaugurated and opened for worship in 1891, and the great dome was well on the way to completion (the cross which surmounts it was formally blessed in 1899). Although the basilica was still viewed as a "provocation to civil war," the prospect for dismantling such a vast work was by now quite daunting. And this time it was none other than Albert de Munn who defended the basilica in the name of a Catholicism that had, by then, seen the virtue of separating its fate from that of a fading monarchist cause. The church was beginning to learn a lesson, and the cult of the Sacred Heart began to acquire a new meaning in response to a changing social situation. By 1899, a more reform-minded pope dedicated the cult to the ideal of harmony among the races, social justice, and conciliation.

But the socialist deputies were not impressed by what they saw as maneuvers of cooptation. They pressed home their case to bring down the hated symbol, even though almost complete, and even though such an act would entail indemnifying eight million subscribers to the tune of thirty million francs. But the majority in the chamber blanched at such a prospect. The motion was rejected by 322 to 196.

This was to be the last time the building was threatened by official action. With the dome completed in 1899, attention switched to the building of the campanile, which was finally finished in 1912. By the spring of 1914, all was ready and the official consecration set for October 17. But war with Germany intervened. Only at the end of that bloody conflict was the basilica finally consecrated. A victorious France – led by the fiery oratory of Clemenceau – joyfully celebrated the consecration of a monument conceived of in the course of a losing war with Germany a generation before. GALLIA POENITENS at last brought its rewards.

Muted echoes of this tortured history can still be heard. In February 1971, for example, demonstrators pursued by police took refuge in the basilica. Firmly entrenched there, they called upon their radical comrades to join them in occupying a church "built upon the bodies of communards in order to efface the memory of that red flag that had for too long floated over Paris." The myth of the incendiaries immediately broke loose from its ancient moorings, and an evidently panicked rector summoned the police into the basilica to prevent the conflagration. The "reds" were chased from the church amid scenes of great brutality. Thus was the centennial of the Paris Commune celebrated on that spot.

And as a coda to that incident, a bomb exploded in the basilica in 1976, causing quite extensive damage to one of the domes. On that day, it was said, the visitor to the cemetery of Père Lachaise would have seen a single red rose on August Blanqui's grave.

Rohault de Fleury had desperately wanted to "place a cradle where [others] had thought to dig a grave." But the visitor who looks at the mausoleum-like structure that is Sacré-Coeur might well wonder what it is that is interred there. The spirit of 1789? The sins of France? The alliance between intransigent Catholicism and reactionary monarchism? The blood of martyrs like Lecomte and Clément Thomas? Or that of Eugène Varlin and the twenty thousand or so communards mercilessly slaughtered along with him?

The building hides its secrets in sepulchral silence. Only the living, cognizant of this history, who understand the principles of those who struggled for and against the embellishment of that spot, can truly disinter the mysteries that lie entombed there and thereby rescue that rich experience from the deathly silence of the tomb and transform it into the noisy beginnings of the cradle.

8

The Urbanization of
Consciousness

Capitalist urbanization occurs within the confines of the community of money, is framed by the concrete abstractions of space and time, and internalizes all the vigor and turbulence of the circulation of capital under the ambiguous and often shaky surveillance of the state. A city is an agglomeration of productive forces built by labor employed within a temporal process of circulation of capital. It is nourished out of the metabolism of capitalist production for exchange on the world market and supported out of a highly sophisticated system of production and distribution organized within its confines. It is populated by individuals who reproduce themselves using money incomes earned off the circulation of capital (wages and profits) or its derivative revenues (rents, taxes, interest, merchant's profits, payments for services). The city is ruled by a particular coalition of class forces, segmented into distinctive communities of social reproduction, and organized as a discontinuous but spatially contiguous labor market within which certain distinctive quantities and qualities of labor power may be found.

The city is the high point of human achievement, objectifying the most sophisticated knowledge in a physical landscape of extraordinary complexity, power, and splendor at the same time as it brings together social forces capable of the most amazing sociotechnical and political innovation. But it is also the site of squalid human failure, the lightning rod of the profoundest human discontents, and the arena of social and political conflict. It is a place of mystery, the site of the unexpected, full of agitations and ferments, of multiple liberties, opportunities, and alienations; of passions and repressions; of cosmopolitanism and extreme parochialisms; of violence, innovation, and reaction. The capitalist city is the arena of the most intense social and political confusions at the same time as it is a monumental testimony to and a moving force within the dialectics of capitalism's uneven development.

How to penetrate the mystery, unravel the confusions, and grasp the contradictions? The question is important for two reasons. Firstly, we know, as Lefebvre puts it, that capitalism has survived into the twentieth century through the production of space and that it has been an increasingly urbanized space that has been produced. A study of the urban process tells us much, therefore, about the mechanisms of capitalism's successful self-reproduction. Secondly, increasing urbanization makes this the primary level at which individuals experience, live out, and react to the changes going on around them. To dissect the urban process in all of its fullness is to lay bare the roots of consciousness formation in the material realities of daily life. It is out of the complexities and perplexities of this experience that we build elementary understandings of the meanings of space and time; of social power and its legitimations; of forms of domination and social interaction; of the relation to nature through production and consumption; and of human nature, civil society, and political life.

Curious ways of thinking, seeing and acting arise out of the confusions of that experience. These cannot be interpreted directly by appeal to polarized or even complex class structures. Nor can they be dismissed as false. I shall, however, insist that they are fetishistic; common sense representations of daily experience obscure inner meanings, even though the surface appearance to which they respond is real enough. If it appears that decaying housing produces crime and that the automobile produces the suburb, then we have to recognize the material correlations between such things, even though the social forces that produce them remain hidden. And for purposes of daily life it is often sufficient and even necessary to accept the surface appearances as the basis for action. To live in the suburbs without a car is as foolish as strolling in a slum oblivious of the higher probability of criminal behavior. The consciousness produced by a fetishistic reading of daily urban life is not bourgeois or capitalistic. It exists on a quite different plane. Failure to demystify it can, however, lead to actions fraught with all manner of unintended consequences. Avid defenders of capitalism can undermine what they most desire to defend, while socialists can end up supporting that which they decry.

Within that confusion, all kinds of other sentiments, illusions, and distortions can flourish. The ferment of discontent and opposition, of understandable and entirely reasonable misrepresentations, of unintended consequences, is always part of the urban brew. Therein lies an extraordinary though often latent energy for social transformation. Capitalist urbanization gives rise to forces that, once put in place and set in motion, can just as easily threaten as support the perpetuation of capitalism. We have, in short, to confront the urbanization of consciousness as a key political problem.

It is the virtue of thinkers like Simmel, Wirth, and Sennett to address that problem directly rather than leaving it, as do Marx, Weber and Durkheim, for example, on the periphery of their thought. Their defect is that they get so enmeshed in surface appearances that either they fail to penetrate the fetishisms or they produce partial rather than integrated interpretations. Simmel (1971), in his famous essay, "The Metropolis and Mental Life," could not get much further than the alienated individualism and limited coordinations of action in space and time. Wirth (1964), though more complex, could not free himself from the ecological presuppositions of the Chicago school. Compared to that, the peripheral vision of a Marx or a Weber at least provides a grounding for interpretation in some overall conception of civil society and its mode of production or organization. The problem is to build into the Marxian perspective the kinds of detailed sophistication that writers like Simmel and Wirth achieved. The urbanization of consciousness has to be understood in relation to the urbanization of capital.

The strategy I propose for attacking that question is simple enough — perhaps overly so. I begin with five primary loci of power and consciousness formation. Individualism attaches to money uses in freely functioning markets. Class under capitalism reflects the buying and selling of labor power and the social relations embodied in the sociotechnical conditions of production under conditions of surplus value extraction. Community, as we shall see, is a highly ambiguous notion that nevertheless plays a fundamental role in terms of the reproduction of labor power, the circulation of revenues, and the geography of capital accumulation. The state exists as a center of authority and as an apparatus through which political-economic power is exercised in a territory with some degree of popular legitimacy. The family (to which I should add all other forms of domestic household economy), finally, has a profound effect upon ways of thought and action simply by virtue of its function as the primary site of social support and of reproduction activities such as child-rearing.

I now want to modify this conception in two very important ways. First of all, no one locus of power and consciousness formation in this nominalist schema can be understood independently of the urbanization of capital; nor can the latter be understood without the former. The task for historical materialist interpretation of the urban process is, therefore, to examine how the ways of seeing, thinking and acting produced through the inter-relations between individualism, class, community, state, and family affect the paths and qualities of capitalist urbanization that in turn feed back to alter our conceptions and our actions. Only in that way can we understand the urbanizing dynamic through which capitalism survives, in spite of all of its internal contradictions, as a viable mode of production and consumption.

How is an urbanized consciousness produced, and with what political effects? Consider, firstly, the relation between money and capital, the communities of which intersect to define much of what the urbanization process and the urban experience are about. Money, I showed in chapter 6, functions as a concrete abstraction, imposing external and homogeneous measures of value on all aspects of human life, reducing infinite diversity to a single comparable dimension, and masking subjective human relations by objective market exchanges. The achievement of urbanization, as Simmel so correctly observes, rests on an increasing domination of the cash nexus over other kinds of human interactions and as such promotes exactly that kind of alienated individualism that Marx and Engels highlight in the *Communist Manifesto*. Money used as capital, however, subsumes all production processes as well as labor and commodity markets under a single, class-bound, profit-seeking logic. Marx shows us that such a mode of production has to expand, that it must simultaneously engage in continuous revolutions in productive forces and in the social relations of production through reorganizations of the division of labor. Here lies much of the dynamic force that produces vast, high-density urbanization and heterogeneity of the sort that Wirth describes.

Money and capital therefore confront us as double alienations, the compounding of which should surely produce energy of revolt sufficient to dispose quickly of both. Yet the alienations can also confound and confuse each other. Class-bound political movements against the power of capital hesitate or fail if they appear to threaten real and cherished, though necessarily limited liberties given by possession of money in the marketplace. Even the poorest person can relish the kind of liberty that even the minutest amount of money power can give. Workers may even connive or accede to their own exploitation in production in return for increased money power that gives them greater market freedoms and greater ability to control a portion of their own space (through home or car ownership) and their own time (so-called "free" time).

The sense of class derived out of the experience of earning money runs up against the experience of limited but important individual freedom in the spending of that money. The urban condition is typically one in which that clash looms large. The liberty and diversity of choice that come with the possession of money in the city's market place provides a locus for experience, thought and action very different indeed from that which attaches to the massing of a proletariat in the work places of a capitalist city. The separation of place of residence from place of work symbolizes the break as does the shift of a role from a seller of labor power to buyer of commodities. Since every effort is made to conceal the history of commodities behind the mask of fetishism (advertising, for example, rarely indicates any truth as to how commodities are produced) the separation between the two worlds of production and consumption becomes complete. Capitalists caught in the throes of violent and often debilitating class struggle have learned to use these confusions and separations creatively. It was the genius of Fordism and of the New Deal (with its Keynesian strategies of state management and its support for trade union consciousness) to offer greater market freedoms in return for diminished class struggle in production. The effect as we saw in chapter 1, was to change the face of capitalist urbanization dramatically and to likewise change the relations between individualism, class, community, family, and the state, in urban contexts.

Consider, secondly, the consciousness of community. The communities of money and capital are communities without propinquity in the broadest sense. The particular kinds of communities we call cities, towns, or even neighborhoods are in contrast, definite places constructed by a way of definite socioeconomic and political process (see, for example, chapter 9).

From the standpoint of the "communities" of money and capital, such places are no more than relative spaces to be built up, torn down, or abandoned as profitability dictates. But from the standpoint of the people who live there, such places may be the focus of particular loyalties. We see again conflicting material bases for consciousness formation and political action. Individuals can internalize both aspects. A pensioner might want maximum return on pension fund investments but struggle against the abandonment of his or her community that the crass logic of profit maximization might imply.

That tension can be resolved in ways advantageous to capital. In chapter 5 I showed how local "growth machines" and ruling class alliances, attempt to attract capitalist development and to defend a local economy against unemployment and the devaluation of assets. This defines much of what local politics is about. Interurban competition – a process in which place-bound loyalty to community and community boosterism has an important role – helps to structure the uneven geographical development of capitalism in ways conducive to overall accumulation. The efficient geographical articulation of capitalism depends on innumerable communities evolving corporatist strategies toward capitalist development. But in so doing, cities have to advertise and sell themselves as prime locations for production, consumption and command and control functions. The production of an urban image, through, for example, the organization of spectacles of the sort described in chapter 9, becomes an important facet of interurban competition at the same time as it becomes a means to rally potentially alienated populations to a common cause.

Images of knowable and affective communities can also be marketed as commodities. That technique is often used in association with speculative housing development. Examples can be found as long ago as the seventeenth century and abound in the nineteenth century (cf. Warner's 1962 study of Boston and Dyos's 1961 study of Camberwell). But the phenomenon became more general after 1945. The Keynesian style of urbanization depended upon the strong mobilization of the spirit of consumer sovereignty in an economy where purchasing power was broadly though unevenly distributed among households. The sovereignty, though fetishistic, was not illusory. It allowed individuals to mobilize all kinds of marks of distinction through differentiations in consumption as a response to the bland universalisms of money (cf. Simmell 1978) above, chapter 6). New kinds of communities could be constructed, packaged, and sold in a society where who you were seemed to depend more and more on how money was spent rather than on how it was earned. Living spaces could be made to represent status, position, and prestige in ways that made Weberian concepts of consumption classes look legitimate. The search to produce and control symbolic capital (see chapter 9) has become an even more salient feature in the organization of urban life in recent years with movements like gentrification, post-modernism and urban revitalization gaining pace. Furthermore, the degraded relation to nature in production has increasingly been supplanted by a relation to nature packaged as a consumption artifact. Suburbanization typically promised access both to nature and to community, each packaged as a commodity (Walker 1981).

None of this was necessarily antagonistic to monetized individualism or to traditional forms of organization of household economies and family life. The desire to enhance or preserve the value of personal property and access to life chances suggests economically rational forms of community participation for individuals and households (Olson 1965). But the outcome is a particular kind of community, totally subservient to monetized individualism and family property relations. Such communities could also function as breeding grounds for different types of labor power and hence as sites of basic processes of class reproduction (see chapter 4).

Community, it transpired, could be constructed in ways entirely consistent with capital accumulation. Demand-side urbanization meant a shift in relations. Greater emphasis was put upon the spatial division of consumption relative to the spatial division of labor so as to generate the surface appearance of consumption classes and status groupings (identified by life-style or mere position in social space) as opposed to class definitions achieved in the realm of production. The social spaces of distraction and display became as vital to urban culture as the spaces of working and living. Social competition with respect to life-style and command over space, always important for upper segments of the bourgeoisie, became more and more important within the mass culture of urbanization, sometimes even masking the role of community in processes of class reproduction. It also meant new relations to the state, the individual, and the family in a society where consumer sovereignty was mobilized to ensure consumption for consumption's sake to match capitalism's incessant drive toward production for production's sake and accumulation for accumulation's sake. The qualities of the urban experience and the conditions for consciousness formation shifted accordingly, as did the whole dynamic of capitalist urbanization.

Yet it is also within these spaces that active community building can take place in ways deeply antagonistic to the individualism of money, to the profit-seeking and class-bound logic of capital circulation, and even to particular views of the family and the state. Utopian movements (anarchist, feminist, socialist, ecological) abound, as do religious attempts to define an alternative sense of community. Urban uprisings like the Paris Commune, the Watts and Detroit rebellions of the 1960s, and the vast swathe of urban social protest movements (Castells 1983) testify to the powerful urge to escape the dominations of money power, capital, and a repressive state. Such movements are not confined to the underprivileged either. As consumers, even upper echelons of the bourgeoisie may be forced to seek collective protection against the ravages of some greedy developer. Peculiar kinds of consumer socialism, using local government power to check growth machine politics and the destruction of the environment, can take root in even the most affluent of areas (like Santa Monica or Santa Cruz). Consumer sovereignty, if taken seriously, presupposes, after all, a certain popular empowerment to shape the qualities of life directly and to drive beyond the pathologies of urban anonymity, monetized individualism, a degraded relation to nature, and profit maximization. But that also means the creation or imposition of a culture of community solidarity and bonding that goes far beyond that tolerable to pure individualism or the pure logic of capital accumulation. The seeds of conflict then are scattered across the social landscape.

Alternative communities find it hard, if not impossible, to survive as autonomous entities. They cannot seal themselves off from the rest of the world (though some try by moving to remote regions). It is hard to keep the "dissolving effects" of monetization at bay. The community domination of a particular place often entails the imposition of a repressive rigidity in the functioning of social relations and moral codes. There is, therefore, much that is repressive about this sort of community (Sennet 1970). New England townships may have been models of community, but they were also bastions of intolerance. Compared to that, the dissolving effects of money and the anonymity of urban life may appear as welcome relief; and the incoherencies of entrepreneurial capitalism, positively stimulating.

The construction of community within the frame of capitalist urbanization contains a tension. Movements against the power of concrete abstractions like money, capital, space and time may spiral into fierce struggles to create an alternative kind of community (see chapter 6). But there are also processes of community construction and community empowerment that integrate only too well into the dynamics of capital accumulation through the production of space. How the tension between these two dimensions of community formation is resolved cannot be exactly predicted in advance, but the historical record indicates how frequently they intersect. The capitalist selling of community as an opportunity for self-realization sparks alternative movements, while the latter can be coopted and used for the selling of community and proximity to nature as consumption goods. All kinds of intermediate mixes are possible. A community may be organized as a sophisticated coping mechanism that wards off the worst aspects of class domination and alienated individualism but in so doing merely makes the domination of money and capital more acceptable. But capitalists, in seeking to promote community for exactly such reasons, can also help create centers of guerrilla warfare against their own interests. Community, therefore, has always to be interpreted as a specific resolution of this underlying tension worked out in the context of relations to the family, the individual, class, and the state, under specific conditions of urbanization.

The family (or household economy) is a very distinctive locus of power and consciousness formation. The intimacy and affectivity of social relations and the importance of gender and child-rearing make for very special qualities of daily experience. The problem has been to unravel its relations to the other loci of consciousness formation. Engels (1942) argued, for example, that the family as a reproductive unit (as well as its internal structure) could be understood only through its relation to a dominant mode of production as well as to forms of state power. Marx (1967, 490) even went so far as to predict the rise of less patriarchal and more egalitarian family forms through industrialization and the increasing participation of women in the labor force. Simmel more closely replicated the argument in the *Communist Manifesto* that the family disintegrated with monetization and became entirely subservient to the individualism of bourgeois interests. But such arguments are controversial and still not resolved.

The rise of the family as an economic unit independent of community predates the rise of capitalism though not of monetization or, probably, of private property relations. It was later characterized by increasing privatization and the insulation of individuals (particularly children) from external influences, making reliance on the protective powers of community even less pressing. The transition of "family production economies" into "family wage economies" occurred with capitalist industrialization and urbanization, but was nowhere near as disruptive of traditional relations as Marx or Engels thought (Tilly and Scott 1978, 227–32). Indeed, the family, with some internal adjustment, managed to preserve itself as an institution at the same time as it played a vital role in the adaptation of individuals to conditions of wage labor and the money calculus of urban life (Tilly and Scott 1978; Hareven 1982; Sennett 1970; Handlin 1951). But it has been subject to considerable external pressure. While it may protect individuals against the alienations of money, it is perpetually threatened by the individualism that money power promotes (arguments over money still being a primary cause of family break-up). It becomes an object of bourgeois and state surveillance (Donzelot 1977) precisely because its insulated environment can become a breeding ground for all kinds of social relations antagonistic to money and to capital. Paradoxically, the family through its protections helps mollify such antagonisms, making for a most interesting intersection with the functions of community. To the degree that the latter provides a framework for coping, adaptation, and control, so the emphasis upon the family may diminish. But the more the capitalist form of community prevails (consistent with accumulation and monetized individualism), the more important the family may become as a protective milieu outside of the cold calculus of profit and the class alienations of wage labor. The family can also substitute for community as a primary agent for the reproduction of differentiated labor power and hence of basic class relations. Family authority structures may also be imported into and replicated within the organization of the labor process, thus making family relations a vehicle for class domination. But, again, it is by no means necessarily a passive agent in this regard. Family ambition helps shape social space at the same time as it can be an agent of transformation of class and employment structures.

Though the family may persist as a vital institution, its meanings and functions shift in relation to changing currents within the urbanization of capital. Tilly and Scott (1978), for example, discern a further shift, most pronounced since World War II, toward a "family consumer economy" specializing in reproduction and consumption. Pahl (1984) shows, however, that families have increasingly used that consumption power not only to protect and command space (through home and car ownership) but also to create new forms of household production, using capital equipment and raw materials purchased from the market but arranged according to their own personal tastes, divisions of labor, and temporal rhythms of production. The same phenomenon — the resurgence of household production systems — can be observed at the lower end of the social scale where it has, however, a quite different meaning; households lacking market power are forced to household production as a pure strategy for survival (Redclift and Mingiolne 1985).

The family therefore exists as an island of relative autonomy within a sea of objective bondage, perpetually adapting to the shifting currents of capitalist urbanization through its relations to individualism, community, class, and the state. It provides a haven to which individuals can withdraw from the complexities and dangers of urban life or from which they can selectively sample its pleasures and opportunities. But it is a haven perpetually buffeted by external forces – the loss of earning power through unemployment, squabbles over money rights, the sheer attractions of monetized individualism compared to patterns of familial repression, and the need to orient child-rearing practices to labor market ends are major sources of disruption in family life. The consciousness created behind bolted and barred doors tends, of course, to be inward looking and often indifferent to a wider world. It may encourage withdrawal from struggles to control money, space, and time as sources of social power through community or class action. From this standpoint the family appears to pose no threat to capitalism. But the consciousness forged out of affective family relations can be dangerous if it spills outward as a basis for moral judgment of all aspects of civil society. How to square the values and virtues of family life with the destructive force of money and capital is ever an interesting conundrum for bourgeois ideology. A common difficulty on both sides of the Atlantic in recent years has been to reconcile government policies favorable in individualism and entrepreneurialism with the protection of family virtues.

Consider, finally, the state as a power base and locus of consciousness formation. In the context of the communities of money and capital, the legitimacy of the state has to rest on its ability to define a public interest over and above privatism (individualistic or familial), class struggle, and conflictual community interests. It has to provide a basic framework of institutions backed by sufficient authority to resolve conflicts, impose collective judgments, pursue collective courses of action, and defend civil society as a whole from external assault and internal disintegration. The gains from its interventions are real enough – all the way from mundane matters of sewage disposal and the regulation of traffic flow to more general procedures for countering market failure, articulating collective class interests, protecting against abuses (community intolerance, excessive exploitation, the abuse of family authority), and arbitrating between warring factions. The gains provide a material basis for legitimate pride in and loyalty to the local or national state and to its symbols and representatives. The state loses legitimacy when it becomes or is seen to become captive to some particular individual, community, or class interest, or so totally inefficient as to yield no effective gains to anyone. I say "seen to become" because that state has at its disposal all manner of means for promoting and sustaining its legitimacy through control over information flow and outright propaganda, none of which is innocent in relation to consciousness formation. Furthermore, particular interests form within the state apparatus. The bearers of the scientific, technical, and managerial expertise that the state relies upon may use the state apparatus as a vehicle to express their power and so project a bureaucratic-managerial and technocratic consciousness onto the whole of civil society in the name of the public interest. The techniques, ideologies, and practices of "urban managerialism" are, many rightly argue, fundamental to understanding the contemporary urban process (Pahl 1977; Saunders 1981). The state, therefore, is not only a focus of place-bound loyalties but also an apparatus that propagates specific ways of thinking and acting.

But the state ought not to be viewed too statically, as a perpetual and unchanging locus of authority independent of the elements of individualism, class, family and community. State practices and policies have to adapt to shifting relations between these other loci. They must also react to the changing dynamic of capitalist development and urbanization. The class alliances that form around issues of urban governance, for example, are fluid in their composition and by no means confine their field of action to formal channels. Indeed, the latter are often institutionalizations of long-established practices of collective decision making on the part of some ruling-class alliance (see chapter 5). The history of local government reform movements, of annexations and interjurisdictional coordinations, illustrates how capitalism's urban dynamic is matched by transformations in political and administrative practices. Even the rise of professionalism (political and administrative) and of managerial and technocratic modes of thought can be seen as both a response to and a moving force in the drive to find rational coordinations for the uses of money, space, time, and capital under increasingly chaotic conditions of capitalist urbanization. When the paths of capital circulation are dominated by the pure individualism of money and the traditional solidarity of communities almost totally dissolves, then a powerful state apparatus becomes essential to the proper management of capitalist urbanization. Conversely, conditions may arise in which a ruling class alliance, faced with burdensome state expenditures, will try to force certain kinds of social provision back into the frameworks of family and community (as, for example, with mental health care in recent years). But even then, the political process of class alliance formation within the urban region take precedence over the particular forms of state power through which that alliance may exercise its influence. When an urban region functions as a competitive unit within the uneven geographical development

The Urban Experience

of capitalism, it necessarily deploys a mix of informal mechanisms (coordinated by such groups as a local chamber of commerce or a businessmen's round table) and local state powers (tax breaks and infrastructural investment). The celebrated public-private partnership, rather than pure urban managerialism, is a basic guiding force in the urbanization of capital.

But state action can also be antagonistic to individualism, the family, community, and capital. The dominant rationality embodied in the state apparatus conflicts with the typical modes of behavior and action emanating from other loci. It was, after all, in the name of the public interest that Haussmann reorganized the interior space of Paris only to stir up a hornet's nest of privatistic responses. It was in the name of that same rationality that Robert Moses took the "meat-axe" to Brooklyn in the 1960s, stirring up, as did many a highway planner, severe community opposition to highway construction through traditional communities. Rational urban planning, even of the socialist variety, often entails the same authoritarianism. A too closed coalition between the technocratic rationalism of a managerial elite and the authoritarianism of state power can undermine the legitimacy of both. Whether or not the state can continue to impose its will depends on the strength of the class alliance behind it and the relative power of opposing forces. While the state has a monopoly over institutionalized violence, it is vulnerable to the power of money and capital, as well as to movements of revulsion and revolt centered in the family, the community, or the underprivileged classes. Struggles for control over the state apparatus are therefore paralleled by struggles over what kind of rational action the state is supposed to pursue and what kind of politics the state is supposed to represent and project. The state is both the hope and the despair not only of revolutionary movements (which view it either as the pinnacle of power to be scaled or as the fount of all evil to be destroyed) but of all segments of society, no matter of what political persuasion.

I propose, then, to view the individualism of money, the class relations of capital, the confusions of community, the contested politics and legitimacy of the state and the partially protected domain of the family as the primary material power bases of social life under capitalism. Through our daily experiences of these bases we generate a matrix of conceptions, understandings and predispositions for action which in turn serve to construct the conditions which prevail in each domain. If that matrix tends to support and reinforce the existing order, then we here find a powerful means whereby historical transitions become broadly legislated by historical circumstances rather than by the conscious collective action of individuals seeking to create new social forms.

Paradoxically, such historical determination in no way vitiates the importance of individual freedom and choice. Indeed, as Bourdieu (1977, 79) suggests, "it is because subjects do not, strictly speaking, know what they are doing that what they do has more meaning than they know." To begin with, the five material bases can be so diversely constructed and so differently used and combined in the course of "common sense" actions that social life possesses an almost limitless terrain for experience. Angered by a family feud, for example, an individual can call in the police, spend the family savings on a drunken spree, work twice as hard as normal, or compensate by resorting to the sociality of community. The very next day, that same individual, in trouble with the police, might invoke class privileges or rally community and family to his or her cause. Through the infinite variety of such practices individuals become adjusted and contribute to broader processes of historical replication and transformation of which they are not aware. We all help to build a city and its way of life through our actions without necessarily grasping what the city as a whole is or should be about. This suggests that there is a "hidden hand" of history around which an immense diversity of freely undertaken practices and common sense notions necessarily coalesce.

The unstable contradictions within each base together with the unpredictable manner in which the power sources get combined, guarantee different outcomes from essentially similar objectives. Individuals and groups, furthermore, may construct the different power bases quite differently (see chapter 9) and then use the power so accumulated for very special purposes. Women, for example, may seek to build community of a very special sort and use community for collective purposes which are quite different from those typically pursued by men. Minorities of all sorts can combine the different possibilities in ways that reflect their own wants and needs, utopian or even nihilistic desires. Social action produces quite disparate life styles, cultural forms, political practices and socio-economic conditions out of a quite limited set of possibilities. This lends an air of unpredictability to paths of social change.

This style of analysis has the virtue of helping us understand the confusion of urban and social political movements under capitalism without conceding their total lawlessness. It helps explain the peculiar mix of satisfactions and disappointments; of fragmented ideologies and states of consciousness; the curious cross-cutting of labor struggles, community struggles, and struggles around the state apparatus or the family; and the seeming withdrawal of individuals and families from matters of broader social concern. It helps put in perspective the active moments of sudden participation and revolutionary fervor and of equally sudden fading and collapse of political movements that seemed to have such a broad and solid base. It also helps in understanding the often extraordinary dissonance between opinions expressed and actions taken.

The Paris Commune (see chapter 6 and *Consciousness and the Urban Experience*, chapter 3) illustrates the confusions. The egalitarian individualism of the radical petite bourgeoisie (with its money concerns) was certainly in evidence, but then so was the quest for community outside of the rule of money and capital. A powerful wing of the workers' movement looked to the free association of producers and consumers through mutual cooperation and federalism as the path to social progress, and many within the women's movement concurred because they sought ways fundamentally to modify the family economy. A different kind of class consciousness, internationalist and seeking to combat the community of capital by building a class movement with a universal perspective was particularly evident within the new leadership of the Paris branch of Working Men's International Association. Republican revolutionaries, Jacobin by tradition, looked to a strong centralized state as the prime lever of social and political liberty, while the Blanquists viewed Paris as the revolutionary hearth from which revolution of the greatest purity would diffuse and liberate France from its capitalist and bourgeois chains. Moderate republicans, in contrast, simply wanted self-governance for Paris, the right to command a local state apparatus that had so much command over them. Many women (and some men) saw the Commune as an occasion to build new kinds of family relationships based on free union and cooperative forms of household production and mutualist forms of exchange. And traditional family loyalties brought men and women together on the same barricades.

The alliance of forces ran the gamut from the rank individualism of money, self-government, household autonomy under conditions of equality between the sexes, the self-management of production and consumption in relation to human need rather than profit, and decentralized and centralized versions of revolutionary socialism, to the purest statism possible. Under such conditions the political confusions of the Commune are understandable. Should the Commune respect the spaces of private property in both production and consumption as well as money power (the Bank of France) as counterweights to the absolutism of state power? Should it use arbitrary police power to ensure discipline and counter subversion? Should it centralize or decentralize authority — and if so, how? That all died on the same barricades can be explained only by the ways in which different identities and states of consciousness fused in a given historical moment into a political movement to defend a particular space against those who represented the power of money and the power of capital unalloyed. Yet, in the iconography of the Commune, it is all too frequently forgotten that this was a distinctively urban event. Its multidimensionality can be comprehended only in terms of the urbanized consciousness that it expressed.

Academics, though not prone to die on barricades, exhibit similar confusions. Neoclassical economists privilege entrepreneurial and consumer sovereignties based on the individualism of money; Marxists, the productive forces and class relations necessary to the extraction of surplus value; Weberians, class relations constructed out of market behaviors, urban managerialism, and the organization of the local state; feminists, patriarchy, family, and women at work; representatives of the Chicago school, the ecology of communities in space; and so on. Each particular perspective tells its own particular truth. Yet they scarcely touch each other and they come together on the intellectual barricades with about the same frequency as urban uprisings like the Paris Commune. The intellectual fragmentations of academia appear as tragic reflections of the confusions of an urbanized consciousness; they reflect surface appearances, do little to elucidate inner meanings and connections, and do much to sustain the confusions by replicating them in learned terms.

Does this mean that we have to abandon Marx for some eclectic mix of theoretical perspectives? I think not. By appropriate use of the marxian meta-theory we can understand the links between divergent theoretical concerns and come to grips with the hidden historical hand within the confusions of social change. There are three steps towards fulfillment of that objective. The first, already sketched in, looks at some simple generative principles that underlie the diversity. The five material bases of power (and their contradictions) identify the sources of social change. The second considers how the circulation of capital constructs the different power bases, the interrelations between them and the consciousness that flows therefrom in specific ways. In the third step, we extend the Marxian theory to encompass the production of space and of urbanization and show how those processes in turn affect the circulation of capital as well as the powers which attach to individualism, class, community, family, and state. The general import is that ways of thinking and doing tend to so order capacities and motivations as to limit the range, though not the diversity, of social action. Such limits, exceeded only at moments of breakdown and revolution, constrain the possibilities to change history according to conscious design precisely because consciousness can express only what practical experience teaches.

Consider, first, how the circulation of capital impinges upon the divergent power bases. The circulation of capital can be described as a series of transitions of the following sort: money is used to buy commodities (labor power and means of production), and these are combined in production to create a new commodity that is sold on the market for the original money plus a profit. Schematically, we can depict the circulation of capital thus:

$$M \to C \begin{cases} LP \\ MP \end{cases} \dots P \dots C' \to M + \triangle m \to \text{etc.}$$

Most of the goods which support our daily consumption are produced in this way. A capitalist economy is an aggregate made up innumerable and intersecting circulation processes of this type. From Marx, we know that a capitalist system has to grow (if all capitalists are to earn positive profits); that it is necessarily founded on the exploitation of labor power (understood technically as the difference between what labor gets and what it creates); and that this always implies class struggle of some sort. We also know that the system is technologically dynamic, provoking perpetual revolutions in labor processes, systems of distribution and consumption, space-relations, and the like. It is also unstable and crisis prone (see Harvey 1982; 1985). We should also note how each transition in this circulation process is spatially constrained: the buying and selling of commodities entails a movement (incurring costs) across space and the buying and selling of labor power on a daily basis is contained within a geographically defined labor market (within commuter fields). Production and consumption occur at particular places and their organization as well as the link between them entails some kind of spatial organization. Fixed physical and spatial infrastructures are required if spatial frictions are to be minimized.

Consider how the various material power bases are implicated in the circulation process of capital. To begin with, the individualism of money has its being at each and every moment of exchange. Since money is predominantly used to buy commodities and money is gained either by selling labor power or organizing capital circulation for profit, then the aggregate power of individualism in the market is fixed by the circulation of capital, modified, of course, by the degree to which money power is drawn off to support the other material power bases of state, family, etc. The alienations and freedoms which attach to this moment in circulation (the fact, for example, that laborers have to work in order to live even though they chose who they work for, that they can freely chose what they buy in the market place but only among commodities which capitalists produce) are real enough and deserve examination in their own right, no matter whether we are dealing with laborers expending their wages or entrepreneurs making investment decisions. This is, as it were, the moment of maximum individual liberty and freedom of decision. What we cannot do, and this was Simmel's most glaring error (see chapter 6), is to abstract the money moment of exchange from the rules of capital circulation. Within the latter constraints, however, it is possible to promote powerful

conceptions of individual liberty and freedom, of bourgeois constitutionality, and even to erect entrepreneurialism and individualism into a guiding
ideology and mythology. Concentration on that moment of capital
circulation alone defines an exclusive set of theoretical concerns (such as
those expressed in Adam Smith or neo-classical micro-economics).

But the circulation of capital is at base founded on a class relation. At its
simplest, this means a relation between buyers and sellers of labor power
and a perpetual struggle between them over wage rates and conditions of
labor. In its details, of course, this relation is complicated and the lines of
struggle fractured by the fact that labor requirements come in many shapes
and forms, that labor qualities and skills are highly differentiated and that
failure to organize collectively or the existence of labor surpluses (Marx's
industrial reserve army in part created by the technological and
organizational decisions of capitalists) puts laborers in a disadvantageous
bargaining position. The conflict in labor markets between individualism
and mechanisms for the expression of class interests is always strong and no
simple formula exists to determine which interest will prevail. Aggregate
requirements for, say, balancing consumption and production tend,
however, to put pressure for the formation of some kind of equilibrium
wage rate, around which a range of specific wage rates tend to cluster
depending upon skills, relative scarcities, technical requirements and
differential organization of class and intra-class interest. The class relation
and the class struggle element here come to the fore as central if not
determinant features within capitalism's dynamics, regulating the volume of
money available to be spent as individual wages, collective goods, and the
like. An equilibrium condition of that class struggle from the standpoint of
capital accumulation is one in which the intensity and productivity of labor
and the total wage bill serve to balance aggregate output with effective
demand.

Consumption together with the social reproduction of labor power occurs
for the most part within the household or community supported, at least in
recent times, by strategic interventions from the state. The circulation of
revenues (wages, interest, rents, etc.) is essential to the circulation of
capital, since goods produced have to be consumed by someone who can pay
for them. This circulation of revenues provides abundant opportunities for
different structures of distribution and secondary forms of exploitation (e.g.
shopkeepers or landlords versus consumers) to arise. Perhaps as compensation for the alienations of monetized individualism, the search for expressive
means to mark individualism (through, say, fashion) or to shape symbolic
capital in the realms of consumption can lead to the formation of
consumption classes and distinctive communities of consumption. Seen
from the standpoint of the circulation of capital, the diversity of

consumption communities or of individual or family lifestyles must somehow cluster to shape an aggregate demand for output that matches continuously increasing productive capacity. Since innovations in production require parallel innovations in consumption, so the competition over life-styles, symbolic capital, and the expressive order in general are essential to the dynamics of capitalism.

The reproduction of labor power within spatially structured labor markets depends on household and family action and the social infrastructures of community, both supported out of the circulation of capital and revenues. The quantities, qualities and value of labor power depend crucially on the nature of family household economies and community structures. Resources generated through the circulation of capital flow into the support of these material power bases and get used in ways that tend in turn to support the circulation of capital. Again, the range of individual or community choice is considerable. But at the end of the day labor power has to be reproduced so as to supply the needs of a capital circulation process that generates the resources to ensure familial and communal conditions of reproduction. While the opposition between these two spheres is a constant source of conflict, agitation and dissonance, any rupture between them indicates a condition of crisis or revolution that must (one way or another) be surmounted as a matter of survival.

The state, finally, has to be omnipresent within (and not external to, as many theories of the state seem to propose) all facets of this circulation process. It has to guarantee the systems of legal and contractual obligation and property rights of constitutional rule and non-violent reciprocities of market exchange through its monopoly over legalized and institutionalized forms of violence. It uses its powers of taxation to sustain itself out of the circulation of capital. The state is always disciplined by money, credit and financial requirements and cannot form an autonomous sphere of authoritative power. Since money is both political and economic, however, the state's regulation of and policy towards money puts it at the center of political-economic life. At the same time, the state has to adopt (by active policy or default) some kind of accumulation strategy to compensate for market failure, ensure long-term (public) investments and regulate the money supply. It also intervenes in class struggle, in the family and community, and regulates individual liberties as to ensure the appropriate reproduction of labor power and the stability of institutions of power in civil society. As a territorial entity, the state becomes a primary agent in the uneven geographical development of capitalism and consolidates its powers through appeal to territorial-based class alliances (see chapter 5) which integrate the production of places within the relative spaces of an increasingly global capitalist economy. To the degree that capitalism survives through the production of space, the corporatist (sometimes bordering on mercantilist) behavior of territorially based class alliances (including those that arise within urban regions) is a key to understanding the self-perpetuation of capitalism. Inter-spatial competition between states, city regions, and localities in turn becomes a vital expressive dimension to consciousness formation, provoking nationalism, regionalism and localisms within a universal and global framework. Political and geopolitical theoretical concerns come to the fore.

All the elements I have described – individual, class, community, family and state – can be given an explicit interpretation in relation to the dynamics of capital accumulation through an appropriate expansion of the Marxian meta-theory. Furthermore, it is possible to see how and why the different power centers might cohere or cluster around the rule-bound requirements of the capital accumulation process without surrendering freedom of manoeuvre and of action. Both theoretical preoccupations and social practices become more readily explicable. The accumulation of capital is, however, the driving force and it is precisely from that quarter that the hidden hand of history operates. Within a capitalist society all other power centers draw their sustenance from and are ultimately accountable to processes of capital accumulation except under conditions of breakdown and revolution. To the degree that the accumulation of capital is, as Marx puts it, "the historical mission of the bourgeoisie," we do indeed have to appeal to a meta-theory of class relations, even though actual, daily-life and specific class relations exist as one power center in a matrix also occupied by individuals, communities, families, and state apparatuses. From this it follows that the hidden hand of history cannot be identified simply in terms of this or that hegemonic class interest as it is constituted in a given time and place. Here, too it is precisely because capitalists as subjects do not, to reiterate Bourdieu's formulation, "strictly speaking know what they are doing that what they do has more meaning than they know."

This second step in the argument locates the orientations of different power centers within an overall theory of a capitalist mode of production. The argument has been schematic, but nevertheless useful from the standpoint of identifying the sorts of inner connexions we might look for in tracking the historical and geographical dynamics of a socio-economic system such as capitalism. But now I want to take a third step and look more closely at the urban context since it is there that firmer connexions between the rules of capital accumulation and the ferment of social, political and cultural forms can be identified. In so doing, I reiterate that the urban is not a thing but a process and that the process is a particular exemplar of capital accumulation in real space and time.

In chapter 5 I showed how the history of the urban process could be framed in terms of the relations between money, time and space under conditions of commodity exchange and capital accumulation. The imperatives of the latter impel changes in our experience of space and time. If the urban experience is at root a particular experience of space and time, then it, too, is subject to powerful forces of change. This has implications for cultural as well as for social and political life. Berman (1982) argues, for example, that the culture of modernity derives from a "certain experience of space and time" while Bradbury and Macfarlane (1976) provide an account of the origins of modernism as a cultural force that dwells strongly upon its urban origins. Jameson (1984) has more recently argued that the rise of post-modernism (see chapter 9) is associated with a crisis in our experience of space and that it, too, has strong urban associations. The urban origins of cultural ferments such as post-modernism is similarly asserted by Chambers (1987):

Post-modernism, whatever form its intellectualizing might take, has been fundamentally anticipated in the metropolitan cultures of the last twenty years: among the electronic signifiers of cinema, television and video, in recording studios and record players, in fashion and youth styles, in all those sounds, images and diverse histories that are daily mixed, recycled and "scratched" together on that giant screen which is the contemporary city.

It was, furthermore, one of Simmel's most powerful contributions to recognize how the organization of space and time and the objective social relations between individuals that urbanization promoted, altered the conditions of mental and cultural life in profound ways.

There is, it seems, a widespread if rather subterranean acceptance of the general significance of the organization of time (labor and leisure time, turnover time, etc.) and space in shaping the expressive worlds of cultural and political life. Pursuing the matter further, I shall propose a connexion not only between capital accumulation and the production of space but also between what I shall call a "hierarchy of spatialities" within the city form.

The space of the body (and all that this implies) is the space of the individual whose spatial movements and gestures make up, for us, one irreducible element of social action in time and space. Many writers (Foucault, for example) have concentrated on the body as the ultimate source of power. The motivations and aspirations of individuals can be explored with the tools of psychology and psycho-analysis, ethnography and linguistics. Individual movements in space and time (which can be tracked and mapped like those of any other bodies) give meaning to the city's spaces and places. Every time I walk the city, I construct and reconstruct it for myself. Individual activities, furthermore, always lie at the nexus of both production and reproduction. Yet the individual space in modern society is always vulnerable to and invaded by the social power of money. The latter, as a universal source of social power appropriable by private persons, becomes the prime individual means to both practical and expressive ends at the same time as we carry our relation to the world of global production in our pocket. Herein lies a link between the personal and other significant spatialities of social action. The space of the family also has special attributes. It is typically partitioned in ways that have much to say about individual gender roles and age, money power and its penetrations into the realms of social relations, with distinctive impacts upon the sense of security and insecurity, oedipal relations and fears of "the other." The external relations of individual within the household likewise express spatial powers of access touched by money power. The collecting together of household units for the reproduction of labor power creates an entirely different level of spatial differentiation – that of neighborhood and community – within the urban frame. Here, too, money is the prime resource to purchase location and associated life chances (see chapter 4) the construction of neighborhood and community spaces takes on different aspects depending upon who is engaging in the constructing and why (see chapter 9 below). The spaces of work are organized as micro elements (office, shop floor, posts, etc.) within macro-complexes (factories, office blocks urban agglomerations) all of which bear the marks of class relations of domination as well as those of hierarchically ordered labor powers, occupations and managerial skills. The money attached to practices in such spaces can be re-cast in communities as so many different expressive domains of status and prestige. The hierarchical orderings of administrative and political space (wards, districts, urban units, regions, nations as well as informally established zones of influence) completes a system of spatial orderings of the five power centers which we have identified as fundamental to social life under capitalism. And all of them are linked together by an intricate network of transport and communications. The city's spaces are organized, interlinked and structured according to a distinctive social logic.

The role and functioning of the different power centers cannot be separated from the spaces they occupy. The construction of the system of spatialities becomes a prime means to articulate power systems. Practices and experiences within these spaces provide the grist for consciousness formation. Forbidden spaces, feared spaces, ignored spaces, redundant spaces contain the materials of our own ignorance in the same way as shared spaces, comfortable or challenging spaces, needed spaces, become the proving ground for defining who or what we are.

The spaces of the city are constructed through the mobilization of the sources of power in particular configurations. Once constructed, the spatial organization of the city assumes the qualities of a text that we have to learn to read and interpret correctly, not simply according to our own needs, wants and desires. The labyrnthine qualities of the city's spaces, their hierarchical orderings and often hidden significations, form a symbolic world which is as imposing as it is imponderable. We can, in turn, fetishise the text and its spaces, treat the symbolic world of the city as a thing in itself to which we must perforce respond. It is sometimes enough to enter the space of the factory, the state, or a community to conform to its supposed requirements in ways that are both predictable and unthinking. Thus does the symbolic order of a city's spaces impose upon us ways of thinking and doing which reinforce existing patterns of social life. A study of the hierarchy of spatialities within an urban form helps reveal how individualism, class relations, community and family obligations and state action relate. The urbanization of capital, by virtue of its powers to create space, thereby finds a tacit means to entrain an urbanized consciousness.

A number of disruptive forces are ranged against such a repressive system for the reproduction of the status quo. To begin with, the accumulation of capital entails the perpetual re-shaping of urban spaces to match the requirements of growth in production and consumption, of expansion and transformation of labor markets, of new physical and social infrastructures, to say nothing of the imposition of new technological forms. Extension of working class home-ownership, for example, changes the spatial organization of the city and its symbolic meanings at the same time as it transforms the mechanisms of consumption. Spatial transformations such as agglomeration, suburbanization, urban renewal, rehabilitation and gentrification have to be understood in terms of the expansionary thrust of capital accumulation. Such transformations are wrought through the "creative destruction" of the landscapes that went before. The tensions and contradictions entailed in the continuous pressure to reorganize the city's spaces make for complex and unpredictable interactions. This becomes all the more evident when fetishistic readings of the city's spaces take hold. Fierce loyalties to this or that place within the city's spaces (the place of community, of commodity exchange, of state symbolism, or whatever) become barriers to spatial transformation. Curiously, capitalism creates conditions in which the spaces of the city are almost certain to be fetished in this way at the same time as it sets in motion processes of creative destruction which reveal all too clearly what the hidden historical hand is made of. When working class communities built up over many years are torn apart through property development, gentrification, and the like, we can hardly avoid seeing ourselves as victims of accumulation rather than as its avatars.

There are, however, other ways in which the ordered systemics of reproduction dissolve into a dynamic of uncertainty. A complicated, labyrinthine and in any case perpetually shifting text such as that presented by a city's spaces cannot be read unambiguously. It is open to all manner of interpretations and misinterpretations precisely because its rules of composition cannot be understood in advance of what experience teaches. Learning the language of a city's spaces is, for most of us, at best a partial experience (the veteran cab driver is probably the most learned of us all) and in any case subject to our own conjunctural needs, wants and passions. The symbolic securities of the city's text are open to disruption by an unstable semiotic of desire. This is the fundamental force to which Lefebvre so frequently points in his search to identify how a city's spaces might be liberated in ways that surmount the bounded and restrictive spaces of state and capital, even of community, family and monetized individualism.

Configurations of individuals, families, communities, classes, and state apparatuses within a spatialized hierarchy which itself is open to fetishization or misinterpretation, does not produce an effect automatically consistent with capital accumulation. Sharp discontinuities and conflicts erupt within the urban process. Tensions of this sort form the basis for odd configurations of personal and political consciousness that conceal as much as they reveal of underlying dynamics. It is all very well to insist, as Marxists and even sensible bourgeois are wont to do, that the system has to be understood as a totality. But most economic agents have neither the opportunity nor the luxury (even if they had the predisposition, experience and education) to penetrate the fetishisms of daily life. And even if they did, their reflections (as many a radical thinker finds) are hard to translate into actions that do much more than address immediate needs and hence support the fetishisms rather than dissolve them.

Where, then, does this leave those of us who, for whatever reason, look to the transformation of capitalism into some saner, less life-threatening mode of production and consumption? We know that capitalism has survived into the twentieth century in part through the production of an increasingly urbanized space. The result has been a particular kind of urban experience, radically different quantitatively and qualitatively from anything that preceded it in world history. Capitalism has produced a "second nature" through the creation of built environments and spatial forms and flows. It has also produced a new kind of human nature through the production of social spaces and interrelations between the different loci of consciousness formation. But these second natures, though produced out of the capitalist mode of production and circulation, are not necessarily consistent with capital accumulation and its dominant class relations. Indeed, with time they may become barriers. The urban process then appears as both fundamental to the perpetuation of capitalism and a primary expression of its inner contradictions. Capitalism has to confront the consequences of its urban structurations at each moment in its history. The produced second natures become the raw materials out of which new configurations of capitalist activity, new productive forces, and new social relations must be wrought.

The search for alternatives has to confront exactly that situation and be prepared to transform, not only that vast constructed second nature of a built environment shaped to accommodate capitalist modes and spatial divisions of both production and consumption, but also an urbanized consciousness. Failure to do so has, I suspect, lain at the root of many of the difficulties of socialist attempts to transform capitalism. Socialism has to show that the creative destruction of revolution is in the long run more creative and less destructive than that inherent in capitalism. It has to find a path toward a radically different kind of urban experience – one that confronts the multiple sources of alienation and disaffection while preserving the minimal liberties and securities achieved. A study of the urbanization of capital and of consciousness helps identify some of the traps into which proposals for social transformation can all too easily fall. It can also help avoid the multilayered fetishisms that attach to the daily experience of urban living and suggest a political way to confront the hidden hand of history.

Can a coordinated attack against the power of capital be mounted out of the individualism of money, the more radical conceptions of community, the progressive elements of new family structures and gender relations, and the contested but potentially fruitful legitimacy of state power, all in alliance with the class resentments that derive from the conditions of labor and the buying and selling of labor power? The analysis of the conditions that define the urbanization of consciousness suggests that it will take the power of some such alliance to mount a real challenge to the power of capital. But there is no natural basis of such an alliance and much to divide the potential participants.

Consider, for example, the distinction between money and money used as capital. Failure to make that distinction has led many Marxists to view the abolition of price-fixing markets and of price signals as a precondition for the abolition of class relations in production. It has taken the experience of totally centralized planning, with its highly rationalized, disciplined, and repressive coordinations of production and consumption in a universalized space and time, to suggest that perhaps the equation of money and capital was an error and that blind control of money uses amounted to the abolition of the modicum of admittedly constrained individual freedom that bourgeois society has achieved. The space of the body cannot be absorbed within that of the state without enslavement. The bourgeoisie has pioneered a path toward greater individual liberty. The problem is to liberate that individual liberty from its purely capitalist basis. The price system is the most decentralized of all decision-making mechanisms for coordinating the social and geographical division of labor with a degree of individual liberty unrealizable in centralized planning or collective community control. Individuals plainly value the limited freedoms given by money uses, and price coordinations yield a more open kind of urban society than that which might otherwise arise.

The problem, therefore, is to get beyond the pure money basis of bourgeois individualism, to curb the use of money power to procure privileged access to life chances, without falling prey to the repressions of community or the authoritarian state. The argument that private property offers one of the few protections against the arbitrariness of the state or the repressive intolerance of community must also be accorded a certain weight. But social democracy, which has shown itself sensitive at least to certain of these issues, has never been able to contain the forms of domination that arise when private property and money power are combined as capital. Nor has it ever dealt with the alienated individualism that pure money coordinations produce except through welfare statism. The path to socialism has to run the gauntlet of such complicated oppositions and change the hierarchy of spatialities that dominate contemporary urban life.

Nor can the present spatial division of labor and of consumption be totally abandoned without almost total destruction of the material bases of contemporary life. The spatial organization of production can, however, be severed from the roving calculus of profit. Some balance should be struck between respect for the history, tradition, and accumulated skills of working communities and innovative probing for new techniques and more efficient spatial configurations. Abundant sentiment can be mobilized behind that idea. The search for less oppressive sociotechnical conditions and social relations of production is, after all, what class struggle in the workplace is all about. Yet it is hard to define the exact meaning of such a project in a world of such intricate interdependence that money power cannot help but dominate as a concrete abstraction that rules our lives. One first step is to curb interurban competition and facilitate interurban cooperation. Beyond that lies the problem of determining some acceptable and dynamic balance between centralization and decentralization of economic decision making. The power of finance capital and the state with respect to production has to be redefined and controlled in ways that promote codevelopment rather than competition.

On the surface, the spatial division of consumption appears an easier issue to address. The direct reorganization of the urban landscape to redistribute access to social power and life chances is essential. Those forms of interurban competition that generate subsidies for the consumption of the rich at the expenses of the social wage of the poor also deserve instant attack. But this is, I suspect, a more dangerous arena than most socialists are wont to admit. The experience of demand-side urbanization (see chapter 1) bit deep into political consciousness. It played upon the fuzzy boundary between the selling of community and the striving for real community, real cultural and personal freedoms exercised collectively. The mass merging of consumerist narcissism and the desire for self-realization has been an important aspect of the urbanization of consciousness. It is a volatile mix, dangerous to provoke and hard to confront. Yet it increasingly appears as one of the key problems and opportunities for political mobilization. Here exists a major base for political agitation, a guerrilla base from which to mount a broader war, but one which is in perpetual danger of degenerating into mild forms of localized consumer socialism that feed rather than heal dissension. The problem is to sever the tight connection between self-realization and pure consumerism. That battle has to be fought if socialism is ever to stand a chance in the advanced capitalist world.

Failure to win battles of this sort leaves us at the mercy of an urban process that internalized capitalist principles of production for production's sake, accumulation for accumulation's sake, consumption for consumption's sake, and innovation for innovation's sake. It also presages a future of accelerating creative destruction and abandonment that will implicate more and more people and places.

Emile Zola closes *La Bete Humaine* with a terrifying image. Engineer and fireman, locked in mortal combat out of their own petty jealousies, tumble from the train to be severed limb from limb beneath its juggernaut wheels. The train, driverless and ever accelerating, rushes toward Paris, while the soldiers it carries, intoxicated and drunk with excitement at the prospect of the grand war with Prussia to come, bellow the loudest and bawdiest of songs with all their energy and might. It was, of course, the Second Empire careering toward war with Prussia and the tragedy of the Commune that Zola sought to symbolize. But the image has perhaps a broader application. The global urbanization of capital entrains a total but also violently unstable urbanization of civil society. The consequent urbanization of consciousness intoxicates and befuddles us with fetishisms, rendering us powerless to understand let alone intervene coherently in that trajectory. The urbanization of capital and of consciousness threatens a transition to barbarism in the midst of a rhetoric of self-realization.

If the urbanization of capital and of consciousness is so central to the perpetuation and experience of capitalism, and if it is through these channels that the inner contradictions of capitalism are now primarily expressed, then we have no option but to put the urbanization of revolution at the center of our political strategies. There is enough supporting evidence for that. Any political movement that does not embed itself in the heart of the urban process is doomed to fail in advanced capitalist society. Any political movement that does not secure its power within the urban process cannot long survive. Any political movement that cannot offer ways out of the multiple alienations of contemporary urban life cannot command mass support for the revolutionary transformation of capitalism. A genuinely humanizing urban experience, long dreamed of and frequently sought, is worth struggling for. Socialism has therefore to address the problem of the simultaneous transformation of capitalism and its distinctive form of urbanization. That conception is, of course, ambiguous. But I prefer to leave it so. Unraveling its meanings is what contemporary political-economic life has to be about.

9

Flexible Accumulation through Urbanization: Reflections on "Post-Modernism" in the American City

"Proletarian revolution is the critique of human geography through which individuals and communities have to create places and events suitable for their own appropriation, no longer just of their labour, but of their total history" (Guy Debord – *Society of the Spectacle*)
"Times are hard, but (post) modern" (Adaptation of an Italian saying)

I. INTRODUCTION

Christopher Jencks (1984, 9) dates the symbolic end of modernist architecture and the passage to the post-modern as 3.32 p.m. on July 15th, 1972, when the Pruitt-Igoe Housing development (a version of Le Corbusier's "machine for modern living") was dynamited as an unlivable environment for the low-income people it housed. Shortly thereafter, President Nixon officially declared the urban crisis over.

1972 is not a bad date for symbolizing all kinds of other transitions in the political economy of advanced capitalism. It is roughly since then that the capitalist world, shaken out of the suffocating torpor of the stagflation that brought the long postwar boom to a wimpering end, has begun to evolve a seemingly new and quite different regime of capital accumulation. Set in motion during the severe recession of 1973–5 and further consolidated during the equally savage deflation of 1981–2 (the "Reagan" recession) the new regime is marked by a startling flexibility with respect to labor processes, labor markets, products, and patterns of consumption (see Armstrong, et al. 1984; Aglietta 1974; Piore and Sabel 1984; Scott and Storper 1986; and Harvey 1988). It has, at the same time, entrained rapid shifts in the patterning of uneven development, both between sectors and geographical regions – a process aided by the rapid evolution of entirely new financial systems and markets. These enhanced powers of flexibility and mobility have permitted the new regime to be imposed upon a labor force already weakened by two savage bouts of deflation that saw unemployment rise to unprecedented post-war levels in all the advanced capitalist countries (save, perhaps, Japan). Rapid displacements, for example, from the advanced capitalist countries to the newly industrializing countries or from skilled manufacturing to unskilled service jobs, hammered home the weakness of labor and its inability to resist sustained levels of high unemployment, rapid destruction and reconstruction of skills, and modest (if any) increases in the real wage. Political economic circumstances also undermined the power of the state to protect the social wage, even in those countries with governments seriously committed to defense of the welfare state. Though the politics of resistance may have varied, austerity and fiscal retrenchment sometimes accompanied by the resurgence of a virulent neo-conservatism, have become widespread in the advanced capitalist world.

What is remarkable about cultural and intellectual life since 1972 is how it, too, has been radically transformed in ways that appear to parallel these political-economic transformations. Consider, for example, the practices of "high modernity of the international style" as practised in 1972. Modernism had by then lost all semblance of social critique. The protopolitical or Utopian program (the transformation of all of social life by way of the transformation of space) had failed (Jameson 1984a) and modernism had become closely linked to capital accumulation through a project of Fordist modernization characterized by rationality, functionality, and efficiency. By 1972, modernist architecture was as stifling and torporous as the corporate power it represented. Stagflation in architectural practice paralleled the stagflation of capitalism (perhaps it was no accident that Venturi, Scott Brown and Izenour published *Learning from Las Vegas* in 1972). Critics of modernity had been around for a very long time (think of Jane Jacobs' *Life and Death of Great American Cities*, published in 1961) and there was a sense, of course, in which the revolutionary cultural movement of the 1960s was fashioned as a critical response to rationality, functionality, and efficiency in everything. But it took the 1973 crisis sufficiently to shake up the relationship between art and society to allow post-modernism to become both accepted and institutionalized.

"Post-modernism" is, however, a most contentious term. Most agree that it entails some kind of reaction to "modernism." But since the meaning of that term is a muddle, the reactions to it are doubly so. There appears, however, to be some kind of consensus "that the typical post-modernist artefact is playful, pluralist, self-ironizing and even schizoid; and that it reacts to the austere autonomy of high modernism by impudently embracing the language of commerce and the commodity." Furthermore, "its stance towards cultural tradition is one of irreverent pastiche, and its contrived depthlessness undermines all metaphysical solemnities, sometimes by a brutal aesthetics of squalor and shock." (Eagleton 1987). But even in a field like architecture, where the "artefact" is clearly in view and writers like Jencks (1984) have sought to define what post-modernism is about, the meaning and definition of the term still remains in contention. In other fields, where post-modernism has become intertwined with post-structuralism, deconstruction, and the like, matters have become even more obscure (see Huyssen 1984). In the urban context, therefore, I shall simply characterize post-modernism as signifying a break with the idea that planning and development should focus on large scale, technologically rational, austere and functionally efficient "international style" design and that vernacular traditions, local history, and specialized spatial designs ranging from functions of intimacy to grand spectacle should be approached with a much greater eclecticism of style.

This kind of post-modernism, it seems to me, seeks some kind of accommodation with the more flexible regime of accumulation that has emerged since 1973. It has sought a creative and active rather than a passive role in the promotion of new cultural attitudes and practice consistent with flexible accumulation, even though some of its defenders, such as Frampton (1985), see it as containing potentialities for resistance as well as conformity to capitalist imperatives. The institutionalization and hegemony of "post-modernism" rests, therefore, upon the creation of a distinctive "cultural logic" in late capitalism (Jameson 1984b).

One other element to the picture must be considered. Not only have capitalism and its associated cultural and ideological practices together undergone a sea change, but our "discourses" (to use the current buzz-word) have likewise shifted. The deconstruction of structuralist interpretations, the abandonment of theory for empiricism in much of social science, the general backing away from Marxism (for both political and intellectual reasons) and the sense of futility in the realm of real representation (the impenetrability of "the other" and the reduction of all meaning to a "text") make it very difficult to preserve any sense of continuity to our understanding of that transformation that set in around 1972. We talked about the world in a different way, used a different language then, compared to now. Yet here, too, I think a case can be made that the political-economic transformation achieved through a succession of economic crises and working class defeats have affected discourses as well as cultural and ideological practices (see Harvey and Scott, forthcoming). That sounds like, and is, old-fashioned Marxian argument. But I cannot help but be impressed at the way in which a whole world of thought and cultural practice, of economy and institutions, of politics and ways of relating, began to crumble as we watched the dust explode upwards and the walls of Pruitt-Igoe come crashing down.

II. FLEXIBLE ACCUMULATION THROUGH URBANIZATION

An understanding of urbanization, I have argued elsewhere (Harvey 1985a, 1985b) is critical for understanding the historical geography of capitalism. It has partly been through shifts in the urban process that the new systems of flexible accumulation have been so successfully implanted. But also, as various historians of the rise of modernism have pointed out, there is an intimate connection between aesthetic and cultural movement and the changing nature of the urban experience (Berman 1982, Bradbury and McFarlane 1976, Clark 1984, Frisby 1986). It seems reasonable, therefore, to look at transitions in the urban process as a key point of integration of the political-economic move towards flexible accumulation and the cultural-aesthetic trend towards post-modernism.

Urbanization has, like everything else, dramatically changed its spots in the United States since 1972. The global deflation of 1973–5 put incredible pressure on the employment base of many urban regions. A combination of shrinking markets, unemployment, rapid shifts in spatial constraints and the global division of labor, capital flight, plant closings, technological and financial reorganization, lay at the root of that pressure. The geographical dispersal was not only to other regions and nations. It included yet another phase of urban deconcentration of populations and production beyond the suburbs and into rural and small-town America in a way that almost seemed like the fulfillment of Marx's prediction of the "urbanization of the countryside". Fixed capital investments and physical infrastructures in existing locations were consequently threatened with massive devaluation, thus undermining property tax base and fiscal capacity of many urban governments at a time of increasing social need. To the degree that federal redistributions also became harder to capture (this was the import of Nixon's declaration in 1973), so social consumption was reduced forcing more and more governments to a political-economy of retrenchment and disciplinary action against municipal employees and the local real wage. It was exactly in such a context that New York City went into technical bankruptcy in 1975, presaging a wave of fiscal distress and radical restructuring for many US cities (Szelenyi 1984; Clavel, et al. 1980; Fainstain, et al. 1986; Tabb 1982).

Ruling class alliances in urban regions were willy-nilly forced (no matter what their composition) to adopt a much more competitive posture. Managerialism, so characteristic of urban governance in the 1960s, was replaced by entrepreneurialism as the main motif or urban action (Hanson 1983; Bouinot 1987). The rise of the "entrepreneurial city" meant increased inter-urban competition across a number of dimensions. I have elsewhere argued (see chapter 1, above) that the competition can best be broken down into four different forms: (a) competition for position in the international division of labor, (b) competition for position as centers of consumption, (c) competition for control and command functions (financial and administrative powers in particular), and (d) competition for governmental redistributions (which in the United States, as Markusen (1986) has shown, focussed heavily these last few years on military expenditures). These four options are not mutually exclusive and the uneven fortunes of urban regions have depended upon the mix and timing of strategies pursued in relation to global shifts.

It was in part through this heightened inter-urban competition that flexible accumulation took such a firm hold. The result has been, however, rapid oscillations in urban fortunes and in the patterning of uneven geographical development (see Smith 1984). Houston and Denver, both boom towns in the mid-1970s, are suddenly caught short in the collapse of oil prices after 1981, Silicon Valley, the high-tec wonder of new products and new employment in the 1970s, suddenly loses its competitive edge while New York and the once-jaded economies of New England rebound vigorously in the 1980s on the basis of expanding command and control functions and even new-found manufacturing strength. Two other more general effects have then followed.

First, inter-urban competition has opened spaces within which the new and more flexible labor processes could be more easily implanted and opened the way to much more flexible currents of geographical mobility than was the case before 1973. Concern for a favorable "business climate", for example, has pushed urban governments to all kinds of measures (from wage-disciplining to public investments) in order to attract economic development, but in the process has lessened the cost of change of location to the enterprise. Much of the vaunted "public-private partnership" of today amounts to a subsidy for affluent consumers, corporations, and powerful command functions to stay in town at the expense of local collective consumption for the working class and the impoverished. Secondly, urban governments have been forced into innovation and investment to make their cities more attractive as consumer and cultural centers. Such innovations and investments (convention centers, sports stadia, disney-worlds, downtown consumer paradises, etc.) have quickly been imitated elsewhere. Inter-urban competition has thus generated leap-frogging urban innovations in life-style, cultural forms, products, and even political, and consumer based innovation, all of which has actively promoted the transition to flexible accumulation. And herein, I shall argue, lies part of the secret of the passage to post-modernity in urban culture.

This connection can be seen in the radical reorganization of the interior spaces of the contemporary US city under the impulsions of inter-urban competition. I preface the account, however, with some general remarks on the class content of spatial practices in urban settings.

III. THE CLASS CONTENT OF SPATIAL PRACTICES IN URBAN SETTINGS

Spatial practices in any society abound in subtleties and complexities. Since they are not innocent with respect to the accumulation of capital and the reproduction of class relations under capitalism, they are a permanent arena for social conflict and struggle. Those who have the power to command and produce space possess a vital instrumentality for the reproduction and enhancement of their own power. Any project to transform society must, therefore, grasp the complex nettle of the transformation of spatial practices.

I shall try to capture some of the complexity through construction of a "grid" of spatial practices (Table 1). down the left hand side I range three dimensions identified in Lefebvre's *The Production of Space*:

1. *Material spatial practices* refer to the physical and material flows, transfers, and interactions that occur in and across space in such a way as to assure production and social reproduction.

2. *Representations of space* encompass all of the signs and significations, codes and knowledge, that allow such material practices to be talked about and understood, no matter whether in terms of everyday common sense or through the sometimes arcane jargon of the academic disciplines that deal with spatial practices (engineering, architecture, geography, planning, social ecology, and the like).

3. *Spaces of representation* are social inventions (codes, signs, and even material constructs such as symbolic spaces, particular built environments, paintings, museums and the like) that seek to generate new meanings of possibilities for spatial practices.

Lefebvre characterizes these three dimensions as the *experienced*, the *perceived*, and the *imagined*. He regards the dialectical relations between them as the fulcrum of a dramatic tension through which the history of spatial practices can be read. The relations are, however, problematic. A "vulgar Marxist" position would presumably hold that material spatial practices directly determine both the representations of space and the spaces of representation.

Table 1.   Spatial Practices

	Accessibility & distanciation	Appropriation & use of space	Domination & control of space
MATERIAL SPATIAL PRACTICES *(EXPERIENCE)*	Flows of goods, money, people, labor power, information, etc.; transport & communications systems; market and urban hierarchies; agglomeration	Urban built environments social spaces of the city & other "turf" designations; social networks of communication & mutual aid	Private property in land, state & administrative divisions of space; exclusive communities & neighborhoods; exclusionary zoning & other forms of social control (policing and surveillance)
REPRESENTATIONS OF SPACE *(PERCEPTION)*	Social, psychological and physical measures of distance; map-making; theories of the "friction of distance" (principle of least effort, social physics, range of a good, central place & other forms of location theory)	Personal space; mental maps of occupied space; spatial hierarchies; symbolic representation of spaces	Forbidden spaces; "territorial imperatives"; community; regional culture; nationalism; geopolitics; hierarchies
SPACES OF REPRESENTATION *(IMAGINATION)*	"Media is the message" new modes of spatial transaction (radio, t.v., film, photography, painting etc.); diffusion of "taste"	Popular spectacles-street demonstrations, riots; places of popular spectacle (streets, squares, markets); iconography and graffiti	Organized spectacles; monumentality & constructed spaces of ritual; symbolic barriers and signals of symbolic capital

Marx (1967; 1973) did not hold such a view. He depicts knowledge as a material productive force in the *Grundrisse* (pp. 699–701) and writes in a justly famous passage in *Capital* (vol 1: 178): "What distinguishes the worst of architects from the best of bees is this, that the architect raises his structure in imagination before he erects it in reality." The spaces of representation, therefore, have the potential not only to affect representation of space but also to act as a material productive force with respect to spatial practices.

But to argue that the relations between the experienced, the perceived, and the imagined are dialectically rather than causally determined leaves things much too vague. Bourdieu (1977) provides a clarification. He explained how "a matrix of perceptions, appreciations, and actions" can at one and the same time be put to work flexibly to "achieve infinitely diversified tasks" while at the same time being "in the last instance" (Engels' famous phrase) engendered out of the material experience of "objective structures" and therefore "out of the economic basis of the social formation in question." Bourdieu accepts the "well-founded primacy of objective relations" without, however, making the false inference that the objective structures are themselves endowed with a power of autonomous development independent of human agency.

The mediating link is provided by the concept of "habitus" – a "durably installed generative principle of regulated improvisations" which "produces practices" that in turn tend to reproduce the objective conditions which produced the generative principle of habitus in the first place. The circular (even cumulative?) causation is obvious. Bourdieu's conclusion is, however, a very striking depiction of the constraints to the power of the imagined over the experienced:

Because the habitus is an endless capacity to engender products – thoughts, perceptions, expressions, actions – whose limits are set by the historically and socially situated conditions of its production, the conditioning and conditional freedom it secures is as remote from a creation of unpredictable novelty as it is from a simple mechanical reproduction of the initial conditionings (Bourdieu 1977: 95)

I accept that theorization and will later make considerable use of it.

Across the top of the grid (Table 1) I list three other aspects to spatial practice drawn from more conventional understandings:

1. *Accessibility and distanciation* speaks to the role of the "friction of distance" in human affairs. Distance is both a barrier to and a defense against human interaction. It imposes transaction costs upon any system of production and reproduction (particularly those based on any elaborate social division of labor, trade, and social differentiation of reproductive functions). Distanciation (cf. Giddens 1984: 258–9) is simply a measure of the degree to which the friction of space has been overcome to accommodate social interaction.

2. The *appropriation of space* examines the way in which space is used and

occupied by individuals, classes, or other social groupings. Systematized and institutionalized appropriation may entail the production of territorially bounded forms of social solidarity.

3. The *domination of space* reflects how individuals or powerful groups dominate the organization and production of space so as to exercise a greater degree of control either over the friction of distance or over the manner in which space is appropriated by themselves or others.

These three dimensions to spatial practice are not independent of each other. The friction of distance is implicit in any understanding of the domination and appropriation of space, while the persistent appropriation of a space by a particular group (say the gang that hangs out on the street corner; amounts to a *de facto* domination of that space. Furthermore, the attempt to dominate space, insofar as it requires reductions in the friction of distance (capitalism's "annihilation of space through time," for example) alters distanciation.

This grid of spatial practices tells us nothing important in itself. Spatial practices derive their efficacy in social life only through the structure of social relations within which they come into play. Under the social relations of capitalism, the spatial practices become imbued with class meanings. To put it this way is not, however, to argue that spatial practices are derivative of capitalism. The spatial practices take on specific meanings and these meanings are put into motion and spaces used in a particular way through the agency of class, gender, or other social practices.[1] When placed in the context of capitalist social relations and imperatives (the accumulation of capital), therefore, the grid can help us unravel some of the complexity that prevails in the field of contemporary spatial practices.

My purpose in setting up the grid was not, however, to set about a systematic exploration of the positions within it, though such an examination would be of considerable interest (and I have penned in a few controversial positionings within the grid for purposes of illustration). My purpose is to find a way to characterize the radical shifts in the class content and the nature of spatial practices that have occurred over the last two decades. The pressure to reorganize the interior space of the city, for example, has been considerable under conditions of flexible accumulation. The vitality of the central city core has been reemphasised, themes such as the quality of urban living (gentrification, consumption palaces and

---

[1] The gender, racial, ethnic and religious contents of spatial practices also need to be considered in any full account of community formation and the production of social spaces in urban settings. A beginning has been made on the gender aspect in works by Stimpson (1981); Rose (1984); Shlay and Di Gregorio (1985); and Smith (1987).

sophisticated entertainment), and enhanced social control over both public and private spaces within the city, have been of widespread significance. But the urban process has also had to cope with increasing impoverishment and unemployment, under conditions where the social wage could not be increased. Here, too, spatial practices have shifted in part towards an increasing control through a return to ghettoization (a practice that was never, of course, severely dented let alone overcome) and the rise of new spaces where the homeless wander, the schizophrenics and discharged mental patients hang out, and the impoverished practice both new and well-tried survival strategies. How, then, are we to make sense of all this shifting and conflict prone spatialization of class polarities? Are there ways, furthermore, to address the question of spatial empowerment of the segregated, oppressed and impoverished populations increasingly to be found in all urban areas?

IV. CLASS PRACTICES AND THE CONSTRUCTION OF COMMUNITY[2]

Different classes construct their sense of territory and community in radically different ways. This elemental fact is often overlooked by those theorists who presume *a priori* that there is some ideal-typical and universal tendency for all human beings to construct a human community of roughly similar sort, no matter what the political or economic circumstances. A study of class agency with respect to community construction under conditions of contemporary urbanization illustrates how essentially similar spatial practices can have radically different class contents.

Let us look, more closely, for example, at the class practices through which communities are typically constructed in urban settings. We here encounter all the flexibility and adapatability of perceptions, appreciations, and actions that Bourdieu insists upon. But the contrast between community construction in low income and disempowered and in affluent and empowered strata of the population is indeed striking.

Low income populations, usually lacking the means to overcome and hence command space, find themselves for the most part trapped in space. Since ownership of even basic means of reproduction (such as housing) is restricted, the main way to dominate space is through continuous appropriation. Exchange values are scarce, and so the pursuit of use values for daily survival is central to social action. This means frequent material and interpersonal transactions and the formation of very small scale

---

[2] I am here deeply indebted to the research work of Phillip Schmandt.

communities. Within the community space, use values get shared through some mix of mutual aid and mutual predation, creating tight but often highly conflictual interpersonal social bonding in both private and public spaces. The result is an often intense attachment to place and "turf" and an exact sense of boundaries because it is only through active appropriation that control over space is assured.

Successful control presumes a power to exclude unwanted elements. Fine-tuned ethnic, religious, racial, and status discriminations are frequently called into play within such a process of community construction. Furthermore, political organization takes a special form, generally expressive of a culture of political resistance and hostility to normal channels of political incorporation. The state is largely experienced as an agency of repressive control (in police, education, etc.) rather than as an agency that can be controlled by and bring benefits to them (see Willis 1977). Political organizations of a participatory sort are, as Crenson (1983) observes, weakly developed and politics of the bourgeois sort understood as irrelevant to the procuring of the use values necessary for daily survival. Nevertheless, the state intervenes in such communities since they are vital preserves of the reserve army of the unemployed, spaces of such deprivation that all sorts of contagious social ills (from prostitution to tuberculosis) can flourish, and spaces that appear dangerous precisely because they lie outside of the normal processes of social incorporation.

Contrast this with the practices of affluent groups, who can command space through spatial mobility and ownership of basic means of reproduction (houses, cars, etc.). Already blessed with abundant exchange values with which to sustain life, they are in no way dependent upon community-provided use values for survival. The construction of community is then mainly geared to the preservation or enhancement of exchange values. Use values relate to matters of accessibility, taste, tone, aesthetic appreciation, and the symbolic and cultural capital that goes with possession of a certain kind of "valued" built environment. Interpersonal relations are unnecessary at the street level and the command over space does not have to be assured through continuous appropriation. Money provides access to the community, making it less exclusionary on other grounds (residential segregation by ethnicity and even race tends to weaken the further up the income scale one goes). Boundaries are diffuse and flexible, mainly dependent upon the spatial field of externality effects that can effect individual property values. Community organizations form to take care of externality effects and maintain the "tone" of the community space. The state is seen as basically beneficial and controllable, assuring security and helping keep undesirables out, except in unusual circumstances (the location of "noxious" facilities, the construction of highways, etc.)

Distinctive spatial practices and processes of community construction – coupled with distinctive cultural practices and ideological predispositions – arise out of different material circumstances. Conditions of economic oppression and socio-political domination generate quite different kinds of spatial practices and styles of community formation than will typically be found under other class circumstances.

V. INFORMALIZATION, THE PRODUCTION OF SYMBOLIC CAPITAL, AND THE MOBILIZATION OF THE SPECTACLE

Flexible accumulation has deeply affected class structures and political-economic possibilities so as to modify the processes of community production, while re-emphasising the importance of the class content of spatial practices. I will look briefly at three aspects of this transformation.

Impoverishment and Informalization

The United States have experienced an increase in the sheer numbers of the urban poor since 1972. The composition of this poverty population has also changed. Unemployed blue-collar workers thrown on the street by de-industrialization and the flood of displaced people out of depressed rural or regional economies or from third-world countries, have been piled on top of what Marx called the "hospital" of the working class, left to fend for itself in the cities. In some cases, particular urban communities tied to a dominant local employment source have been plunged as a whole into a condition of impoverishment by a single plant closing. In other instances, particularly vulnerable groups, such as female-headed households, have been plunged deeper into the mire of poverty, thus creating zones where phenomena like the feminization of poverty become dominant. Fiscal constraints of which neo-conservativism has made a political virtue rather than an economic necessity, have at the same time undercut the flow of public services and hence the life-support mechanisms for the mass of the unemployed and the poor.

Learning to cope and survive in urban settings on almost no income is an art that takes a while to learn. The balance between competition, mutual predation and mutual aid has consequently shifted within low income populations. The growth of impoverishment has, paradoxically, led to a diminution of the power of some of the more positive mechanisms to cope with it. But there has also been one other dramatic response – the rise of what is known as the "informal sector" in American cities (focussing on illegal practices such as drug-trafficking, prostitution, and legal production and trading of services). Most observers (see Castells and Portes 1987) agree that these practices expanded in scope and form after 1972. Furthermore, the same pheneomena were observed in European cities, thus bringing the urban process in the advanced capitalist countries as a whole much closer to the third-world urban experience (Redclift and Mingione 1985).

The nature and form of informalization varies greatly, depending upon the opportunities to find local markets for goods and services, the qualities of the reserve army of labor power (its skills and aptitudes), gender relations (for women play a very conspicuous role in organizing informal economies) the presence of small-scale entrepreneurial skills, and the willingness of the authorities (regulatory and oversight powers like the unions) to tolerate practices that are often outside the law.

Low income communities present, in the first place, a vast reserve of labor power under strong pressure in these times to find a living of almost any sort.

Under conditions of government laxness and trade union weakness, new kinds of production of goods and services can arise sometimes organized from outside the community but in other instances organized by entrepreneurs within the low-income community itself. Homework has become much more prominent allowing women, for example, to combine the tasks of child-rearing and productive labor in the same space, while saving entrepreneurs the costs of overhead (plant, lighting, etc.). Sweatshops and the informal provision of services began to emerge as vital aspects of the New York and Los Angeles economies in the 1970s and by now have become important throughout the US urban system. These have been paralleled by an increasing commodification of traditional mutual aid systems within low-income communities. Baby-sitting, laundering, cleaning, fixing up, and odd jobs, which used to be swapped more as favors are now bought and sold, sometimes on an entrepreneurial basis.

Social relations within many low income communities have, as a consequence, become much more entrepreneurial, with all of the consequences of excessive and often extraordinary exploitation (particularly of women) in the labor process. The flow of incomes into such communities has increased but at the expense of traditional mutual aid systems and the stronger implantation of social hierarchies within the communities themselves. The flow of value out of such communities has also increased substantially. This has led many to look with surprise at the local dynamics of urban development and to argue for the toleration, acceptance, and even encouragement of informalization, thus lending credence to the neo-conservative argument that private entrepreneurial activity is always the path to economic growth and success – as if that could solve the problems of all the poor rather than those of just a select few. Nevertheless, the growth of informalization — and the emergence of unregulated urban spaces within which such practices are tolerated — is a phenomenon thoroughly consistent with the new regme of flexible accumulation.

The Production of Symbolic Capital

The frenetic pursuit of the consumption dollars of the affluent has led to a much stronger emphasis upon product differentiation under the regime of flexible accumulation. Producers have, as a consequence, begun to explore the realms of differentiated tastes and aesthetic preferences in ways that were not so necessary under a Fordist regime of standardized accumulation through mass production. In so doing they have reemphasized a powerful aspect of capital accumulation: the production, and consumption of what Borrdieu (1977, 171–97; 1984) calls "symbolic capital." This has had important implications for the production and transformation of the urban spaces in which upper income groups live.

"Symbolic capital" is defined by Bourdieu as "the collection of luxury goods attesting the taste and distinction of the owner." Such capital is, of course, a transformed kind of money capital, but "produces its proper effect inasmuch, and only inasmuch, as it conceals the fact that it originates in "material" forms of capital which are also, in the last analysis, the source of its effects." The fetishism involved is obvious, but it is here deliberately deployed to conceal, through the realms of culture and taste, the real bases of economic distinctions. Since "the most successful ideological effects are those which have no words, and ask no more than complicitous silence," so the production of symbolic capital serves ideological functions, because the mechanisms through which it contributes "to the reproduction of the established order and to the perpetuation of domination remain hidden." (Bourdieu 1977: 188).

It is instructive to bring Bourdieu's theorizations to bear upon the production of upper class communities and their built environments. It has a lot to tell us about the material processes of gentrification, the recuperation of "history" (real, imagined, or simply re-created as pastiche) and of "community" (again, real, imagined, or simply packaged for sale by producers), and the need for embellishment decoration, and ornamentation that could function as so may codes and symbols of social distinction (cf. Simmel 1978; Firey 945; Jager 1986). I do not mean to argue that such phenomena are in any way new — they have been a vital feature to capitalist urbanization from the very beginning and, of course, bear more than a few echoes of distinctions passed on from older social orders. But they have become of much greater significance since 1972, in part through their proliferation into layers of the population that were hitherto denied them.

Flexible accumulation permits a profitable response to the cultural discontents of the 1960s, which implied rejection of standardized accumulation and a mass culture that provided too few opportunities to capture symbolic capital. To the degree that political economic crisis encouraged the exploration of product differentiation, so the repressed market desire to acquire symbolic capital could be captured through the production of built environments (Smith and Lefaivre 1984). And it was, of course, exactly this kind of desire that post-modernist architecture set out to satisfy. "For the middle class suburbanite," Venturi et al. (1972, 154) observe, "living, not in an antebellum mansion, but in a smaller version lost in a large space, identity must come through symbolic treatment of the form of the house, either through styling provided by the developer (for instance, split-level Colonial) or through a variety of symbolic ornaments applied thereafter by the owner".

Symbolic capital is, however, open to devaluation or enhancement through changes in taste. If symbolic capital contains a hidden power of domination, then power relations are themselves vulnerable to mutations in taste. Since competition between producers and the machinations of consumers render taste insecure, struggles over fashion acquire a certain significance within the urban scene (see, e.g. Zukin's (1982) study of loft living). The power to dominate as well as the ability to convert symbolic into money capital becomes embedded in the cultural politics of the urban process. But that also implies that domination of space within the urban process has an even more vital cultural edge to it under a regime of flexible accumulation. To the degree that domination of whatever sort contains the potentiality of violent response on the part of the dominated, so here, too, a latent domain of conflict has been opened up for explicit articulation.

The Mobilization of the Spectacle

"Bread and Festivals" was the ancient Roman formula for social pacification of the restless plebs. The formula has been passed on into capitalist culture through, for example, Second Empire Paris, where festival and the urban spectacle became instruments of social control in a society riven by class conflict (Clark 1985).

Since, 1972, the urban spectacle has been transformed from counter-cultural events, anti-war demonstrations, street riots and the inner-city revolutions of the 1960s. It has been captured as both a symbol and instrument of community unification under bourgeois control in conditions where unemployment and impoverishment have been on the rise and objective conditions of class polarization have been increasing. As part of this process, the modernist penchant for monumentality – the communication of the permanence, authority, and power of the established capitalist order – has been challenged by an "official" post-modernist style that explores the architecture of festival and spectacle, with its sense of the ephemeral, of display, and of transitory but participatory pleasure. The display of the commodity became a central part of the spectacle, as crowds flock to gaze at them and at each other in intimate and secure spaces like Baltimore's Harbor Place, Boston's Feneuil Hall, and a host of enclosed shopping malls that sprung up all over America. Even whole built environments became centerpieces of urban spectacle and display.

The phenomenon deserves more detailed scrutiny than I here can give. It fits, of course, with urban strategies to capture consumer dollars to compensate for de-industrialization. Its undoubted commercial success rests in part on the way in which the act of buying connects to the pleasure of the spectacle in secured spaces, safe from violence or political agitation. Baltimore's Harbor Place combines all of the bourgeois virtues that Benjamin (1973, 158–65) attributed to the arcades of nineteenth century Paris with the sense of the festival that attached to world expositions, "places of pilgrimage to the fetish Commodity." Debord (1983) would take it further: "the spectacle is the developed modern complement of money where the totality of the commodity world appears as a whole, as a general equivalence for what the entire society can be and can do." To the degree that the spectacle becomes "the common ground of deceived gaze and of false consciousness," so it can also present itself as "an instrument of unification" (Debord 1983). Mayor Schaefer and the urban class alliance ranged behind him in Baltimore, have consciously used the spectacle of Harbor Place precisely in that way, as a symbol of the supposed unity of a class-divided and racially segregated city. Professional sports activities and events like the Los Angeles Olympic Games perform a similar function in an otherwise fragmented urban society.

Urban life, under a regime of flexible accumulation, has thus increasingly come to present itself an "immense accumulation of spectacles." American downtowns no longer communicate exclusively a monumental sense of power, authority, and corporate domination. They instead express the idea of spectacle and play. It is on this terrain of the spectacle that the break into the post-modern urban culture that has accompanied flexible accumulation has partially been fashioned, and it is in the context of such mediating images that the opposition of class consciousness and class practices have to unfold.[3] But, as Debord (1983) observes, the spectacle "is never an image

---

[3] I cannot here resist drawing attention to the way in which Barthes (1975) brought the concept of *jouissance* into philosophical respectability at the same time as the exploration of the city as a theater, as a spectacle, full of play spaces became more prominent in both the theory and practice of urban design. I also suspect that the appreciation of the urban fabric as a "text" to be read and interpreted with pleasure had something to do with the tax advantages that derived to the real estate industry of declaring whole segments of the city "historic preservation districts."

mounted securely and finally in place; it is always an account of the world competing with others, and meeting the resistance of different, sometimes tenacious forms of social practice."

VI. URBAN STRESS UNDER FLEXIBLE ACCUMULATION

Flexible accumulation has had a serious impact upon all urban economies. The increasing entrepreneurialism of many urban governments (particularly those that emphasized "public-private partnership") tended to reinforce it and the neoconservativism and post-modernist cultural trends that went with it. The use of increasingly scarce resources to capture development meant that the social consumption of the poor was neglected in order to provide benefits to keep the rich and powerful in town. This was the switch in direction that President Nixon signalled when he declared the urban crisis over in 1973. What that meant, of course, was the transmutation of urban stresses into new forms.

The internal adaptations within the city likewise played their part in facilitating and fomenting flexible accumulation. Poor populations had to become much more entrepreneurial, adopting, for example, "informal" economic means to survive. Increasing competition for survival under conditions of increasing impoverishment meant serious erosion of traditional mutual aid mechanisms in urban communities that had little capacity to dominate space and were often disempowered with respect to normal processes of political integration. The ability to dominate space through communal solidarity and mutually supportive patterns of appropriation weakened at the very moment that many spaces became vulnerable to invasion and occupation by others. A tension arose between increasing unemployment of workers in traditional occupations and the employment growth triggered by downtown revivals based on financial services and the organization of spectacle. A new and relatively affluent generation of professional and managerial workers, raised on the cultural discontents with modernism in the 1960s, came to dominate whole zones of inner city urban space seeking product differentiation in built environments, quality of life, and command of symbolic capital. The recuperation of "history" and "community" became essential selling gimmicks to the producers of built environments. Thus was the turn to post-modernist styles institutionalized.

There are serious social and spatial stresses inherent in such a situation. To begin with, increasing class polarization (symbolized by the incredible surge in urban poverty surrounding islands of startling and conspicuous wealth) is inherently dangerous, and given the processes of community construction available to the poor, it also sets the stage for increasing racial, ethnic, religious, or simply "turf" tensions. Fundamentally different class mechanisms for defining the spatiality of community come into conflict, thus sparking running guerilla warfare over who appropriates and controls various spaces of the city. The threat of urban violence, though not of the massive sort experienced in the 1960s, looms large. The breakdown of the processes that allow the poor to construct any sort of community of mutual aid is equally dangerous since it entails an increase in individual anomie, alienation, and all of the antagonisms that derive therefrom. The few who "make it" through informal sector activity cannot compensate for the multitude who won't. At the other end of the social scale, the search for symbolic capital introduces a cultural dimension to political economic tensions. The latter feed inter-class hostilities and prompt state interventions that further alienate low income populations (I am thinking, for example, of the way street corner youths get harassed in gentrifying neighborhoods). The mobilization of the spectacle has its unifying effects, but it is a fragile and uncertain tool for unification, and to the degree that it forces the consumer to become "a consumer of illusions" contains its own specific alienations. Controlled spectacles and festivals are one thing but riots and revolutions can also become "festivals of the people."

But there is a further contradiction. Heightened inter-urban competition produces socially wasteful investments that contribute to rather than ameliorate the over-accumulation problem that lay behind the transition to flexible accumulation in the first place (see Harvey, 1988). Put simply, how many successful convention centers, sports stadia, disney-worlds, and harbor places can there be? Success is often short-lived or rendered moot by competing or alternative innovations arising elsewhere. Over-investment in everything from shopping malls to cultural facilities makes the values embedded in urban space highly vulnerable to devaluation. Down-town revivals built upon burgeoning employment in financial and real estate services where people daily process loans and real estate deals for other people employed in financial services and real estate, depends upon a huge expansion of personal, corporate, and governmental debt. If that turns sour, the effects will be far more devastating than the dynamiting of Pruitt-Igoe ever could symbolize. The rash of bank failures in Texas, Colorado, and even California (many of them attributable to over-investment in real estate) suggests that there has been serious over-investment in urban redevelopment.

Flexible accumulation, in short, is associated with a highly fragile patterning of urban investment as well as increasing social and spatial polarization of urban class antagonisms.

VII. POLITICAL RESPONSES

"Every established order tends to produce," Bourdieu (1977, 164) writes, "the naturalization of its own arbitrariness." The "most important and best concealed" mechanism for so doing is "the dialectic of the objective chances and the agent's aspirations, out of which arises the *sense of limits*, commonly called the *sense of reality*" which is "the basis of the most ineradicable adherence to the established order." Knowledge (perceived and imagined) thereby "becomes an integral part of the power of society to reproduce itself." The "symbolic power to impose the principles of construction of reality – in particular, social reality – is a major dimension of political power."

This is a key insight. It helps explain how even the most critical theorist can so easily end up reproducing "adherence to the established order." It explains Tafuri's (1976) conclusion (based on the history of avant-gardism and modernity in architecture) of the impossibility of any radical transformation of culture and therefore of any radical and transforming architectural practice in advance of any radical transformation in social relations. The insight compels scepticism towards those who have recently embraced post-modernism (or radical individualism or some other aspect of contemporary practice) as a radical and liberating break with the past. There is strong evidence that post-modernity is nothing more than the cultural clothing of flexible accumulation. "Creative destruction" – that centerpiece of capitalist modernity – is just as central in daily life as it ever was. The difficulty, therefore, is to find a political response to the invariant and immutable truths of capitalism in general while responding to the particular forms of appearance that capitalism now exhibits under conditions of flexible accumulation. From that standpoint, therefore, let me explore some modest proposals.

Consider, first, exploring the interstices of present processes for points of resistance and empowerment. Decentralization and deconcentration taken together with the cultural concern with the qualities of place and space creates a political climate in which the politics of community, place, and region can unfold in new ways, at the very moment when the cultural continuity of all places is seriously threatened by flexible accumulation. It is out of that sort of tension that Frampton (1985) advocates a regional architecture of resistance to the homogenizing forces of global capitalism and Rossi (1984) pursues an architecture expressive of the continuity of neighborhood tradition and collective memory.[4] The cultural theses of post-

---

[4] Rossi (1984), it is intersting to note, bases his theory of architectural practice on the ideas of several geographers, notably Vidal de la Blache, regarding the importance of neighborhoods as settings for the continuity of "genres de vie" and sites of collective memory. From my

modernity are, evidently, open to radical interpretation in the cause of greater empowerment of the poor and underprivileged. But that is small beer compared to the "creative destruction" with which flexible accumulation typically scars the fabric of the city.

Flexible accumulation also opens up new paths of social change. Spatial dispersal means much greater geographical equality of opportunity to lure in new activities to even the smallest towns in the remotest region. Position within the urban hierarchy becomes less significant and large cities have lost their inherent political economic power to dominate. Small towns that have managed to lure in new activities have often improved their position remarkably. But the chill winds of competition blow hard here too. It proves hard to hang on to activities even recently acquired. As many cities lose as gain by this. The ferment in labor markets has also undermined traditional union powers and opened up opportunities for migration, employment, and self-employment for layers in the population once denied them (though under much more competitive circumstances leading to low wages and deteriorated work conditions for women, new migrants, and ghettoized minorities). Flexible production opens up the possibility of cooperative forms of labor organization under a modicum of worker control. Piore and Sabel (1984) emphasize this argument and see this as a decisive moment in the history of capitalism when totally new and much more democratic forms of industrial organization can be implanted. This style of organization can also arise through the social consolidation of "informal sector" activities as cooperative and worker controlled endeavors.

Conditions of flexible accumulation, in short, make worker and community control appear as a feasible alternative to capitalism. The emphasis of political ideology on the left has therefore shifted towards a "feasible" decentralized socialism, thus drawing much more inspiration from social democracy and anarchism than from traditional Marxism. This corresponds with the vigorous external attack and internal critique of centralized planning mechanisms in the socialist countries (e.g. Nove 1983).

Political parties on the left have evolved in much the same direction. Municipal socialism in Britain, economic democracy and community control in the United States, and community mobilization by the "Greens" in West Germany illustrate the trend. There is plainly much that can be done, at both local and regional levels, to defend and empower local

---

standpoint, Rossi chose the wrong geographer because Vidal was notoriously reluctant, at least until the very end of his life and his seminal but much neglected *Geographie de l'Est*, to explore the dynamic transformations of social and physical landscapes wrought under capitalist social relations.

interests. Community and religious organizations actively support plant buy-outs, fight plant closure, and otherwise support the mutual aid mechanisms of traditional low-income community solidarity. Institutions can also be persuaded to support the thrust for greater empowerment of the populations that surround them. A sympathetic state apparatus can find ways to support cooperatives (in service provision, housing provision, and production) and perhaps find ways to encourage the formation of skills through the tapping of local talent. Financial institutions can be pressured into supporting community reinvestment, cooperative endeavors, and neighborhood development corporations. Even spectacles can be organized in a political cause. Planners can try to ensure that the transformations of neighborhood will preserve rather than destroy collective memory. Far better that a deserted factory be turned into a community center where the collective memory of those who lived and worked there is preserved rather than being turned into boutiques and condos that permit the appropriation of one people's history by another.

But there are acute dangers. Both the theory and the practices have the effect of reinforcing the fragmentations and reifications. It is invidious to regard places, communities, cities, regions, or even nations as "things in themselves" at a time when the global flexibility of capitalism is greater than ever. To follow that line of thinking is to be increasingly rather than less vulnerable in aggregate to the extraordinary centralized power of flexible accumulation. For it is just as geographically unprincipled and naive to ignore the qualities of a global process as it is to ignore the distinctive qualities of place and community. Practices fashioned only in the latter terms define a politics of adaptation and submission, rather than of active resistance and of socialist transformation.

Yet a global strategy of resistance and transformation has to begin with the realities of place and community. The problem is to discover a centralized politics that matches the increasingly centralized power of flexible accumulation while remaining faithful to the grass-roots of local resistances. The "Greens" in West Germany and the Rainbow Coalition in the United States appear to be taking up such questions. The difficulty is to merge these freshly minted ideologies with a more traditional oppositional politics shaped in response to a previous regime of accumulation (without, however, embracing radical individualism, neo-conservativism, or post-modernism as signs of liberation). There is plenty of scope here for progressive forces, at both local, regional and national levels to do the hard practical and intellectual work of creating a more unified oppositional force out of the maelstrom of social change that flexible accumulation has unleashed.

This is mainly to speak, however, of the politics of resistance. What of the politics of some more radical transformation? While capitalism is always in a state of pre-socialism, it is scarcely on anyone's agenda these days to think about something as daring as the transition to socialism. Bourdieu (1977, 168), perhaps, provides a clue as to why:

The critique which brings the undiscussed into discussion, the unformulated into formulation, has as the condition of its possibility objective crisis, which in breaking the immediate fit between subjective structures and the objective structures, destroys self-evidence practically.

Only under conditions of crisis do we have the power to think radically new thoughts because it then becomes impossible to reproduce "the naturalization of our own arbitrariness". All major social revolutions have been wrought in the midst of breakdown in the bourgeois ablity to govern.

There are abundant cracks in the shaky edifice of modern capitalism, not a few of them generated by the stresses inherent in flexible accumulation. The world's financial system — the central power in the present regime of accumulation — is in turmoil and weighed down with an excess of debt that puts such huge claims on future labor that it is hard to see any way to work out of it except through massive defaults, rampant inflation, or repressive deflation. The insecurity and power of creative destruction unleashed by flexible accumulation takes a terrible toll, often on many segments of a population, thus generating acute geopolitical rivalries. These could easily spin out of control (as they did in the 1930s) and break up the West as a coherent political-economic unit (protectionist and financial "wars" have been part of our daily diet of news for some time now). Though crisis prone, however, the capitalist system is not *in* crisis and few of us care to consider how life would be if it were. Indeed, the system is so shaky that even to talk about its shakiness is to be seen to rock it in unseemly ways.

This brings me to my second major point. Objective crisis may be a nesssary but it is never a sufficient condition for major social transformations. The latter depend upon the rise of some political force capable of stepping into the vacuum of power and doing something truly creative with it. The nature of that political force does indeed make a difference; between, to use Marx's own polarities, a transition to barbarism or socialism. If the presently disempowered are to have a voice in that then they must first possess "the material and symbolic means of rejecting the definition of the real that is imposed on them." (Bourdieu 1977: 169). As Willis (1977) shows, however, the disempowered evolve their own means of symbolic representation that in many respects represent their social world more accurately than that which educators would impose upon them. "Drop out" and oppositional inner-city sub-cultures, with their distinctive languages, are as widespread and vibrant as they have ever been. But that language, if only because it is the language of those trapped in space, is adaptive rather than transformative with respect to global processes that preclude empowerment for the mass of the population.

Critical theory here has a role. But only if it, too, is self-critical. To begin with, all critical theory emerges as the practice of a group of "organic intellectuals" (to use Gramsci's phrase) and its qualities therefore depend upon the class and territory in which the practitioners have their being. Academics and professionals are not exempt. Our critical theory therefore has certain qualities that differentiate it from the critical theory expressed in working class cultural and political practices. True empowerment for the presently disempowered must be won by struggle from below and not given out of largesse from above. The modes of class and under-class opposition to flexible accumulation must therefore be taken seriously. The problem, on all sides, is to find practices that define a language of class and territorial alliances from which more global oppositional strategies to flexible accumulation can arise.

Even that kind of critical theory cannot contain the answers. But it can at least pose the questions and in so doing reveal something of the material realities with which any transition has to cope. That is, to be sure, a small contribution. But it is out of the assemblage of such small contributions that meaningful transformations must be wrought. A critical appraisal of the current regime of flexible accumulation, of the cultural practices of post-modernity, and of the re-shaping of physical and social space through urbanization, together with reflection on the ideologies through which we understand such processes, appears as one small but necessary preparatory step towards the reconstitution of a movement of global opposition to a plainly sick and troubled capitalist hegemony.

References

Aglietta, M. 1974. *A Theory of Regulation*. London.

Allison, J. 1932. *Monsieur Thiers*. New York.

Albert, W. 1972. *The turnpike road system in England*. London.

Armstrong, P., A. Glyn, and J. Harrison 1984. *Capitalism since World War II*. London.

Barthes, R. 1975. *The Pleasure of the Text*. New York.

Baudelaire, C. [1857] 1983a. *Les fleurs du mal*. Trans. R. Howard. Boston.

―――. [n.d.] 1983b. *Intimate journals*. Rev. ed., reprint, trans. C. Isherwood. San Francisco.

Becker, G., ed. 1969. *Paris under siege. 1970–71: From the Goncourt journal*. Ithaca.

Benjamin, W. [1969] 1973. *Charles Baudelaire: A lyric poet in the era of high capitalism*. Trans. H. Zohn. London.

Berman, M., 1982. *All that is solid melts into air*. New York.

Berry, B., and E. Neils. 1969. Location, size, and shape of cities as influenced by environmental factors: The urban environment writ large. In *The quality of the urban environment*, ed. H. Perloff. Baltimore

Blaut, J. 1974. The ghetto as an internal neo-colony. *Antipode* 6, no. 1: 37–41.

Bouinot, J., ed., 1987. *L'Action Economique des Grandes Villes en France et à l'Etranger*. Paris.

Bourdieu, P. 1977. *Outline of a Theory of Practice*. Cambridge.

Bourdieu, P. 1984. *Distinction: A Social Critique of the Judgement of Taste*. London.

Bradbury, M. and J. McFarlane 1976. *Modernism; 1890–1930*. Harmondsworth.

Braudel, F. [1979] 1984. *The perspective of the world*. Trans. S. Reynolds. New York.

Braudel, F. and E. Labrousse, eds. 1976. *Histoire économique et sociale de la France*, vol. 3. Paris.

Bruhat, J., J. Dautry, and E. Tersen. 1971. *La Commune de 1871*. Paris.

Castells, M. 1972. *La question urbaine*. Paris.

―――. 1983. *The city and the grassroots*. Berkeley and Los Angeles.

―――― and A. Portes 1986. World underneath: the origins, dynamics, and effects of the informal economy. *Conference on the Comparative Study of the Informal Sector*. Baltimore.

Cerf, M. 1971. *Edouard Moreau*. Paris.

Chambers, I. 1987. Maps for the metropolis: a possible guide to the present. *Cultural Studies* 1:1–22.

Chinitz, B. 1958. Contrasts in agglomeration: New York and Pittsburgh. *American Economic Review* 51:279–89.

Chevalier, L. [1958] 1973. *Laboring classes and dangerous classes*. Trans. F. Jellinek. Princeton.

Clark, T.J. 1985. *The Painting of Modern Life: Paris in the Art of Manet and his followers*. New York.

Clavel, P., J. Forester and W. Goldsmith 1980. *Urban and regional planning in an age of austerity*. New York.

Cobb, R. 1975. *A sense of place*. London.

Cohen, R. 1981. The new international division of labor, multinational corporations, and urban hierarchy. In *Urbanization and urban planning in capitalist society*, ed. M. Dear and A. Scott. London.

Coing, H. 1982. *La ville, marché de l'emploi*. Paris.

Crenson, M. 1983. *Neighborhood politics*. Cambridge, Mass.

Dansette, A. 1965. *Histoire religieuse de la France contemporaine*. Paris.

Day, R. 1976. The theory of long waves: Kondratieff, Trotsky, Mandel. *New Left Review* 99:67–82.

de Certeau, M. 1984. *The practice of everyday life*. Berkeley.

Deane, P., and W. Cole. 1967. *British economic growth, 1688–1959*. London.

Dear, M. ed. 1988. Reconsidering social theory: a debate. *Society and Space* 5:363–434.

Debord, G. 1983. *Society of the spectacle*. Detroit.

Dickens, C. [1854] 1961. *Hard times*. Reprint. New York.

———. [846–48] 1970. *Dombey and son*. Reprint. Harmondsworth.

Donzelot, J. 1977. *La police de familles*. Paris.

Dreyfus, R. 1928. *Monsieur Thiers contre l'Empire, la guerre et la Commune*. Paris.

Duclos, D. 1981. The capitalist state and the management of time. In *City, class, and capital*. ed. M. Harloe and E. Lebas. London.

Durkheim, E. 1965. *The elementary forms of religious life*. New York.

Dyos, H.J. 1961. *Victorian suburb: a study of the growth of Camberwell*. Leicester.

Eagleton, T. 1987. Awakening from modernity. *Times Literary Supplement* February 20th, 1987.

Edwards, S. 1971. *The Paris Commune*. Chicago.

Engels, F. [1872] 1935. *The housing question*. International Publishers, New York.

——— [1845] 1971. *The condition of the working class in England in 1844*. 2nd ed., trans. and ed. W.O. Henderson and W.H. Challoner. London.

Fainstain, S., N. Fainstain, R. Hill, D. Judd and M. Smith 1986. *Restructuring the city*. New York.

Fine, B. 1979. On Marx's theory of agricultural rent. *Economy and Society* 8:241–78.

Firey, W. 1945. Sentiment and symbolism as ecological variables, *American Sociological Review* 10:145–60.

Fischer, C. 1982. *To dwell among friends: Personal networks in town and city*. Chicago.

Foster, J. 1974. *Class struggle in the industrial revolution*. London.

Foulon, M. 1934. *Eugène Varlin*. Clermont Ferrand.

Frampton, K. 1985. Critical regionalism: speculations on an architecture of resistance. In C. Johnson ed. *The City in conflict*. London.

Fried, M. 1963. Grieving for a lost home. In *The urban condition*, ed. L. Duhl. New York.

———— and P. Gleicher. 1961. Some sources of residential satisfaction in an urban slum. *Journal of the American Institute of Planners* 27:305–15.

Friedmann, J., and G. Wolff. 1982. World city formation: An agenda for research. *International Journal of Urban and Regional Research* 6:309–44.

Frisby, D. 1986. *Fragments of modernity*. Oxford.

Giddens, A. 1984. *The Constitution of society*. Oxford.

————. 1973. *The class structure of the advanced societies*. London.

————. 1981. *A contemporary critique of historical materialism*. London.

Giglioli, P., ed. 1972. *Language and social context*. Harmondsworth, Middlesex.

Girard, L. 1952. *Les politiques des travaux publics sous le Second Empire*. Paris.

Godelier, M. [1966] 1972. *Rationality and irrationality in economics*. Trans. B. Pearce. London.

Goode, J. 1978. *George Gissing: Ideology and fiction*. London.

Goodman, R. 1971. *After the planners*. New York.

————. 1979. *The last entrepreneurs*. Boston.

Gottlieb, M. 1976. *Long swings in urban development*. New York.

Gramsci, A. 1971. *Selections from the prison notebooks*. Trans. and ed. Q. Hoare and G.N. Smith. London.

Guillemin, H. 1956. *Cette curieuse guerre de 1870*. Paris.

————. 1971. *L'avènement de M. Thiers et réflexions sur la Commune*. Paris.

Handlin, O. 1951. *The uprooted*. New York.

————. 1982. *Family time and industrial time*. London.

Harvey, D. 1973. *Social justice and the city*. London.

————. 1975. The political economy of urbanization in the advanced capitalist societies – the case of the United States. In *The social economy of cities*, ed. G. Gappert and H. Rose, Annual Review of Urban Affairs no. 9. Beverly Hills.

————. 1982. *The limits to capital*. Oxford.

————. 1985. The geopolitics of capitalism. In *Social relations and spatial structures*, ed. D. Gregory and J. Urry. London.

————. 1985a. *The Urbanization of Capital*. Oxford.

————. 1985b. *Consciousness and the Urban Experience*. Oxford.

————. 1988. The geographical and geopolitical consequences of the transition from fordist to flexible accumulation. In *America's new market geography*, ed. G. Sternlieb and J.W. Hughes. New Brunswick, N.J.

———— and A. Scott (Forthcoming) The practice of human geography, theory and specificity in the transition from fordism to flexible accumulation. In W. Macmillan, ed. *Remodelling Geography*. Oxford.

Hawley, A., and O. Duncan. 1957. Social area analysis. *Land Economics* 33:340–51.

Hayden, D. 1981. *The grand domestic revolution: A history of feminist designs for American homes, neighborhoods, and cities*. Cambridge, Mass.

Holton, R. 1984. Cities and the transition to capitalism and socialism. *International Journal of Urban and Regional Research* 8:13–37.

Houdeville, L. 1969. *Pour une civilisation de l'habitat*. Paris.

Huyssen, A. 1984. Mapping the post-modern. *New German Critique* 33:5–52.

Isard, W. 1942. A neglected cycle: The transport building cycle. *Review of Economics and Statistics* 24:149–58.

Jackson, J.B. 1972. *American space*. New York.

Jacobs, J. 1961. *The life and death of great American cities*. New York.

Jacobs, J. 1969. *The economy of cities*. New York.

———. 1984. *Cities and the wealth of nations*. New York.

Jager, M. 1986. Class definition and the esthetics of gentrification. In N. Smith and P. Williams eds. *The Gentrification of the city*. London.

James, J. [1907] 1946. *The American scene*. Reprint. New York.

Jameson, F. 1984a. The politics of theory: ideological positions in the post-modernism debate. *New German Critique* 33:53–65.

———. 1984b. Post-modernism, or, the cultural logic of late capitalism. *New Left Review* 146:53–92.

Jencks, C. 1984. *The Language of post-modern architecture* (fourth edition). London.

Jonquet, R.P. (n.d.) *Montmartre. autrefois et aujourd hui*. Paris.

Katznelson, I. 1981. *City trenches: Urban politics and the patterning of class in the United States*. New York.

Kern, S. 1983. *The culture of time and space, 1880–1918*. London.

Kerouac, J. 1955. *On the road*. New York.

Kropotkin, P. [1898] 1968. *Fields, factories, and workshops*. New and rev. ed. new York.

Landes, D. 1983. *Revolution in time: Clocks and the making of the modern world*. Cambridge, Mass.

Lasch, C. 1977. *Haven in a heartless world*. New York.

Lazare, L. 1872. *La France et Paris*. Paris.

Lefebvre, H. 1970. *La révolution urbaine*. Paris.

———. 1972. *Le droit à la ville*. Paris.

———. 1974. *La production de l'éspace*. Paris.

———. [1973] 1976. *The survival of capitalism*. Trans. F. Bryant. London.

Le Goff, J. [1977] 1980. *Time, work, and culture in the Middle Ages*. Trans. A. Goldhammer. Chicago.

Lepidis, C., and E. Jacomin. 1975. *Belleville*. Paris.

Lesourd, P. 1973. *Montmartre*. Paris.

Lissagaray, P.O. 1976. *Histoire de la Commune*. Paris.

Lewis, J.P. 1965. *Building cycles and Britain's growth*. London.

Lukács, G. [1923] 1968. *History and class consciousness*. Trans. R. Livingstone. London.

Lyotard, J. 1984. *The postmodern condition*. Manchester.

McPherson, C.B. 1962. *The political theory of possessive individualism*. London.

Malthus, T. [1836] 1951. *The principles of political economy*. Reprint. New York.

Mandel, E. [1972] 1975. *Late capitalism*. Trans. J. de Brés. London.

Marcuse, H. 1968. *Negations: Essays in critical theory*. Boston.

Markusen, A. 1986. Defense spending: a successful industrial policy. *International Journal of Urban and Regional Research* 10:105–22.

Marx, K. [1852] 1963. *The eighteenth brumaire of Louis Bonaparte.* International Publishers, New York.

———. 1963. *The poverty of philosophy.* International Publishers, New York.

———. 1964b. *The economic and philosophic manuscripts of 1844.* International Publishers, New York.

———. 1967. *Capital.* 3 vols. International Publishers, New York.

———. 1972. *Theories of surplus value.* vol. 3. Lawrence and Wishart, London.

———. 1973. *Grundrisse.* Penguin Publishers, Harmondsworth.

———. 1976. The results of the immediate process of production. Appendix to *Capital*, vol. 1. Penguin Publishers, Harmondsworth.

Marx, K., and F. Engels. 1955. *Selected correspondence.* Progress Publishers, Moscow.

Marx, K., and V.I. Lenin. 1968. *The civil war in France: The Paris Commune.* International Publishers, New York.

Marx, L. 1964. *The machine in the garden.* London.

Massey, D., and A. Catelano. 1978. *Capital and land: Land ownership by capital in Great Britain.* London.

Massey, D., and R. Meegan. 1982. *The anatomy of job loss.* London.

Merrington, J. 1975. Town and country in the transition to capitalism. *New Left Review* 93:73–92.

Miliband, R. 1968. *The state in capitalist society.* London.

Mollenkopf, J. 1983. *The contested city.* Princeton.

Molotch, H. 1976. The city as a growth machine: Toward a political economy of place. *American Journal of Sociology* 82:309–32.

Newson, E., and J. Newson. 1970. *Four years old in an urban community.* Harmondsworth.

Norris, P. [1903] 1981. *The octopus.* Reprint. New York.

Nove, A. 1983. *The Economics of Feasible Socialism.* London.

Ollman, B. 1971. *Alienation: Marx's conception of man in capitalist society.* London.

———. 1973. Marxism and political science: A prolegomenon to a debate on Marx's method. *Politics and Society* 3:491–510.

Olson, M. 1965. *The logic of collective action.* Cambridge, Mass.

Pahl, R. 1984. *Divisions of labour.* Oxford.

Pinkney, D. 1958. *Napoleon III and the rebuilding of Paris.* Princeton.

Piore, M. and C. Sabel 1984. *The Second Industrial Divide.* New York.

Pollard, S. 1965. *The genesis of modern management.* Cambridge, Mass.

Postan, M. 1935. Recent trends in the accumulation of capital. *Economic History Review* 6:1–12.

Postel-Vinay, G. 1974. *La rente foncière dans le capitalisme agricole.* Paris.

Poulantzas, N. [1968] 1973. *Political power and social class.* Trans. and ed. T. O'Hagen. London.

Pred, A. 1973. *Urban growth and the circulation of information in the United States system of cities, 1790–1840.* Cambridge, Mass.

Price, R. 1975. *The Economic modernization of France.* London.

———. 1983. *The modernization of rural France.* London.

Redclift, N., and E. Mingione, eds. 1985. *Beyond employment: Household, gender, and subsistence.* Oxford.

Rey, P-P. 1973. *Les alliances de classes*. Paris.

Robson, B. 1969. *Urban analysis: A study in city structure*. London.

Rohault de Fleury, H. 1903–7. *Historique de la basilique du Sacré-Coeur*. 3 vols. Unpublished. Bibliothèque Nationale. Paris.

Rorty, R. 1979. *Philosophy and the mirror of nature*. Princeton.

Rose, D. 1984. Rethinking gentrification; beyond the uneven development of marxist urban theory. *Society and Space* 2:47–74.

Rossi, A. 1984. *Architecture and the city*. Cambridge, Mass.

Rougerie, J. 1968. Remarques sur l'histoire des salaires à Paris au dix-neuvieme siècle. *Le Mouvement Sociale* 63:71–108.

Saunders, P. 1981. *Social theory and the urban question*. New York.

Scott, A. and M. Storper, eds. 1986. *Production, work, territory: The geographical anatomy of industrial capitalism*. London.

Sennett, R. 1970. *The uses of disorder: personal identity and city life* New York.

Sharp, C. 1981. *The economics of time*. Oxford.

Shlay, A. and D. Di Gregorio 1985. Same city, different worlds: examining gender and work-based differences in perceptions of neighborhood desirability. *Urban Affairs Quarterly* 21:66–86.

Simmell, G. 1971. The metropolis and mental life. In *On individuality and social forms*, ed. D. Levine. Chicago.

———. [1920] 1978. *The philosophy of money*. Trans. T. Bottomore and D. Frisby. London.

Smith, N. 1984. *Uneven development: nature, capital, and the production of space*. Oxford.

Smith, N. 1987. Of Yuppies and housing; gentrification, social restructuring, and the urban dream. *Society and Space* 5(2): 151–72.

Smith, N. and M. Lefaivre. 1984. A class analysis of gentrification. In J. Palen and B. London, eds. *Gentrification, displacement and neighborhood revitalization*. Albany.

Stein, G. 1974. *Gertrude Stein's America*. New York.

Stilgoe, J. 1983. *Metropolitan corridor: Railroads and the American scene*. New Haven.

Storper, M., and R. Walker. 1983. The theory of labor and the theory of location. *International Journal of Urban and Regional Research* 7:1–43.

———. 1984. The spatial division of labor: Labor and the location of industries. In *Sunbelt/Snowbelt*, ed. L. Sawers and W. Tabb. New York.

Szelenyi, T. ed. 1984. *Cities in recession: Critical responses to the urban policies of the new right*. Beverly Hills.

Tabb, W. 1982. *The Long default*. New York.

Tafuri, M. 1976. *Architecture and utopia*. Cambridge, Mass.

Tarbell, I.M. 1904. *The history of the Standard Oil Company*, vol. 1, New York.

Tarr, J. 1973. From city to suburb: the "moral" influence of transportation technology. In *American urban history*, ed. A. Callow. New York.

Thomas, B. 1972. *Migration and economic growth: A study of Great Britain and the Atlantic economy* 2d ed. rev. London.

Thomas, E. 1967. *Rossell (1844–1871)*. Paris.

Thompson, E.P. 1967. Time, work-discipline, and industrial capitalism. *Past and Present* 38:56–97.

————. 1968. *The making of the English working class*. Harmondsworth.

Thrift, N. 1981. Owner's time and own time: The making of a capitalist time consciousness, 1300–1850. In *Space and time in geography*, ed. A. Pred. Lund.

Tilly, L.A. and J.A. Scott. 1978. *Women, work, and family*. New York.

Timms, D. 1971. *The urban mosaic: Towards a theory of residential segregation*. London.

Venturi, R., D. Scott-Brown and S. Izenour. 1972. *Learning from Las Vegas*. Cambridge, Mass.

Walker, R.A. 1976. The suburban solution, Ph.D. diss., Department of Geography and Environmental Engineering, Johns Hopkins University, Baltimore.

————. 1981. A theory of suburbanization. In *Urbanization and planning in capitalist society*, ed. M. Dear and A. Scott. New York.

Ward, J.R. 1974. *The finance of canal building in the eighteenth century*. London.

Warner, S.B. *Streetcar suburbs*, Cambridge, Mass.

Webber, M. 1963. Order in diversity: Community without propinquity. In *Cities and space: The future use of urban land*, ed. L. Wingo. Baltimore.

————. 1964. Culture, territoriality, and the elastic mile. *Papers, Regional Science Association* 11:59–69.

Willis, P. 1977. *Learning to Labor*. Farnborough.

Williams, R. 1960. Introduction to C. Dickens, *Dombey and son*. Harmondsworth.

————. 1973. *The country and the city*. London.

Wirth, L. 1964. *On cities and social life*, ed. A.J. Reiss, Jr. Chicago.

Zeldin, T. 1973, 1977. *France, 1848–1945*. 2 vols. London.

Zola, E. [1885] 1954a. *Germinal*. Trans. L. Tancock. Harmondsworth.

————. [1871] 1954b. *The kill (La curée)*. Trans. A. Texiera de Mattos; intro. Angus Wilson. New York.

————. [1885] 1967. *L'argent*. Pléiade, Paris.

————. [1876] 1970. *L'assommoir*. Trans. . Tancock. Harmondsworth.

———— [1877] 1980. *The earth*. Trans. D. Parmée. Harmondsworth.

Zukin, S. 1982. *Loft living*. Baltimore.

Index